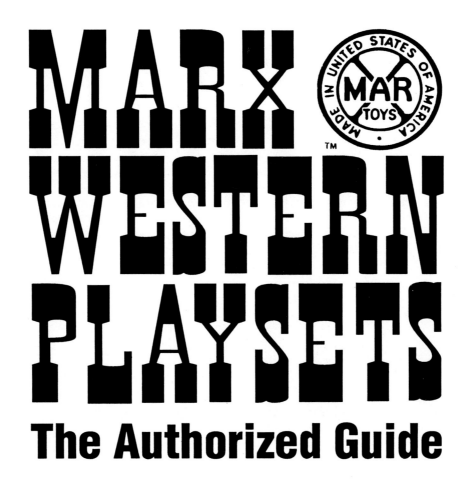

MARX™ WESTERN PLAYSETS

The Authorized Guide

Jay Horowitz

GREENBERG
PUBLISHING COMPANY, INC.

Greenberg Publishing Company, Inc.
7566 Main Street
Sykesville, Maryland 21784
(410) 795-7447

First Edition

Manufactured in the United States of America

Greenberg Publishing Company, Inc. publishes the world's largest selection of American and European toy train publications as well as books on Marx, Aurora, Buddy L, pressed steel and firefighting toys. For a complete listing of current Greenberg publications, please call 1-800-533-6644 or write to Kalmbach Publishing Company, 21027 Crossroads Circle, Waukesha, Wisconsin 53187.

Greenberg Shows, Inc. sponsors *Greenberg's Great Train, Dollhouse and Toy Shows*, the world's largest of its kind. The shows feature operating train layouts, dollhouses, and collectible toys. Shows are scheduled along the East Coast each year from Massachusetts to Florida. For a list of our current shows please call (410) 795-7447 or write to Greenberg Shows, Inc., 7566 Main Street, Sykesville, Maryland 21784 and request a show brochure.

Greenberg Auctions, a division of Greenberg Shows, Inc., offers nationally advertised auctions of toy trains and toys. Please contact our auction manager at (410) 795-7447 for further information.

ISBN 0-89778-291-7 (Hardback)

Library of Congress Cataloging-in-Publication Data

Horowitz, Jay.
Marx western playsets : the authorized guide / Jay Horowitz. — 1st ed.
p. cm.
Includes Index.
ISBN 0-89778-291-7 : $45.95
1. Louis Marx & Co. — Collectibles — Catalogs. 2. Toys — Collectors and collecting — United States — Catalogs. I. Title.
NK9509.65.U64L682 1992
688.7'2'097471 — dc20 92-9914
CIP

CONTENTS

THE COLLECTOR'S POINT OF VIEW: A FOREWORD

Privileged to have read an early draft of the manuscript of this book, I know that you will enjoy the discoveries it offers. I continue to find the narrative of the Louis Marx story fascinating. Imagine a sixteen-year-old venturing into the world of big business! And only a few years later, starting what became one of the most famous toy manufacturing companies in the world — Louis Marx & Co., Inc., later known as Marx Toys.

It all began when Louis Marx learned that a former employer considered the tin toys he manufactured obsolete after they saturated the immediate market (and therefore the manufacturer deemed the stamping dies that had been made for the production of these toys unusable). Marx arranged to purchase the dies and went on to show him and the world a thing or two! During the decades that followed, the Marx company grew to lead the industry. To my way of thinking, the first thirty years were preparatory. They laid the groundwork so that Marx could, in the early 1950s, produce the Marx playsets that we have come to love and revere.

The attention to detail and quality that the Marx company insisted on helped Marx both lead the way and dominate the field. In fact, without Marx, playsets virtually disappeared in the 1980s. That is why today the concept of playsets is synonymous with Marx.

Undoubtedly it was the technology of plastic-injection molding, developed following World War II, that allowed the playset as we know it to come into being. The first Marx playsets that contained plastic-injection molded figures were Western sets. Appropriately this book focuses on them, but it also goes behind the scenes — to the edification and delight of the great number of collectors of Marx toys, and of those who are not collectors but who have at one time in their lives owned a toy that was produced by Louis Marx & Company. Until now only a few people have had access to the information you are about to read. What I have learned by being fortunate enough to review the manuscript of the book and also by being a consultant on the manufacture of the new Marx playsets has enlightened me as to the complexities of making just one set. What I have gained through my association with Marx Toys is the fulfillment of a dream.

The most memorable moment for me was the first conversation that I had with Charles Marx, the nephew of Louis Marx. Being such an avid Marx playset collector, I was thrilled to hear Charles Marx speak of the old days and of working in the trenches. A lot of what Charles had to say, especially on the different Marx playsets, is right here in this book. He spoke not only of Louis Marx's business life but also of his personal life and his friendships with leaders from the ranks of the military and the political sphere. Until my contact with Charles, Louis Marx was only an image. Now he is brought to life with human qualities.

Also of interest is the quiet, seldom-heard voice of David Marx. Before reading the manuscript, I had heard very little about him, but now I know that David Marx was brother Louis's right hand. While Louis Marx was more in the public eye, David was working hard to see that the job got done, and done right. It required both Louis and David to make the Marx toy company successful.

As a child I spent many hours, days, weeks, months, and years playing with my Marx playsets. As an adult, I have been studying and collecting Marx playsets for twenty years. Each of my Marx sets is exhibited in the basement of my home. I have recently added new sets: "The Gold Rush," "Desert Storm Air," "Desert Storm Liberation," and, of course, "The Flintstones" thirtieth-anniversary commemorative set. This last contains everything that the original had plus a lot more — even updated figures. I can't wait to see what is next.

Before the publication of this book, we collectors had to rely upon memory, discussion with other playset collectors, the instruction sheets, or general rumor, which all proved unreliable or incomplete sources. At best, they did not allow us precisely to distinguish one set from another, and, in the worst case, they were conjecture and inaccurate. Now, however, we are able to consult the most complete and accurate information available, direct from the Marx Toys archives.

The final chapter of this book gives a detailed list of the Western playsets, and of the variations of each set, with their distinguishing characteristics and years of production. At least one version of each playset is featured; for these, reproductions of several kinds of documentation have been extracted from the archives. By studying the listings and pages from the actual Marx catalog, as well as factory bills of material, we can determine exactly which set we have, verify whether it is complete, and learn what may be missing. Furthermore, we may be able to tell which retail outlet it was sold by. (Marx made many special sets for large and small chains.) Also of interest are the various mold information sheets that are included, each providing a list of every part made in the mold; this is especially helpful in determining what accessories and furnishings should be included with each playset. Many of the illustrations included are actual promotion photos that were used by the Marx company years ago in its marketing of new playsets. Additional photos of playsets have been added by Greenberg Publishing; I am proud to say some of them were taken right from my own basement collection.

There are hours of very enjoyable and informative reading ahead, as well as puzzles to answer. For example, one of the facts I learned is the very existence of playset #4238 (Official Legend of Jesse James), listed for 1966. Was it ever in production? Or was a limited quantity made as a special order for a very influential customer? Charles Marx himself is not sure, and I have never seen one. Perhaps we can unravel this mystery.

I would like to thank Jay Horowitz, for including me in the preparation of this informative book; Charles Marx, for bringing the legend to life; and also, especially, a very big thank you to the memory of the "Toy King" himself, Louis Marx, for all of the fabulous playsets and other toys that were produced and sold for the enjoyment, the education, and now the collections of so many.

Happy Collecting!

Gary J. Linden

PREFACE

Of the many congratulatory phone calls and business propositions I received upon acquiring the physical assets of Louis Marx & Company in 1982, one in particular stands out. The attorney for a major toy manufacturer telephoned and repeatedly expressed his relief at locating me. It had taken considerable detective work on his part to trace me from the defunct Marx Toy Company to my office in Florida. I was amazed at his persistence! He spoke at length before coming to the point. "What type of a big deal was he leading up to?" I wondered.

"I am calling," he said, "because I wish to acquire a Goofy."

"What?" I replied, almost falling out of my chair.

"A Goofy," he reaffirmed with determination.

This must be a joke, I thought. My company, American Plastic, sells or rents tooling to plastic toy and houseware manufacturers. Over the last ten years, we've purchased most of the Marx toy tooling and dies, which makes us the modern-day Marx source. Goofy is a Marx toy figure, but I had never had anyone call to buy a single toy. (Now they do, on a daily basis.)

He further explained that he was a *toy collector* who, by hard work and good luck, had acquired the entire array of Marx Disney figures, except Goofy. Now he was willing to do or pay almost anything to complete his collection.

I reiterated that American Plastic mass-markets toys and that, although we had the mold for Goofy in storage, it would not be practical to make just one for him. Because of the high set-up cost and the fact that the mold would make not only Goofy, but thirty-seven other Disney characters, the cost of Goofy would equal the start-up expense plus the cost of thirty-eight Disney figures — about $250 for a figure once mass-produced for a cost of 2½ cents. To me, *that* was goofy!

He insisted that he was willing to pay the cost. Logic had little to do with his decision. What a nut, I thought. Today, I know better — he was simply a typical toy collector. This incident was my introduction to the serious (and sometimes goofy) world of toy collecting.

Given the pace, competition, volume, and ever-changing demands for toys for different ages and cultures, the world of the toy manufacturer is both very serious and very crazy. Toy collectors individually seem just as intense and daring. They are very different from the industry's regular customers: the collector is not the child for whom the toy was originally manufactured. He is the grown-up child, now pursuing an adult's passionate quest. Along the way he reminisces about the toys he had dreamed of having as a child and can now purchase — if he can find them. He can be coolly methodical in the pursuit of his passion.

Take, for example, collector Paul Gailey, an ardent student of Marx toys, who has systematically examined every gear and spring within Marx pieces. He takes pride in understanding how they function and how to repair them. Paul has often assisted Bruce Greenberg — a publisher of books about toys and toy trains — compile collector guides to Marx.

In April 1990 Paul and Bruce invited me to be their guest at the fabulous semi-annual York, Pennsylvania, Train Collectors Association (TCA) meet. Here, tens of thousands of train collectors fill the fairgrounds for two days — buying, selling, swapping, and enjoying round-the-clock activities. Once there, I was amazed at how many of them were Marx collectors.

While at the York meet, I accepted an invitation from John Fox, organizer of the Marx Train Collectors Club, to speak to its members there. Initially, the atmosphere in the meeting room seemed cool (collectors can be *very* protective when it comes to their investments in antiques, and therefore concerned about efforts to revive a manufacturer). Later, however, the club members showed me, by their rousing, standing ovation, that they were just as excited as I to learn more about the Marx Toy Company. Their questions revealed their thirst for factual information. They crowded around as I showed the original black-and-white promotional photographs of Marx playsets (many of which appear in this book). From the interest shown there and at subsequent meetings with other collectors, I realized how helpful a book documenting Marx playsets would be.

During my tour of the York meet, I overheard many collectors swapping stories and information about Marx. I soon realized that what was accepted as history and technical fact in many cases was based on hearsay and conjecture. One could call it collector lore or "Marx mythology," although I knew that the individuals engaged so earnestly in conversation really sought accurate and comprehensive data. With this in mind, I determined to set the record straight, as well as give the collectors insight into the manufacturing process so that they can better understand how Marx and other toys were developed and sold.

Sources of Information

The purpose of this book is to supply as much accurate, comprehensive information as is currently available. The product data was extracted from the records of the Marx archives; it has been unavailable to the public until now. This valuable information is enhanced by the personal recollections of former Marx employees and other contemporaries.

Undoubtedly, the highlight for me in preparing this book is my new friendship and association with Charles Marx and the Marx family. Charles is the son of David Marx, Louis Marx's brother and lifelong partner. As such, Charles is a walking, talking, living Marx history book. His charming mother, Charlene, lived the Marx years first-hand, and she also shared her memories.

The product information in Chapter Four describes the standard and crossover Western playsets and their usual or intended set contents. All of the information about the Western playsets was carefully extracted from the records found in September 1982 at the Marx factory in Girard, Pennsylvania. These records include consolidated data from the Glendale, West Virginia, and Erie, Pennsylvania, plants. Gene Rocco, long-time Marx employee, has advised me that virtually all of the playsets were made at the Glendale plant. Therefore, nearly all the information obtained from the Marx records for use in this book came from the original Glendale volumes. (American Plastic moved the records to Miami, Florida, via railroad in 1984; the records are now located there, intended for use in the proposed Marx museum.) Unless otherwise credited, all illustrative material in this volume is from the Marx Toys archives.

The following Marx records served as a basis for my research:

Assembly Information: Taken from product folders, this indicates the assembly line flow, time-and-motion studies, the individual operations, job descriptions, and dedicated equipment.

Bills of Material: Lists of each part used in a product, indicating its material, quantity, and source.

Blueprints: Detailed scale drawings of the molds, dies, and parts.

Catalog Sheets: Taken from published Marx catalogs which were circulated within the industry for the toy buyers and salespeople.

Distributor Catalogs: The actual annual or periodic consumer catalogs of the major retail chains and representatives offering Marx toys.

Mold Sheets: The description sheets of each mold. These include a mold's origin, date of construction, builder, drawing number, product used in, machine designed for, the all-important list of cavities contained, and very often even a photograph of the complete shot as it comes out of the mold.

Operation Manuals: Description of the special and specific processes used for any given product, excluding the standard, or generic processes such as injection molding (see Chapter Three), steel stamping, assembly, etc.

Part Drawings: Accurate, professional mechanical drawings of each part, fabricated or purchased.

Photographs: A number of promotional photographs in the Marx archives serve as excellent records. We have reproduced herein some of the original 8" x 10" glossies of the Western playsets used by Marx. Found in a large blue looseleaf binder, these have never before been seen by the public. It was this binder that I brought to the York, Pennsylvania, meet; its reception inspired this book.

Product Numbers: This guide lists the various product numbers under which each playset was manufactured, according to the archival records, so that the collector can evaluate his or her own set, or one to be purchased. The *years* of manufacture shown are based only on those years printed on the Specification Sheets, and/or Bills of Materials, indicating that a particular playset was made at least in the year shown. The same spec sheet was often reprinted several years in a row; we have indicated the first year for which the archives produced documentation. When reproducing documents in this book, we do not repeat the duplicate sheets, as they would be superfluous.

Specification Sheets: Lists of the parts for each toy and the tool used to make each part.

Current Distribution of Products and Information

Since purchasing most of the Marx tools and dies in 1982, American Plastic has become increasingly aware of the interests and needs of Marx collectors. As a result, we have launched four projects:

1. The Marx Vintage Collector Series

A new Marx company has been formed to manufacture limited editions of a few later-issue toys. Each toy will be produced according to the original Marx specifications and will be certified as "original." In many cases the mold core will be marked with a Roman numeral indicating the first year of the reissue, i.e., "XC" for 1990. This numeral will readily distinguish original from reissue toys. These toys will be offered to subscribers and will be numbered and reasonably priced.

2. "Re-Marx"

Limited edition reissues of 1940s and 1950s products will be manufactured and offered to hobby shops and dealers. These toys will be simple in scope and will not be individually numbered.

3. Books

Marx will develop books and other material based on the production records found in the Marx archives. This book is our first such project.

4. Marx Toy Newsletter

A new quarterly newsletter geared specifically to collectors of Marx toys will be mailed free of charge to those who call American Plastic or Marx Toys and ask to be put on the Marx mailing list.

We are committed to serving the Marx customers and collectors, and we will continue to explore additional services, such as providing popular molds for spare parts — which is now under study. It is my personal goal to maintain the high standards for quality, durability, and service originally established by Louis Marx & Company many years ago. I sincerely hope that this book serves to bridge the industrial world of toy manufacturing and the intense, nostalgic world of toy collecting and appreciation.

Jay Horowitz

Beginning with plain, economical packaging for mail-order customers in the early days of Marx Western playsets, the product line has been presented in many ways. Gary J. Linden Collection.

ACKNOWLEDGMENTS

I wish to extend my gratitude to many people without whose information and skills this book would not have been possible. **Bruce Greenberg**, my sponsor and publisher, provided professional guidance. Attorney **Andrew Lewin**, my first "goofy" contact with a true Marx collector, enlightened my firm to the serious needs of collectors. **Nadine Laham's** ideas and perseverance inspired me to start this complex project. **Lora Siegel** gathered the initial external research, putting in long hours, including holidays and weekends.

Other Marx fans who helped me with this book were **Charlene Marx**, whose recollections enhanced what would have been a far less interesting and comprehensive book; and **Maxine Pinsky**, whose books on Marx toys have contributed so much to the world of the Marx collector.

In gathering information and ideas for the content of this book, several people deserve special thanks. **Joel Wildman**, general manager of the Marx Vintage Collector Series, furnished many helpful ideas. **John Fox**, founder and president of the Marx Train Collectors Club, initiated my first real contact with Marx collectors. **Bill Murphy** provided initial direction toward collectors. **Nick Argento**, one of my first contacts with Marx collectors, was also one of the first to spark my personal interest. **Paul Gailey**, my sponsor to York, helped me catch the bug for collecting. **Jim Flynn**, a reporter for *Classic Toy Trains* and one of the most instrumental contributors to this book, located valuable Marx blueprints. And **Debbie Flynn**, his wife, took me to the Chicago Toy Expo. **Michael Denmark**, president of Plastic Toy and Novelty Corp, taught me the business when I was twenty-two and supplied me with my first molds.

Gary Linden, one of the world's most avid Marx playset collectors, shared his vast knowledge, reviewed the manuscript, and allowed us to photograph his personal collection. **Larry Passick**, my personal friend and a Marx historian who formerly worked for Marx Toys and Coleco, has been an important source of Marx information. **Shirley Henschel** spoke with me as a former Marx employee. **Ann Eisenhower** shared with me her memories of Louis Marx at the White House. **Manolo Diaz-Barreiro (Jr.)** and his brother, **Pedro Diaz-Barreiro**, who with their father were integrally involved in the Mexican Marx operations, shed much light on the Golden Years. **Harvey Lepselter** entertained me with an interesting and humorous interview.

Sy Wayne, the man who took over as Marx's chief financial officer from empire-builder **Archie Marcus,** filled in much background and detail. **Frank Rice**, with Marx in 1946-1962 and 1972-1975 and responsible for most aspects of the development of Marx playsets, was of invaluable assistance, chronicling the genesis of the playset concept and sharing many details of their evolution and of the Marx organization itself — as only an insider could. **Ray Lohr**, chief designer who oversaw product development at Marx during thirty-four years and invented the Big Wheel, provided many facts and recollections as he reviewed the manuscript. **Gene Rocco**, the Marx mold curator for over thirty years, continuing under American Plastic, filled in information and located hard-to-find samples.

Gloria Sanchez, the Marx librarian, provided endless assistance in my search for the truth. **Vicky Guajardo,** my personal executive secretary, helped enter much of the data for this book, and is loyal and caring, as always. **Maria Lopez** gathered the internal research with patience and diligence.

Readers of early versions of this book contributed their comments, and to **Joseph Freed**, **Linda Greenberg**, **Marty Johnson**, and **Allan Miller** go my thanks. I appreciate the assistance of the individuals who allowed us to photograph playsets and figures in their collections, and provided additional information: **Ed Bielcik**, **Don Faruolo**, **Mike Poko**, **Tripp Riley**, and **Carl Zambon**, as well as Gary J. Linden.

Deborah George Wright and **Andrea L. Kraszewski** helped move my first rough manuscript along toward the book you now have, working with diligence and imagination. **Elsa van Bergen**, Greenberg staff editor, applied her professionalism as she gave the text its final edit, organized the listings and illustrations, coordinated communication with the consultants and readers, and oversaw the production of this book.

Brad Schwab and **Chris Becker** did the new photography for this book. The front cover photo takes us into the Gunsmoke playset in Gary J. Linden's collection and was set up and shot by Chris Becker and **Jim Bunte**. The back cover photo shows one version of the complete Fort Apache playset, in the collection of Don Faruolo. **Donna Price** proofread, **Maureen Crum** designed the cover, and **Wendy Burgio** planned and executed the interior format. Managing Editor **Samuel Baum** provided guidance and support throughout the production process.

Lois Horowitz, always generous with her motherly love and support, aided me with her research. And **Jack M. Horowitz**, who handled media research and industry relations, introduced me into the world of toys, and into the world.

Charles Marx not only opened a window to the past and provided a personal perspective on the Marx years, but he also gave much enthusiasm and support on this subject. He truly is the only man alive who speaks more Marx than I do! And lastly, my greatest thanks go posthumously to **Louis** and **David Marx**, for their lifelong commitment to the world of fun and fantasy.

Jay Horowitz
June 1992

INTRODUCTION: A WORD FROM CHARLES MARX

The playset has always been one of my favorite products in the Marx toy line. The great stock of molds, dies, and other related tooling provided the versatility that allowed Louis Marx & Co., Inc. to respond to changing trends. My Uncle Lou always felt that for a toy to be successful, a child must be able to relate the toy to life around him.

For example, when the Russians launched the space race with Sputnik, we at Marx made space products, eventually including a Cape Canaveral playset; when a television program became popular, we quickly secured the rights and adapted our existing tooling to the theme. An example was the *Gunsmoke* television series. As soon as this program became popular, we took several of our already existing Western playset molds and built a new mold with the likeness of the featured figures. It was the same for *Rin-Tin-Tin, The Alamo,* and others.

No matter how we changed or created new playsets to reflect the trends and circumstances prevalent at a particular time, one thing was certain: we would always anticipate a sales demand from the major accounts. We expected Sears, for example, would carry Marx playsets. In the years when we offered more desirable sets, overall sales volume increased. Even during uncertain economic times, the playsets remained a highly stable, dependable category.

The number and combination of pieces that a playset required — often over a hundred — allowed Marx to customize a particular set for a major buyer. Hence, an account like Gimbel's was able to order a unique or distinctive toy unavailable to other clients. The variety of units allowed us to play with the contents of a set to supply a customer with a product within his specified price range. I remember the hours spent working with Ed Hjelte and Frank Rice, looking for new ways to combine the molds for different sets. These techniques were established by my father and uncle from the company's earliest days. By checking the specification sheets, one could probably determine whether a particular set was a standard version or an exclusive one, sold only through one of the major chains or department stores such as Sears or Montgomery Ward.

For example, during the Bicentennial celebration Sears introduced the "Heritage" series to American children. We tied our Heritage series to the 1976 Bicentennial by using historical figures representing historic moments. Parents often responded to this theme for educational reasons, but children played with them for their own reasons. Nonetheless, children could not help but learn about history through their exposure to the classic themes used in the "Blue and Gray," "Alamo," "Fort Apache," and the "Revolutionary War Set," to name a few.

My Uncle Lou felt it was a terrific *bonus* effect for the children to learn while playing, but he never lost sight of his number one objective — fun! His priority was *play value.* He would speculate on how long it would take a child to get bored with a particular toy. He felt that playsets provided the child with the basic components for hours, days, or years of enjoyment — enjoyment limited only by the child's imagination. Uncle Lou also liked the fact that a playset could be enjoyed by several children at once, or could keep a single child engaged for hours. My father, David, always stressed the importance of giving great *value* for the price.

All in all, the Marx playset was a favorite for people of all ages. As we reminisce about my wonderful relatives, to properly honor their accomplishments we must remember that they were most proud of the exceptionally talented people that contributed to the organization that they built. Marx was a solid company, supported by very intelligent forceful personalities. Some of the important Marx employees I remember are Bill Kelley, the Erie plant manager; H. D. "Bucky" Livingston, manager at Glendale; Walter Nisperly, Glendale Research and Development; Al Larsen of Glendale; and Chippy Martin at Girard — and of course Ed Hjelte, head of Research and Development; Frank Rice, in charge of playsets and games; and George Payne, who worked on Heritage sets in particular.

As I look back, remembering those days working at Louis Marx & Co., Inc., and considering our accomplishments, I understand why Marx was the industry leader. I also understand why today the Marx name remains prominent in the fondest memories of Americans, still commanding respect within the industry and from collectors. However, back in the 1940s, 1950s, and 1960s, we did not feel we were "living legends"; we were simply regular people, going to work daily and enjoying every minute of it!

Much work and research has gone into making the information contained in this book available to the public. Thanks to Jay Horowitz and his team of coworkers, more people can discover — and rediscover — the fantasy and enduring magic of Marx playsets.

Charles Marx

CHAPTER ONE

THE MEN BEHIND THE TOYS

How did a boy, whose parents could not afford to buy a single toy for their son, grow up to become the world's largest toy manufacturer? The answer is an American success story, like those retold by generations of entrepreneurs throughout the Industrial Age. Louis's special abilities were in sales and marketing; toys simply provided the vehicle with which he made his fame and fortune.

In telling the story of Louis Marx & Company, it is often difficult to separate the men from the company. Many facets of the business overlap with the personalities of the driving forces behind it. Chapter One attempts to provide insight into Louis Marx's background, the early years of the toy company, and the role played by Louis's brother David. The story of the growth and the recent past of Louis Marx & Co., Inc. is narrated in the following chapter.

GROWING UP

The Toy Hall of Fame in New York City displays a plaque honoring Louis Marx. It reads:

> Nicknamed the "Toy King of America" and the "Henry Ford of the Toy Industry," Louis Marx established the Louis Marx Toy Company in 1921. By 1950, it was the world's largest manufacturer. Marx' general philosophy was to offer quality at the lowest possible price, and he believed that there were no new toys, only "old toys with new twists." His popularity with buyers meant that he had virtually no need for salesmen or advertising. Marx was also first to mass-produce mechanical toys in the U. S. and many of his wind-ups are valued collectors' items.

Louis's sales and merchandising techniques were new in the 1920s, but today they are standard trade practices, used world-wide. He led the way.

Louis Marx was born in Brooklyn, New York, on August 11, 1896, to German immigrants Jacob and Clara Marx. Louis's older sister was Rose and his younger brother was David; all three attended Erasmus High School.

Growing up in rough-and-tumble New York, Louis and David spent much time on the streets, where big brother Louis showed David the ways of the world. From an early age, they recognized the value of money, a lesson that served them well in later years. It is difficult now to imagine how poor they were at one time. When young Louis first began his career, it was necessary for him to walk across the bridge from Brooklyn to Manhattan because he could not spare the two-cent carfare for public transportation. What a contrast to later years when the same person, no longer having to pinch pennies, would be chauffeur-driven to work.

EARLY BUSINESS EXPERIENCE

When his father's tailoring business in the Prospect Park section of Brooklyn failed in 1912, Louis, being the eldest son, was forced to help support the family. He was sixteen. On a friend's recommendation, he was hired to work full-time at the Ferdinand J. Strauss

Company. This early mechanical toymaker was later to become known as "the founder of the mechanical toy industry in America."

Although he started as an errand boy, Louis quickly ascended the ranks and was moved into sales. With an appetite for responsibility still unsatiated, and eager to create sales volume, Louis was sent to Strauss's East Rutherford, New Jersey, location. Within months, he was running the plant. Strauss, recognizing Louis's extraordinary talent, took him on the road as his sales assistant. Decades later, veteran toymaker Strauss commented that his former employee, who had since become his largest competitor, came to him as a boy with the brain of a forty-year-old.[1]

By 1917, twenty-one-year-old Louis had become the heir apparent to the Strauss Company. But his precocious concepts caused tension between him and Ferdinand Strauss. There are several versions of why Louis left Strauss. According to one view, Louis saw the opportunities of mass production and mass marketing, but Strauss officials disliked this new approach, viewing it as a threat to their tradition of quality and originality. The board of directors voted against Louis's policy, so he proudly and promptly left the company. Hindsight suggests that Louis's views made more sense than those which Strauss and the board so vigorously defended. By some accounts, Louis left due to dissatisfaction with his pay. In any event, he was ready to move toward new experiences.

He began a stint in the army that year, and this experience contributed much to his future. It gave him the opportunity to learn about the tools of combat — material that would fuel his fascination with the military and with battle scenes.[2] It also afforded him the opportunity to initiate contacts that would serve him in years to come; it especially left him, apparently, deeply impressed by the top brass — their bravado, artistry in action, and result-oriented approach to problem solving. Years later he became friends with many of the great generals of World War II. As a matter of fact, he became so friendly with them that he named each of his five sons from his second marriage after a general (or two), and honored each military namesake as a godfather.

Louis Marx returned to civilian life with drive, determination, and ability. The world at the moment had few doors open to him. He had no money and was not formally educated for a profession. On the other hand, Louis had had years of practical experience and training in every aspect of the mechanical toy business. Working his way up from the bottom, Louis had learned at Strauss the ins and outs of manufacturing, administration, product development and improvement, distribution, and marketing.

It was not long before Louis became a salesman for a Vermont wood products company, where he redesigned a line of toys. Under Louis's guidance, sales reportedly increased from $15,000 per annum to $1,500,000 in two years.[3] While with that company, Louis Marx became friendly with William J. Thompson, Sr., buyer for Woolworth's, and this friendship was to become a key element in the founding of Louis's own firm.

Undoubtedly, Louis's business acumen would have led to success in almost any arena (imagine Louis as the Henry Ford of the *textile* industry instead of the toy industry, with mills around the world). However, Louis chanced upon the great idea of providing toys to the world. And unlike many people who pass up their great ideas — reasoning that if it were so good, someone else would have already done it — Louis seized his opportunity and made history happen.

Timing was on Louis's side. The war was over. And in 1919, Americans wanted to get on with life and pursue the fun awaiting them in what was to become the Roaring Twenties. Because there was no mature American toy industry, the United States had been importing toys from Germany. But at the end of the war, Americans did not want to buy toys from the just-defeated enemy! As nationalism took hold, American products were at a premium. American ingenuity flourished and spawned hundreds of fledgling industries that would soon dominate the world. The movie, business equipment, automobile, and other industries — like toy manufacturing — burgeoned.

LOUIS MARX & COMPANY

Capitalizing on the opportunity of the times, Louis began on his own in 1919 and was joined by brother David a couple of years later. David seems to have been destined from birth to share his big brother's future: he was even born on August 11, 1899, on Lou's third birthday! Like his brother, David received an education in New York City's school of hard knocks: he learned early how to fight for every penny. Growing up, David held a series of jobs, from selling newspapers on street corners to waiting on tables (his last job before entering the toy business). Those who later knew David as an uncompromising adult could not imagine him waiting on anyone. But these experiences provided him with practical skills that served him well in later years.

"Louis Marx & Company" (it became incorporated as Louis Marx & Co., Inc.) was located at 200 Fifth Avenue, where it remained throughout the Marx ownership. As with most new businesses, this one had no capital, assets, sales base, patents, trademarks, products, processes, machinery, suppliers, or customers. Never mind. They had conviction and commitment, good instincts, and Louis's experience and indomitable energy, combined with David's people skills: this provided the firm with all the resources it needed.

While building the funds to undertake his own manufacturing, Marx served as a sales representative for various established manufacturers into the early 1920s, "repping" not only the Vermont Wood Company but the Strauss Company — Louis's former employers — and later the C. E. Carter Company. To Louis's credit, no matter how high he moved up in the world, he never burned his bridges behind him. Past business contacts became resources for further business. An example of this was one of the first product lines his new firm marketed — play dishes and cooking utensils. Louis knew how children liked to imitate adults, and so he had reasoned: What better way for a girl to play house than with kitchenware? As odd as it may seem in today's plastic age, those early dishes were made of wood. And so the relationship Louis had forged with the Vermont wood products company turned into one of his new company's first representation agreements — wooden toys and play kitchenware.

While still in his twenties, Louis Marx worked out a representation agreement with the Girard Model Works (GMW) of Girard, Pennsylvania, which produced model mechanical toys. This agreement provided the young Marx company with an additional, noncompetitive line of products and further expanded its viability as a rep.

In setting themselves up as middlemen, Louis and David not only represented manufacturers to stores, but also specialized in locating mass producers of quality toys for the marketplace. From the outset, Louis Marx intended that the Marx name would stand for products that were well-designed, of high quality, break-resistant, and fun. This applied to the toys he represented for other manufacturers and the toys he later manufactured himself. Louis's business philosophy was simple and direct: "Give the customer more and better toy than your competitor for less than he charges."[4] He never deviated from this philosophy throughout his career. It is a philosophy that, if properly implemented, would work in almost any business.

They chose their products wisely and contracted manufacturing out to existing manufacturers. The formula worked. It enabled the brothers now to sell their *own* products without a major capital investment or the expense of owning a factory. Hence, they could concentrate on the all-important aspect of their business — marketing. The manufacturers, on the other hand, had existing overheads already amortized by certain sales and profit. For them, any additional business Louis Marx & Company generated represented income and profit that they would not otherwise have had. There-

STEEL
MECHANICAL TOYS
CLIMBING MONKEY, Etc.
Send for Catalog
and FREE Samples
LOUIS MARX & CO.
200 Fifth Avenue New York City

Above, an ad from the June 1921 issue of the toy trade journal, Playthings, *documents Louis Marx's early establishment of his place in the marketplace. Below, one of the early patents taken out by the young company, for a mechanical pecking goose.*

GOLDEN GOOSE:

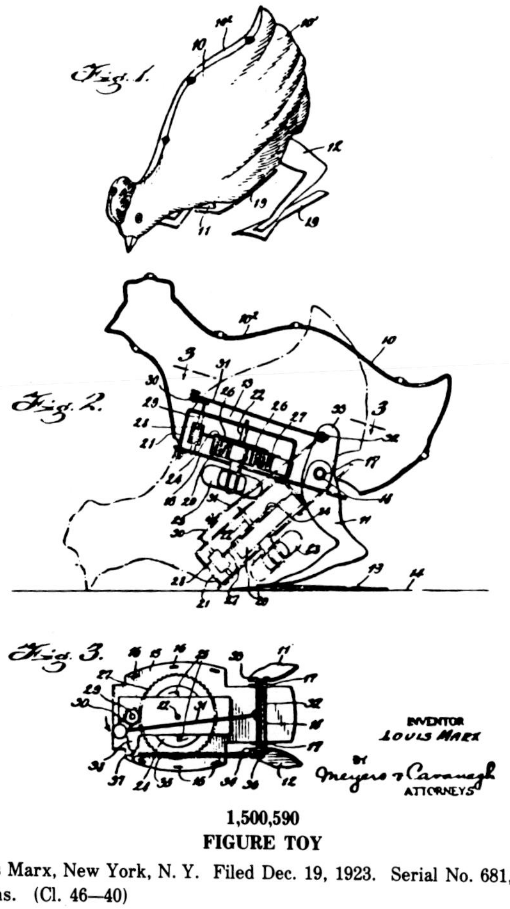

1,500,590
FIGURE TOY

Louis Marx, New York, N. Y. Filed Dec. 19, 1923. Serial No. 681,611. 4 Claims. (Cl. 46—40)

A toy fowl comprising a body member formed in representation of a fowl, a plurality of leg members, the said body member being mounted on the leg members for oscillation movement thereon between a substantially horizontal or normal body position and a downwardly inclined position with the beak of the fowl adjacent a support such as the ground on which the toy is placed, and mechanism carried by the body member and connected to the leg members for oscillation the body member relatively to the leg members in simulation of an eating or pecking action.

fore, this incremental income would produce product at lower cost.

With such mutual benefits to be realized in an apparently booming economy, and with the specialization possible for both parties, Louis Marx & Company took the first step to establish industrial trends for the twentieth century. Some seventy years later, the toy manufacturing world still operates by this system. Many, if not most, of the major toy manufacturers contract for a large portion of their manufacturing.

Marx further developed its original concept with innovations such as its post–World War II lead in making products in the Orient. Today it is not unusual for a toy manufacturer to design a product in New Jersey, build tooling in Portugal, contract the molding in Hong Kong, source components in Japan, assemble in China, and sell to Toys "R" Us back in New Jersey. Louis Marx & Company's early ideas have evolved into an integrated, global process.

The Fledgling Enterprise

Once it was financially able, the company expanded and became almost entirely self-sufficient, beginning its own manufacturing. Marx began by renting space in a factory owned by C. E. (Nick) Carter at Nineteenth and Cascade Streets in Erie, Pennsylvania. But within a year Louis and David realized the need for increased production capability and contracted the C. E. Carter Company to produce mechanical toys at the Nineteenth Street plant.[5]

In 1922 Ferdinand Strauss, about to retire, sold to Louis two sets of tools that were then considered obsolete — the metal stamping dies that made Zippo the Climbing Monkey and the Dapper Dan Minstrel Singer. Both were thought to have already saturated the market. Marx borrowed $500 from his mother and soon proved the contrary. The fledgling toy company updated the presentation of these and, at 25 cents per monkey and 50 cents per dancing minstrel singer, sold a purported 8 million units of each.[6] The profits from these two products made Louis a millionaire. He now had ample working capital to expand his lines and implement his unique marketing techniques.

Early on, Louis worked closely with a young man named Henry Katz to develop metal toy trucks. Katz later went on to become another giant in the industry; indeed, the story of Henry Katz paralleled that of Louis Marx in some ways. He had entered the toy business when he was seventeen and only a decade later was one of the major toy men in the United States. He was also a born salesman and is known in toy history for the work he began in the 1930s promoting the development of Buddy "L" (metal toys and trucks) as well as Western Stamping (toy typewriters and equipment) and Worcester Toys (plastic tea sets and blow-molded ride-on toys much like Marx's) — all direct competitors with Marx. After Katz had gone his own way, Marx continued to design and produce a line of strong steel trucks.[7]

For a number of years, Marx was representing other manufacturers as well as selling its own proprietary products, and Louis Marx continued as the company's most viable salesman. No matter how successful Louis Marx became, he always handled certain accounts personally. After all, a man like Bernard Gimbel (of department store fame) required special attention. Bernie was among the few Louis considered close friends. Once a year they would ceremoniously sit down together to review the Marx merchandise that would be featured in Gimbel's department store for the upcoming Christmas season. It was an event they both looked forward to.

On one such occasion during the 1950s, Louis, who was unhappy with the quantity of the Gimbel order, abruptly opened the door of his private office and barked out in his guttural voice at the unfortunate person who happened to be the handiest: "Get me the Strawbridge and Clothier order!" Ed Fury, the Marx employee within hearing range, leapt to attention. Without seeming to touch the ground, he raced to do Louis Marx's bidding. Unfortunately, Louis had not enunciated clearly, assuming that Fury knew exactly what he had in mind. Louis's purpose, very simply, was to boast to Bernie of the quantity of Marx trains being ordered by a smaller Philadelphia department store, in the hope of intimidating the New York magnate into increasing his order.

About thirty minutes later, Fury returned, huffing and carrying a large bowl of sour cream. Entering Louis's office, he said, "Here is the cream, Mr. Marx, but I am afraid that strawberries are out of season." Louis's reaction changed from bewilderment, to anger, to disgust, to frustration. "The Strawbridge and Clothier order! Not the strawberries and cream order!" Bernie began laughing uncontrollably, and soon that was all Louis could do, too.

THE PERSONA OF LOUIS MARX

In 1955 *Time* magazine ran a feature entitled "Louis Marx: The Little King."[8] It is true that Louis enhanced his hard-working lifestyle with touches of luxury. He was chauffeured to his office or engagements in a stunning vehicle that would be parked at the corner of the building at Fifth Avenue and 23rd Street (in the "No Parking" area), where passersby could gawk at its magnificence. Louis's chauffeur would spend the day polishing the car while awaiting instructions. Some people would point and say "That's Mr. Marx's Rolls Royce!"

The FAB building, now housing the Toy Hall of Fame and its citation of the contribution of Louis Marx, was home to the small firm that grew to be the world's largest toy manufacturer. Louis walked down its lobby to begin his long day on the seventh floor.

(Actually, although it appeared to be a Rolls, and Louis Marx owned at least three of them, a former Marx executive reports that it was an unusual four-door convertible that had a Bentley body with a Rolls Royce grille.)

The Fifth Avenue Building (FAB) was a home to virtually everyone in the U. S. toy industry at one time or another and is a story in itself. It housed the fortunes and frustrations of many and served as a forum for those who engaged in the international exchange of playthings. As Louis entered the FAB lobby, the porter and doormen would bow their heads, "Good Morning, Mr. Marx!" He would nod a quick acknowledgment in passing. And thus began a typical twelve-hour work day.

While other toymakers, employees, and visitors waited for the next elevator within the bank of twelve, Louis walked briskly to his "personal car" — the very first one at the rear left of the lobby. Although the

Louis Marx with the portrait of him by Dwight D. Eisenhower that graced his home in Scarsdale, New York

building housed hundreds of small, one-room companies, along with several large corporations, the Marx company had quickly outgrown its original space and had taken over most of the seventh floor.

Some days he skipped lunch and rode the elevator to the roof of the building where, dressed in shorts and hooded sweatshirt, he jogged. This may not sound strange today, in view of our health-minded society. However, in the 1940s it was highly unusual to see a man in his forties jogging along on the roof of a Manhattan office building in the middle of the business day. Although Louis enjoyed running alone, his competitive streak was even more apparent when he could lure along a friendly companion. Since Louis was already in shape and used to his personal "FAB track," he easily outran his companions. As testament to his fitness, Marx won a handball doubles championship in New York City in the 1930s.

Health was a priority. Coupled with his commitment to exercise was his interest in proper nutrition (one of the traits he shared with Henry Ford). In spite of his emphasis on health and nutrition, he was always seen sporting his trademark cigar.

The complete self-made man, Louis admired all types of mental achievement. Despite his monetary success, Louis made it a priority to complete the formal education that he had been forced to abandon in his youth. *Fortune* magazine, in its January 1946 feature article, offered an anecdote to describe Louis's keen intellectual dedication. It seems that Bernie Gimbel had invited Louis to attend a prizefight one night in 1945. "Can't, Bernie," Louis reportedly said, promptly turning down his close friend and major customer. "It's a school night," Louis explained, referring to his enrollment status as the oldest and only regularly registered millionaire student at New York University.[9]

Always the pragmatic opportunist, Louis found ways to apply the lessons of history and politics to his world of business and finance. He studied liberal arts courses such as "The History of Western Civilization," "American Political Parties," and "The Psychology of Religion." Believing that a sense of culture was critical to one's success, both personally and professionally, Louis made sure that his children were schooled properly in the arts and sciences. He continuously strove to build his vocabulary and would spend hours reading the dictionary. He regularly had his secretary, Miss Roberts, type the words he wished to add to his vocabulary into a series of black books, which he carried wherever he went. He was often seen studying these books in idle moments and even while jogging upon the FAB roof.

It truly is difficult to separate the man and his company, and much of Louis's character is evident in the development of the company in its early years. Part of the Louis Marx mystique was his uncanny foresight. Whether he actually forecast the trends or set them is an unending debate. World events open windows of opportunity that men like Louis recognize and act upon promptly and successfully. Others simply follow the path established by leaders.

Family and Friends

As is often the case with self-made successes, Louis Marx worked and played with intensity. Often he carried his enthusiasm to extremes. When it came to his family, he was a staunch supporter. At a young age, Louis married Rene Freda Saltzman and had four children: Barbara, Louis Jr., Jacqueline, and Patricia. No matter how busy Louis was, he always made time for his family.

When Louis was forty-six, Rene died from cancer. Louis then personally brought up his four children, and he began to contemplate his early retirement in order to spend more time with the children. He was a widower approaching fifty, engaged in the full-time vocation of business, as well as the full-time avocation of rearing his children as a single parent. Little did he suspect at the time that he would remarry, start a second family, and continue to work into his mid-seventies!

Among toy industry magnates, Louis Marx was the closest that a man could be to royalty in the United States. He lived the glamorous life portrayed on Hollywood sets. Home was the largest privately owned estate in Scarsdale, New York. A rambling, white-pillared, three-storied Georgian mansion on close to twenty acres, just off the Hutchinson River Parkway, it included a fenced-in garden that provided Louis's sixteen dogs and innumerable other pets with romping room. Among other amenities were a tennis court, swimming pool, paddle court, and expansive well-manicured grounds. Two paintings by President Eisenhower graced the mansion's interior.

In spite of his rigid personal standards and his prudent business ways, Louis was often surprisingly generous. On Halloween night each year, the neighborhood children would clamor to his Scarsdale estate where Marx toys were given to all trick-or-treaters in lieu of candy. In his obituary, *The New York Times* described Louis as a supporter of many charities, especially those for children, to which he generously donated both cash and toys; and *Time* magazine reported that Louis gave over a million toys a year to the children of poor families, orphanages, and other institutions.

During their formative years, the Marx youngsters met at the mansion. Louis was of course the unofficial family entertainer. He would begin by gathering the children together in one room, to tell them a story. Having their undivided interest, he would engage them in the unraveling of a mystery as he led the young siblings from room to room until — with eyes bulging — they ended up in the basement. The children soon found themselves at the gates of the massive wine cellar where a ghost would appear, or where one of the many horrible villains of the story would end up behind bars. The children's screeches filled the mansion as they scrambled for their rooms.

Some time after Rene's death, Louis met the woman who would become his second wife: Idella Ruth Blackadder. She was a beautiful blond — two inches taller than he, and Louis often boasted that she was twenty-eight years younger than himself. Their wedding in 1948 was a true star-studded event attended by celebrities, including politicians, movie stars, other entertainers, and five-star generals. Their marriage begat five sons, playfully referred to by Marx as the "second shift": Spencer-Bedell, Emmett Dwight, Bradley Marshall, Curtis Gruenther, and Hunter Bernhard, named by Louis after World War II's most famous generals.

Asked in 1945 whether he expected his son Louis Jr., to take over his business, Louis Sr.'s response was that "a toy business cannot be successfully handed on to one's children. 'It requires a certain touch,' he says, 'the kind of judgmental touch you can't teach someone [Further, he said that] there are more important things in the world than making toys.' "[10]

Interestingly enough, Louis Jr., echoed these thoughts when he himself was interviewed: "I soon realized that my father had something — he was born with it — that I could never learn: a feel for what toy would succeed with children next Christmas."[11] It is clear, however, that Louis Marx, Jr., did inherit his father's drive and ability and, like his father, was not one to follow in *anyone's* footsteps. A capable and intelligent man in his own right, and wanting to demonstrate his own abilities and gain independent recognition, he chose a different career path. His area of expertise became venture capital — especially in the oil industry.

The 1950s represented the Golden Years for Louis Marx, as well as for Louis Marx & Company. Having attained a mature age, success in business, strong social standing, educational polish, family fulfillment, fame, financial security, and success in every way possible, the world's largest toymaker was featured on the cover of the December 12, 1955 issue of *Time* magazine, which reported:

> Through the swinging glass doors of Manhattan's "21" Club one night last week popped a roly-poly, melon-bald little man with the berry-bright eyes and beneficent smile of St. Nick touching down on a familiar rooftop. Louis Marx, America's toy king and café-society Santa, was arriving at his favorite workshop. With his beautiful blonde [second] wife Idella — who looks the way sleigh bells sound — 59-year-old Lou Marx toddled regally toward a table in the center of the downstairs room. The table is always reserved for Millionaire Marx by the divine right of toy kings — and the fact is that he has never been known to let anyone else pay the check.[12]

Louis and Idella's marriage ended in divorce, but his taste for beautiful young women did not abate. Though not a tall man, Louis's presence commanded an aura of respect that many women could not resist. This personal aura overflowed into all aspects of his life.

Even outside of "Toydom," Louis was recognized as a celebrity. His peers included heads of state, royalty, celebrities, sports personalities, stage and screen stars, and writers, as well as other industrialists. It has been said that once while Louis was dining at "21", Henry Ford (whom Marx admirers called "the Louis Marx of the Automobile Industry") recognized Louis and came over to greet him.

Employees at the Marx office were often startled by the unannounced visit of a celebrity. In 1969, for example, just prior to Christmas, a tall Texan, intending to purchase toys for his Christmas shopping, appeared at the Marx company's seventh floor escorted by David Marx. Although the Marx employees were accustomed to seeing celebrities, they still made a fuss over Lyndon Johnson. While the newly retired president waited for Lady Bird to complete her shopping, Johnson spent two-and-a-half hours reviewing toys in the Marx office, where he was gingerly fawned over by Marx staff. Louis gave Lyndon a fifteen-minute personal audience, following which Johnson said: "Thank you for your time. I realize that you are a busy man running a large business."

Ray Lohr, who served as Marx's chief toy designer, recalls that the story of how Louis Marx first met this country's leading generals was one Louis loved to tell. Over the years several versions of it have come to light. Here is the way Ray heard it. One Saturday afternoon near Christmas, in the mid-1930s, a man came into the Fifth Avenue office. It happened that Louis Marx, as usual working harder than any employee, was the only one in the office. The visitor said he was looking for a Marx electric train switch for his family. Louis Marx found one and gave it to him, refusing payment, pleading he didn't sell retail.

The man introduced himself as Hap Arnold, an army flying officer. A week later Marx received a pair of tickets to the Army-Navy football game in Philadelphia. On a whim he and his wife Rene decided to go. In seats nearby he found a group of soldiers and their wives celebrating the promotion of a handsome young fellow to Lieutenant Colonel; he was named Dwight Eisenhower. In the party, in addition to Hap Arnold, was Col. George Marshall. Marx was delighted with these personable people and they with him and his lovely wife. He invited them all out to dinner, and thus was born enduring friendships.

Louis's loyalty to the generals of World War II was sincere. Louis was concerned that the great wartime heroes would be forgotten in peacetime and become financially feeble, in spite of their service to their country. Therefore, Louis took it upon himself to subsidize their finances in businesslike fashion. One example was his cosmetic company, called "Charmore," of which he made shares available to the generals at a nominal cost. Louis's generosity to children extended to the children of enlisted men, to whom he donated toys through the army posts.

DAVID MARX

Many believe it is doubtful that Louis Marx could have attained the success he did had he not had such a proficient, complementary, and loyal cohort accompanying him as he began his industrial journey. Louis and David worked as a symbiotic team.

At first *both* Louis and David went out to sell toys manufactured by others. As time passed, it became evident that Louis preferred to do the buying, negotiating, representing, and selling, while David would mind the "store," handling more of the administrative and detail work. David had an almost superhuman memory, with the ability to readily recall the names of customers and business contacts.

Charlene Marx, David's wife, once observed that Lou had the vision to see ten years ahead, while David had the practical capability to focus Louis's long-term vision on the reality of the moment. Sometimes the brothers were referred to in baseball terms (especially appropriate as David's skill and passion for the game made him consider turning professional at one point): Louis was like the famous Babe Ruth, the home-run star who took the bows; David paralleled the "Iron Horse" Lou Gehrig, a great steady player, in the game for the long haul.

In reality, the relationship between the brothers did not always function smoothly. But, despite their differences, Louis and David spent their lives working together without ever having a written contract. Although they sometimes shouted at each other in the privacy of their offices, Louis and David maintained proper decorum in public.

PLAYTHINGS January, 1930

LOUIS MARX & COMPANY
MANUFACTURERS OF
MECHANICAL TOYS
200 FIFTH AVENUE
NEW YORK

PATENT NOTICE ON TRACTION BELT TOYS

We hereby announce to the Trade that we have cured a license from the Wolverine Supply & Manufacturing Company under its Huth Patent #1,334,539 for which we are paying substantial royalties.

We are manufacturing and selling all of our Climbing Toys having Traction belts under this license.

Our customers of these toys are therefore protected under this patent.

We also announce that we have additional patents pending in the U. S. Patent Office on other features of these Climbing Traction Toys.

LOUIS MARX & COMPANY

David H. Marx
Sey

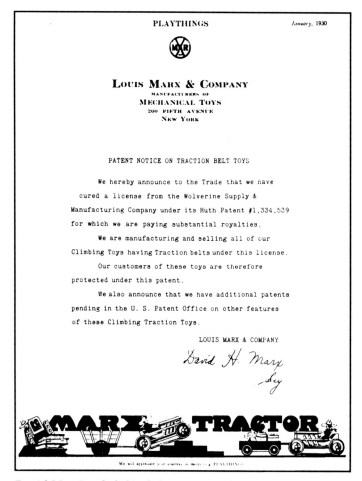

David Marx's role behind the scenes is shown in this page from the January 1930 Playthings.

While Louis eventually encircled the pre–jet set globe, visiting places like Japan, Hong Kong, and Wales, David's life evolved around Manhattan, New Jersey, and Palm Beach. David did not need the attention of national publications, nor the recognition of the masses, and he did not like to travel. David's son Charles, his wife, and former employees have stated that — as incredible as it may seem — David never even visited any of the factories, domestic or foreign, of which he shared ownership.

David often represented the company to the industry, and it was David who was perhaps more personally known throughout the Fifth Avenue Building, since he spent much of his time there orchestrating day-to-day events. He was held in such high esteem by his colleagues in the business community that, independent of his involvement in the Marx toy business, he was invited to join the advisory board of The Chemical Bank of New York.

When the brothers were in their twenties, Louis seemed more concerned with starting a family and settling down with his children, while David seemed more interested in spending his free time out on the town. It was David who often entertained important clients. Once again, the two provided an essential balance.

Remembered by some as a Damon Runyonesque character, David referred to himself as a "Gay Blade" and elegantly dressed the part. His top hat, tails, spats, and fancy walking stick made him look as though he had walked out of a Fred Astaire film. An integral part of New York café society, David, like Louis, became a regular visitor to "21", as well as to Toots Shor's and The Stork Club. His circle of personal friends included Georgie Jessel, Max Baer, Jack Haley, Hank Greenberg, Bugs Baer, Nelson Rockefeller, J. Edgar Hoover, and many others.

A young Ed Sullivan (of future television fame) put an end to David's bachelor years. A newspaper columnist whose job it was to know what was happening about town, Sullivan introduced David, on one auspicious day in 1934, to a pretty young singer from Fort Worth, Texas; she was half of a sister act performing at The Palace Theater. One glance at the striking Charlene Aber, then twenty-two, and the thirty-five-year-old David turned in his top hat.

Their marriage lasted over fifty years and produced four children: Charles, Marlene, Pamela, and Clara Lou. Charles, born March 17, 1936, was the only one of Louis's or David's children to join the Marx toy company.

When David retired, he spent the rest of his days in his Shrewsbury, New Jersey, mansion and Palm Beach winter home. He loved horse racing and had a farm in New Jersey, where he bred thoroughbreds; he raced them at nearby Monmouth Park racetrack. As befitting a true toy man, he died during the annual New York Toy Fair week in February 1985. Still in Louis's posthumous footsteps, David passed away at the same age as his deceased brother.

MEMORIES OF LOUIS MARX

Louis Marx influenced the lives of many people during his eighty-five-year lifetime, including both his personal and professional contacts. Their memories provide an interesting perspective on the industrialist.

Ann Eisenhower, granddaughter of the President, fondly remembers the little old guy who would come to the White House at Christmas to bring toys to her and her brother, David. She recalls that Louis was very friendly with her grandfather, who held the toy wizard in high esteem.

One of Louis Marx & Company's longtime employees from the Golden Era recalls: "Louis Marx was never wrong! Impossible as it may seem, the man had an uncanny ability to look at a new toy or invention and predict with reasonable certainty its degree of success. He would dictate a memo into the file so that it would memorialize his prediction in writing. Therefore, once the product proved its success or failure, anyone could always take the memo labeled 'pre-product' to prove his accuracy." Skeptics of this remarkable ability have suggested that Marx actually would dictate two memos, one predicting failure, one success, so that he could not miss.

Pedro Diaz-Barreiro, son of Mexican Marx partner Manolo Diaz-Barreiro, recalls: "I remember Louis Marx visiting Mexico when we built the new plant in the late 1960s. He stayed in our home. I remember him as an intelligent, generous man who liked to bet at the horse races. He was aggressive and persistent. He always lived like a king, and was obsessed with his family." Louis's family was not his only obsession. According to Diaz-Barreiro (and industry consensus in general), Louis was a workaholic — work was his hobby.

Mickey Denmark, founder and president of Plastic Toy & Novelty Corp., one of the most stable and reliable postwar toy companies, once spotted Louis Marx at the Nuremberg airport. Denmark decided to approach Marx, whom he had never met.

"Hello, Mr. Marx. I just want to shake your hand," proudly spoke the six-foot two-inch, strong, handsome, Dean Martinesque man from Brooklyn.

"Hi," responded Louis. "What is your name?"

"Mickey Denmark," he replied.

"Oh, of Plastic Toy!" affirmed Marx.

About twenty years after the incident, Denmark recalls that Louis's recognition made him feel about ten feet tall: "The Toy King himself knew who I was!" Louis Marx was nobody's fool — he knew his competition.

Another of the old-timers, Les Berger of Cardinal Industries, reminisced and remarked: "Marx built the best molds, and made the best-quality toys."

One of the owners of a major United States toy factory and an industry kingpin (who wishes to remain anonymous), had a different perspective. He once said: "The only man in the entire industry that I am afraid of is Louis Marx." These industry fears were well-founded.

In 1967, after spending the better part of a year and a fortune to purchase the rights from the British inventor, and to design and develop it, Kenner was about to come out with a new toy, the Spirograph. Joseph Steiner, one of the owners of Kenner Toys, flew to England to secure the rights. Somehow, Louis Marx got his hands on a sample. Within days of Kenner's launch of the Spirograph, Marx came out with a nearly exact duplicate — the "Design-O-Marx."

Kenner sued and obtained an injunction to keep Marx from manufacturing his Spirograph look-alike for seventeen years (the life-span of a patent).[13] The #100 Design-O-Marx mold sat on the shelf at the Girard plant from 1968 until 1983. After acquiring the Marx molds in 1982, American Plastic leased the use of the mold to foreign markets not covered by U.S. patent laws. After Kenner's patent expired in 1984, American Plastic leased the use of the mold to Toy Biz, which updated the product and called the result Design-A-Graph. Today it continues as a solid seller. Louis knew a good product when he saw it.

It was said by more than one competitor that Louis was ruthless, notorious; nothing would stop him. One anonymous competitor has said: "When Marx had a good product, which was not an unusual situation, they would protect it by every legal means possible — patent, trademark, copyright, secrecy until the very last second. Then they'd price it very low, with very high quality and a strong product line, making it difficult for others to penetrate their market. If anyone would dare to copy them, Marx would talk down the 'miserable copy.' On the other hand, however, whenever someone else had a good idea, Marx would not even blink before offering a similar but improved product. 'That's good old American competition,' he'd say."

One example of the Marx approach to competition is the story of how Mattel, rapidly growing on the success of Barbie and Hot Wheels by the early 1960s, came out with the "Va-Room." This was a plastic housing in the shape of a motor that would be attached to a bicycle; pushing down a lever would activate an internal flywheel device, which would simulate the roar of a motor. The Va-Room was an instant smash success.

Mattel had avoided exposure of the motor very successfully in this country before the Toy Fair of 1964. However, their French outlet showed a sample at their fair in Lyon, France, in February of that year. Covering the European fairs were Louis Marx; Ralph Leonardson, top toy buyer at Sears, and George Alley, his assistant buyer; Charlie King, the Marx mail order salesman, a humorous man and son of one of Marx's show business friends, musical comedy star of the 1920s and 1930s Charles King; and Ray Lohr, Marx's chief designer and today head of his own design firm. Ray Lohr has shared his recollections of what happened next.

All five men got a look at the item without letting on who they were. All thought it would sell. The next evening, over dinner at the famous Tour d'Argent restaurant in Paris, the designer remarked that such a motor was no big technical problem, that Marx could produce an equivalent item to retail for $3.98, well under the price charged by Mattel, which was burdened by TV advertising costs.[14] There would be no patent problem since a similar motor noise had been made for another model. Marx used a different mechanism. Mattel's was mechanical, the Marx version was battery-operated and motorized.

"For heaven's sake, get going, let's make it. Get back early. I'll phone Dave and tell him we'll have one to sell," was Louis Marx's immediate comment. Charlie King and George Alley immediately began to plan on how many Sears would take, with their order the first to be filled.

The engineer had a model ready within a week and was struck by the beatific smile on the face of David Marx when it was delivered into his hands in New York. The development and tooling departments were well enough organized to refine the item, produce samples, tool it, and get production started in August. A very efficient production line, designed and owned by Cliff Scantlebury, a former Marx engineer, was able to deliver 1,700,000 motors before Christmas at a maximum daily rate of 27,000 pieces from the five sets of duplicate, multiple cavity molds. (For a description of the molding process, see Chapter Three.) Cost was about $1.00, and the item wholesaled for about $1.90.

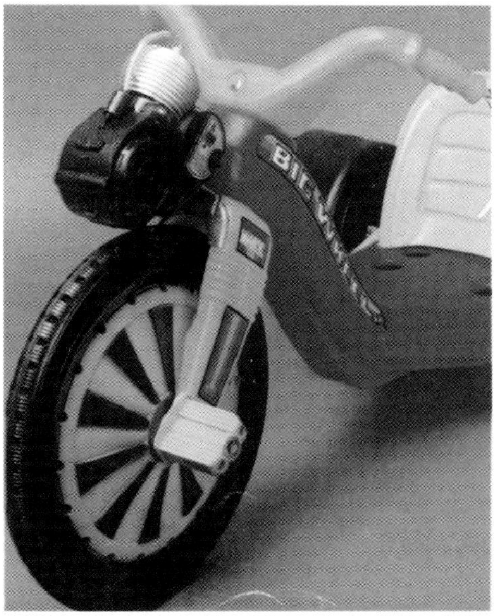

Two D batteries and the Big Wheel acquires big sound from the Za-Zoom motor.

The Sears order was 250,000, of which they sold all but about 10,000. Marx took these back the next year — an indication of how closely and considerately he worked with customers.

The Va-Room and the Marx Za-Zoom motors did not sell well after the first year. Marx also rushed into production a noisemaking dump truck, lawn mower, vacuum cleaner, and motorcycle, and Charlie King, pained by all the roaring in the office, suggested that the big hit for 1966 be "Toys With Silence!"

Mattel later sued Marx for unfair competition but got nowhere except an agreement to change the Za-Zoom name a bit. They could not prove monetary damages, as they had to admit to selling all they could make, as did Marx in 1964.

Mattel executives were later heard to express amazement at the fast competition. It illustrated the effectiveness of Marx's intimate control and fast decisions over the design and the production of the line.

EPILOGUE

The personal story of Louis Marx ended on February 5, 1982, when he died at White Plains Hospital in Westchester County, New York. Ten years earlier Louis and David had sold Louis Marx & Co., Inc. to Quaker Oats for $52 million. After his death, Louis's Scarsdale mansion was sold and the property developed into a housing project known as "Marx Estates." The man behind the company is gone — but his legacy lives on.

Old Marx toys have survived in the loving hands of collectors, and new Marx toys are now being manufactured. The following chapters provide more background on the evolution of the Marx firm, its fate after the sale to Quaker, its processes and marketing efforts, and the current plans of American Plastic Equipment, Inc., which owns most of the Marx molds. The book then turns to detailed descriptions of the Western Playsets — one aspect of the Marx contribution to the pleasure of millions.

NOTES

1. "Louis Marx: Toy King," *Fortune*, January 1946, p. 127.
2. Maxine A. Pinsky, *Greenberg's Guide to Marx Toys,* Vol. I (Sykesville, Md.: Greenberg Publishing Company, Inc., 1988), p. 11. [Author's note: All of my attempts to locate other sources to verify Louis Marx's military history resulted in dead-ends. Information included in this book about his time in the Army is based on M. A. Pinsky's research. J. H.]
3. "The Little King," *Time*, December 12, 1955, p. 96.
4. "Louis Marx: Toy King," p. 127.
5. Eric J. Matzke, *Greenberg's Guide to Marx Trains*, Vol. I. (Sykesville, Md.: Greenberg Publishing, 1989), p. 7.
6. "Louis Marx: Toy King," pp. 127, 163.
7. A full account of Henry Katz's career is provided by Albert W. McCollough, *The New Book of Buddy "L" Toys*, Vol. II. (Sykesville, Md.: Greenberg Publishing, 1991), p. 25ff.
8. Ibid, p. 125.
9. "Louis Marx: Toy King," p. 122.
10. "Louis Marx: Toy King," p. 164.
11. "The Money Men; Dan Lufkin's Partner — Whatsisname?" *Forbes*, April 1, 1974, p. 58.
12. "The Little King," p. 92.
13. Denys Fisher (Spirograph) Limited et al. v. Louis Marx & Co. of W. Va., Inc., No. 68-6-W was decided December 4, 1969 in a West Virginia District Court.
14. The author remembers the retail price as $2.98.

CHAPTER TWO

LOUIS MARX & CO., INC.

As Chapter One focused on the men who founded the firm, this chapter chronicles the evolution of "the world's largest toy manufacturer" in terms of its business philosophies and operations and the teamwork within the organization. In order to graduate from an individual-based company to a dynamic corporate organization, a truly wise businessman must realize that, like the leader of an orchestra, he cannot play all of the instruments simultaneously and therefore must seek additional talent. Louis Marx obviously sought and harnessed such talent.

EARLY EXPANSION

Quickly and decisively formed, Louis and David's strategies were remarkably successful. As the company developed, it moved steadily from repping and contracting to manufacturing. Marx brought Archie B. Marcus on board in the 1920s as the company's accountant. He was a driven, hard-nosed, detail- and organization-oriented administrator — exactly what the two brothers needed. As business increased, so did Marcus's responsibilities. He implemented operational systems that were so complete and coherent, they set the foundation for the development of the Marx empire. It was the inclusion of Archie Marcus into what would be a "royal triumvirate" of management that allowed the company to grow and prosper economically.

Part of the expansion mode enjoyed by the company as early as the 1920s was the start by Louis and David of a separate company, Jaymar Specialty Company, named for their father, Jacob Marx. Jaymar's cardboard and wooden toys were compatible and non-competitive with the Marx company's own metal mechanical line. Jacob's eldest daughter, Rose, and her husband, Mickey Borden, eventually ran the business. Dorothy, their daughter, later married Ralph Kaufman, who operated Jaymar until early 1992. (Jaymar had been in the Borden-Kaufman family until 1990 when it was sold.)

By the mid-1930s, Louis Marx & Company manufactured nearly all of the firm's products at its own facilities. Louis had discovered that the industrial services (such as supplying of components from color separations to wire parts) he needed were not always readily available from other manufacturers. Marx strove to become self-sufficient, often producing all the parts needed for a given toy. As the company became more aggressive in pioneering new production techniques, it became economically sound and dependable, which was vital to creating and controlling virtually all of its component and assembly production processes. In-house production afforded tighter management, on-time delivery, quality control, and rigid security. Soon the company made everything it needed, except for the raw materials and certain standard parts such as rivets and screws, which were then purchased.

These 1937 photographs, provided by William Kalsch, bring us inside the Louis Marx & Company operation. Beside a lithography machine at Erie, Pennsylvania, are employees Roy Hitchcock, William Kalsch, Jack Quirk, and Andy and Nick Marchionna; also shown, an unusual pause in the assembly line, which was in Marx factories typically female-staffed (these women are working on the Honeymoon Express).

DOMESTIC ACQUISITIONS

Erie, Pennsylvania

Louis Marx built on his earlier relationship with the C. E. Carter Company by purchasing and incorporating it under the name of "Louis Marx & Company, Inc., of Pennsylvania" in September 1933. This first Louis Marx & Company subsidiary began with an authorized capital of $250,000. In October 1935 Marx purchased the plant of the defunct Eriez Stove Company, further expanding its Erie-based operation.[1] The Erie plant specialized in metal toys like the Climbing Monkey and various wind-up vehicles, with a big line of climbing tractors. The local people called the plant "The Monkey Works."

Glendale, West Virginia

With an authorized capital of two hundred shares of common stock of no par value, "Louis Marx & Company of West Virginia" was chartered in December 1933. This subsidiary leased and later purchased the Fokker aircraft plant at Glendale and acquired a warehouse a mile or so away at McMechen, West Virginia.[2] The Fokker plant was a huge building with inside rail siding to accommodate a number of railroad cars. Each plant specialized in certain products or lines, and this was the plant that produced playsets, as you will see from the reproductions of Glendale factory documentation in Chapter Four.

Girard, Pennsylvania

Marx also built on its relationship with Girard Model Works. Louis, a passive stockholder of GMW until the owner sold out to local people in 1934, eventually gained control as its largest stockholder. In February 1935 Louis Marx & Company established "The Girard Manufacturing Company" as its train manufacturing site, with an authorized capital of $300,000. This third Marx subsidiary was located about twenty miles from its Erie operations.

As Marx grew, it relied heavily on Girard's excellent "GMW paper" for drafting. In fact, throughout the years, all of the Louis Marx & Company drafting plans carried the insignia "Girard Model Works," until Quaker Oats bought the company and labeled the paper "Marx Toys."

To keep the creative competitive edge, each plant employed its own staff with a well-financed research and development division to design new and better toys. Marx maintained research and development divisions of about thirty people at Girard, sixty at Erie, and twenty-five at Glendale. The Erie division department, which in 1974 included about four draftsmen, thirty-five model makers, and sixteen artists, headed by Ray Lohr, provided much of the toy development work for the entire Marx company and all its affiliates.

Each of the plants — Erie, Girard, and Glendale — had its own systems of organization. This diversity fostered a competition for excellence among the Marx facilities. Even some of the specification sheets, which listed the essential materials to produce a toy, were different at each plant.

Each plant bought its own supplies and managed its own budget. Until the 1950s there was no central purchasing office for the Marx company, which might have bought steel, for example, in bulk quantity for all of the plants. It was not until the conversion to plastics that a centralized purchasing office was established to supply plastics to all the plants.

GOING INTERNATIONAL

Marx's business strategies had led to success and kept company costs down and profits up. As early as the mid-1930s, Louis looked to duplicate abroad the business practices that had proved successful in the United States.

Louis Marx & Company entered foreign manufacture of toy trains with the acquisition of a British plant at Swansea, Wales. Employees of the Girard, Pennsylvania plant reported that electric motors, transformer windings, laminated cores, and control slide mechanisms were shipped to Marx, Ltd. in large lots — as many as 35,000 per shipment. Although the British plant could produce a handsome lithographed train, it still depended on the technical competence of the Girard plant to provide the high-quality motor mechanisms. Marx, Ltd. was the first of many equally successful international operations for Marx.

Archie Marcus, in charge of all systems and controls, oversaw and regularly visited the three main domestic plants. And once Marx acquired or built a foreign operation, Archie Marcus, Vice President for Administration, took over. He regularly visited all subsidiaries and joint-venture locales, traveling constantly. Often the licensees came to New York to consult with Marcus. Marcus's dedication and knowledge helped propel the Marx enterprises toward its extraordinary success.

Marcus also oversaw the shipping of parts and components, such as the practice of sending motors and transformers made in the United States to England or Mexico. This practice of supplying strategic components of high value versus low cubic volume gave Marx complete international control.

By the close of the 1930s, Louis Marx & Company had grown from two young men in a small office to a mature manufacturing company with several thousand employees, three domestic and one foreign manufacturing plants, a nationally known reputation, and a strong and consistent customer base. All of these factors helped it emerge from the 1930s as the world's largest manufacturer of toys!

SOUND BUSINESS STRATEGIES

The success of Marx toys was in large part due to its strong founding managers. Louis and David were not men to stand on ceremony or issue titles. While there never was any doubt that Louis Marx was the ultimate authority, the entire operation was run by the triumvirate. Like the legs of a tripod, it provided perfect balance. Louis was the catalyst, the creative genius responsible for direction, policy making, sales, and marketing who spent much of his time traveling. David was the director, the administrative day-to-day boss who rarely left the floor. Archie Marcus was the iron-fisted controller, a professional accountant who oversaw all operations, including foreign. They achieved the ultimate balance of power.

Later on, the three men were joined by George Dessler, considered by Louis Marx the best salesman in the business, who relieved Louis's shoulders of part of the sales burden. Dessler was a delightful, congenial man beloved by everyone. His stock in trade was a deep roaring laugh, which when in full throttle would set the crowd to joining the uproar.

The company's early-established efficient bare-bones structure set the pattern for the decades that followed. It is widely believed that one of the major flaws committed by Quaker Oats when it acquired Marx Toys was to replace a few reasonably paid, hard-working, loyal, long-term employees with many highly paid, detached, although well-educated executives, who had little or no practical experience, knowledge, or commitment to the toy business.

For example, Louis and David wisely knew that their buyers were simply grown-up kids who ought to have a chance to see and play with the toys they were about to buy in quantity. So, the company's showroom was filled with demonstration tables. For entertainment purposes, Marx used one of the round tables in the showroom at the Fifth Avenue Building. People could walk up, swing a ball in a circular motion, and attempt to have it stop at a particular spot on a raised metal base with a hole in the center. Called Roll Ball, it was based on an ancient game. Executives and clients would play and bet at it. It was a very popular feature of a trip to Marx. Why Marx never produced it as a game remains a good question. The old-time buyers and employees fondly remember it to this day!

The underside of one of these cars reveals the Marx reuse of scrap metal. T. Riley Collection.

Louis Marx's personality drove him to excel. Anything less than number one was unacceptable. In spite of such ambition, many buyers considered Louis an extremely fair man. After all, he made toys better and more affordable than anyone else. Louis used the economy of scale, providing a better product to a much larger segment of the market.

Two basic policies were instilled from the beginning at the Louis Marx & Company: "Give the customer more toy for less money," and "Quality is not negotiable." Louis and David worked long, hard days and nights to turn these policies into realities, setting an example for their staff and the entire industry.

Apart from a few of the original wooden toys, the material used throughout the 1920s and 1930s was metal — especially lithographed steel. To help keep prices down, Marx often designed its products to use "litho rejects" from other companies. This was a relatively standard procedure. It frequently happened that steel litho that had been prepared for use on other products, such as cookie tins, had printing on it that was stamped incorrectly — and was therefore rejected. The material was still of high quality and could be lithographed or printed on the reverse side; the first printing would not be seen since it faced inward in the new product.

This was a standard Marx cost-cutting procedure. Litho rejects in no way defaced or lowered the quality of the product, and represented a saving on material costs. The use of this procedure was discovered through the study of collector train products and was discussed in an article by Jim Flynn in the August 1990 issue of *Classic Toy Trains*, which has stimulated the interest of many novelty collectors.

Quality was always the top priority at Marx, a factor easily verified by the multitude of undamaged Marx toys still available throughout the collector world today. After surviving several years of children's hard play abuse and a half-century of storage and unpredictable handling, a Marx mechanical toy can often be wound up and seem to work like new! This is quite an accomplishment in today's world of planned obsolescence.

Besides assuring quality, the complete in-house Marx operation of the 1930s, which allowed it to make sub-assembly or component parts for a fraction of what they would have cost if purchased outside, was another means of achieving high value at low cost. The Marx company limited its outside purchases to raw materials where production process was patented or cost-effective.

To achieve even higher profitability, the Marx company used what we shall call the "elimination of the compound reserve." Briefly, Marx's cost analysis process identified how various component manufacturers, assemblers, and other suppliers increased the *actual hard cost* of a product at each stage of manufacture by calculating their markups on the basis of the previous supplier's price to them — and it then eliminated these increases.

For example, the *hard cost* of a component is increased when the component manufacturer adds on a percentage for overhead, profit, and other factors. The component manufacturer then arrives at a *selling price*, which may be then increased by adding a sales commission or a finance percentage. The component producer's *full price* to the assembler then becomes the assembler's *hard cost* of the component. The assembler then adds his own costs to cover his overhead, profit, commissions, etc., and arrives at a *real cost*. And then packaging, marketing, advertising, distribution, sales commissions, and other expenses are added. Eventually, the assembler arrives at a *full sales price* for the manufacturer, who in turn adds his margins and sells to the wholesaler, who adds his overhead and profit margins. Finally, the retailer adds a healthy markup to cover his overhead and profit (if any). The consumer then purchases the product at the fair competitive *retail price*.

The economic reality of the toy business in the 1930s was that, due to these compounded and multiple factors, a toy with a hard cost of $.10 might have retailed for $1.00! However, at the Louis Marx & Company of the 1930s, a toy with an original hard cost of $.10 sold to a distributor for about $.15, and retailed for about $.19. This was possible because Marx did it all; the middlemen and their layers of overhead and profit were eliminated, leaving only the producer and the retail outlet.

Low overhead, direct cost, high quality, and high value were among Marx's mottos. Furthermore, since David and Louis did not believe in large advertising budgets during those early years, little money was spent on promotion. The company's reputation for quality sold the products.

The last public balance sheet of the parent company, Louis Marx & Co., Inc., for the year ending December 31, 1937, appeared as a consolidated statement about the company and its three U. S. subsidiaries. Current assets: $3,218,428; current debt: $524,358; tangible net worth: over $2 million. According to the statement, the cash value alone exceeded the firm's liabilities — an amazing feat when one considers that these were Depression-era figures. Louis Marx & Co., Inc. owned practically all of the stock of its foreign and domestic subsidiaries.

Communication was fundamental to Louis and David's management of the many Marx locations. Although the company's factories were located in Pennsylvania and West Virginia, Louis directed their daily operation by letter and telephone from his Fifth Avenue office in New York City. He kept a twenty-four-hour hotline open to the factories. It has been reported that Louis visited the three main plants annually in February; however, employees state that they rarely, if ever, saw him. Nonetheless, Louis and David were extremely well informed of their operations and kept abreast of new toy possibilities and potential markets. Archie Marcus, Marx's business manager and controller, helped make this possible through his regular visits.

Marx made the maintenance of safe and efficient factory equipment a top priority. For example, even the punch press, which stamped out and formed the toy parts, had safety guards that knocked an operator's hand out of the way if he or she inadvertently left it in the impact area when the press was cycling. While the original presses at Glendale did not have this feature, it was added on in response to employee suggestions. It is interesting to note that much of the safety equipment was also designed at Marx. Hence, Marx was independently and voluntarily safety-conscious on its own long before the advent of the Occupational Safety and Health Administration (OSHA). Incidentally, this would help to avoid unexpected liability costs that undoubtedly would have arisen had the company not had this foresight.

Another key to success was that Marx never borrowed money for expansion and tooling (or any other reason), but preferred to finance investments from its own capital. This afforded the company more flexibility without the cost of interest and the time delays and other obligations inherent in borrowing. Moreover, it enabled the Marx factories to automate — and thereby

A 1929 Montgomery Wards catalog ad

run more smoothly and produce more toys faster and at less expense.

Time magazine reported: "Since most toy makers . . . copy their competitors' products, new toys are as elaborately guarded and as inevitably filched as Detroit's new car designs."[3] Infamous for copying the designs of competitors' successful products, Marx was always careful to distinguish between patent infringement (or violation) and toy piracy, the difference being whether or not one got away with it! The former could cost the violator hundreds of thousands of dollars (in 1945); the latter could net a company twice that.

The trick was to alter a competitor's successful design just enough to avoid infringement. The Marx company was a master of modification. Marx's secret was that not only was the design altered, but small improvements were made. This gave the company a double edge: it sold an improved version of a product consumers already wanted; and it avoided the initial expense of research, development, and marketing. Marx then tripled its advantage by offering the product at a reduced price.

High volume was Marx's strongest competitive edge. Ninety percent of its products were sold to the large chain stores and mail-order houses. The remaining 10 percent was sold to distributors who supplied the smaller retailers, such as novelty and book stores. Marx recognized that the high volumes of each order helped keep the price down; cut distributor, marketing, and sales costs; and permit it to give more toy for the price.

When roller skates retailed at $2.50 per pair, the Marx company mass-produced ball-bearing skates that retailed at $1.00. Taking the concept even further, it later made plain-bearing skates available for $.50 per pair. As with the roller skates, the Marx company was able to mass-produce model railroads at a much lower cost; prior to the 1930s, toy trains were a fairly expensive and exclusive product.

The company also optimized its production by shipping the dies for staple items to its factories in Great Britain, running off thousands of units for sale in the commonwealth before shipping the dies back to the States to resume production for the market year. Similarly, it was expedient to keep the dies for novelty items here until the American fad had passed, and then send them to Europe to supply a new market. This eliminated the high cost of shipping finished goods and the expense of tariffs.

Always attuned to every opportunity that would give him the competitive edge, Louis often purchased the companies that provided him services, thus turning the expenditure of one division into the income of another. Sometimes he purchased a company for no other reason than to remove from the market a competitor such as the Unique Art Manufacturing Company, which made mechanical toys similar to Marx's Lincoln Tunnel. His purchase of Wyandotte tools and dies and Lojo Trucks were other examples.

Louis Marx was to toys what Henry Ford was to cars. At a time when automobiles were made almost entirely by hand, one-by-one, at a cost of thousands of dollars each, Ford introduced the "Model T." He mass-produced it by the millions, retailing it at about one-tenth the cost of the then-typical car (in the neighborhood of $7000); Ford offered cars that ranged from $395 to $795. No wonder Louis became known as "The Henry Ford of the Toy Industry." Louis Marx espoused principles that continue to make for sound business strategies today.

SALES AND MARKETING

One of the mightiest sales boosts for the company came in 1924 when Sears, Roebuck & Co., the largest American mail-order house, began regularly cataloging Marx toys and became one of the principal Marx accounts. Soon other mail-order houses picked up the

Marx line. The large-volume buyers appreciated the opportunity to customize and order their own individual sets. Playsets especially lent themselves to this concept. A creative customer could practically design his own playset.

By the early 1950s, the large chain stores such as Sears, Montgomery Ward, J. C. Penney, Macy's, and Woolworth sold 90 percent of Marx's United States production. Marx's toy trains were often transported to their distributors on real trains, and were often sold in carload lots.

The post–World War II years represented a revitalization of American industries. It was a period that saw the great expansion into world empire building, with the industrialization of Japan, Hong Kong, Mexico, and England; the introduction of television and its implications for promotion; the advent of plastic and its production opportunities; and ultimately the rise of global marketing.

At this time C. E. (Ed) Hjelte was hired away from an important post with the Abraham & Straus department stores to be head of marketing for Marx. This was viewed as quite a coup, and the personable and talented Hjelte went on to prove his merit through his significant contributions to the growth of Marx after World War II. Among those reporting to him were chief designer Ray Lohr; Francis (Frank) Rice, who was in charge of playsets; C. W. (Chip) Martin; Bud Bedell; Walter Nisperly; Harold (Bucky) Livingston; and, later, Al Bagg.

While at A & S, Hjelte became famous for his many successful promotions, especially a fall promotion of a doll and carriage at a sensational price. Upon joining Marx, he worked to redirect the firm from a merchandising orientation toward boys to one that included girls' items. Frank Rice remembers the fabulous introduction of a dollhouse at an amazing price; it "set the stage." Marx was given the back page of the Sears Christmas catalog, traditionally reserved for a fruit cake, and through the complete cooperation and efforts of Sears buyer Ralph Leonardson, Louis Marx & Company had a smash. Mr. Leonardson had underestimated the sales potential, but in backing him up, at considerable expense, to meet his orders, Louis Marx and Ed Hjelte helped build the reputation of Marx as a supplier which could be trusted to deliver on promise. The happy relationship with Sears opened the door to a whole new line of mail-order merchandise — especially playsets. (The playset saga will be told more fully in Chapters Three and Four.)

Appreciating that Marx had provided them with a major hit, Sears placed early, guaranteed purchase orders, which always carry weight with a manufacturer. One of the main problems inherent in the toy business is its seasonal nature. Manufacturers work all year long to produce toys that sell during the few weeks before Christmas. In the early years, Marx curtailed production between January and April, practically shutting down operations during these months. Although by the mid-1920s Louis Marx & Company was known throughout the United States, it was not until the late 1940s, when Marx was a world-wide name, that the sales volume warranted continuous year-round production. It is likely that almost every child growing up in the United States, Great Britain, or Canada during these years had at least one Marx toy. Despite occasional problems with labor or material, Marx never left the customer — wholesale or retail — stranded.

In 1955, for the first time in history, more than $1 billion worth of toys were sold in the United States. According to *Time* magazine, "since 1919, when 644 domestic toy makers produced goods with a retail value of $150 million, U. S. toydom has grown to include some 2,000 manufacturers."[4] As a point of comparison, it took another decade for industry-wide sales to reach $2 billion. And at the time of this writing, 1992, industry-wide sales are reported to be approximately $14 billion. There are even a few individual companies whose sales surpass $1 billion yearly.

Louis Marx & Company reported in 1955 that it would gross more than $50 million, net $5 million, and produce 10 percent of all toys sold in the United States.[5] These figures did not include income from foreign operations, such as the one in Mexico, which at that time was reported as the most profitable. The firm's product lines at that time included almost every type of toy imaginable, except bicycles and dolls (it later did experiment with plastic bicycles and at least two types of dolls).

Citing the Marx company business statistics for 1955, *Time* magazine included, apart from the U. S. factories:

Foreign Subsidiaries:
- 1 wholly-owned British
- 1 wholly-owned Canadian

Foreign Manufacturing Interests:

Germany	Japan
France	Australia
Mexico	Brazil
South Africa	

Employees:
- 8,000 U. S. (peak)[6]

By the 1960s, Marx toys were globally manufactured and marketed, and had become a household name. Marx had reached the pinnacle. There was nowhere else to go. Louis was in his sixties, a mature and accomplished self-made success.

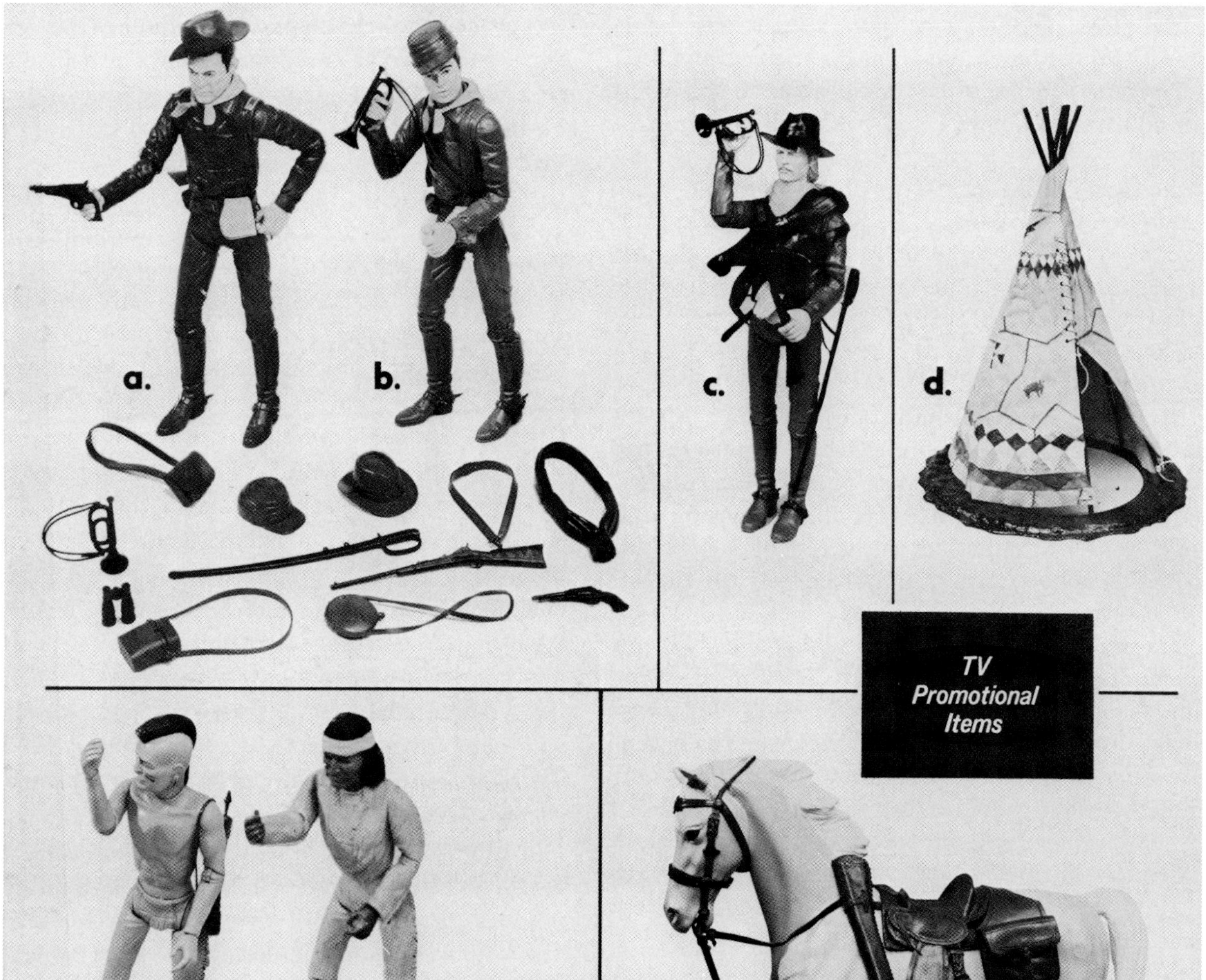

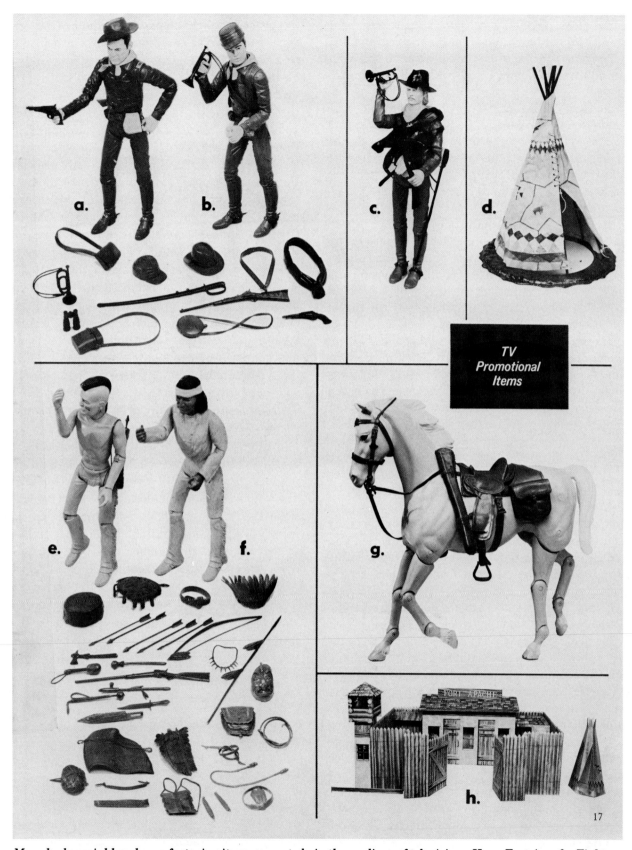

Marx had special brochures featuring items promoted via the medium of television. Here, Fort Apache Fighters: a. #1865: Captain Tom Maddox; b. #1862: Zeb Zachary; c. #1866: General Custer; d. #1867: Fighting Indian's Tepee; e. #1864: "Fighting Eagle"; f. #1863: "Fighting Geronimo"; g. #1861B: "Commanche"; h. #1875: Fort Apache.

Changing Promotional Philosophies

Marx did not need to employ salespeople to seek new business in the early years — the large retailers such as Bernard Gimbel came to Marx. Louis often traveled with certain buyers, like his close friend Bernie, in search of new products to develop. Often, before Louis had contacted his designers with a new toy idea, he had a buyer with an advance order.

Louis often boasted that the quality of his products let the toys sell themselves. While the younger, smaller companies began to invest heavily in advertising, national news media carried statements like: "Toycoon Marx is his own walking ad agency; he spent only $312 for advertising in 1955."[7] Why should he spend money on promotion when he had his sales in his hip pocket?

On the average, Marx rarely spent over $2,500 a year for advertising.[8] Marx's meager salesforce and advertising approach worked well in the 1920s, when the company was small; in the 1930s, when personal service was at a premium; in the 1940s, because of the war; and in the 1950s, with the influx of new money and opening of new markets. The popularity of Marx Toys during this period is illustrated by the following. One October in the late 1950s, there was a fire in the Glendale, West Virginia plant. It came at the peak of the Christmas shipping season. Marx toys were in such great demand that the customers said they would take the orders *whenever* available (even in January)!

But by the 1960s, advertising — especially television commercials — became instrumental to mass promotion. Marx could no longer afford to depend on its momentum of success alone for new business, in light of the late-1950s advertising craze that spawned mega-sales for upstarts. Mattel and Remco doubled and tripled their sales, eroding the Marx-dominated market.

The 1950s represented a time of change. Where the Marx company continued to stress emphasis on individual one-time-sale products, other companies forged ahead with "concept marketing." New products encouraged the desire in children to collect the relatives, friends, and accessories for toys like Barbie and G. I. Joe. Meanwhile, Marx continued to rely heavily on its past successful standard products — which had served it so well during the 1930s, 1940s, and 1950s — although it was introducing new items.

As television promotion gained popularity, many toy companies devoted as much as fifteen seconds of a one-minute commercial to identifying the company name in the hope of fostering brand recognition. Many of the companies came up with their slogans and jingles at that time. Mattel not only sponsored commercials during the Mickey Mouse Club show but also sought the use of its products on the show. Firm believers in the tried-and-true methods of what seemed a perpetual moneymaking machine, David and Louis were slow to accept the need for expensive television advertising and were not convinced that television advertising could produce enough profit to offset its cost. But during the 1960s, a team of Marx executives — including Hjelte, Edward Kelly, who became sales manager when George Dessler retired, and David Marx — brought their collective business and production experience together in a team to deal with the television issue. The Ted Bates advertising agency was hired and "Magic Marxie" was created. A pixie character, he proudly chanted:

"Make sure you get the very best
Look for the letters on my chest
M-A-R-X,
Magic Marxie!"

The first few years of television advertising were not successful for the Marx company. "The Train with the Brain" was the first of seven forgettable early promotions. (This concept has since been exploited by another toy company; apparently it was ahead of its time.) Eventually, Marx became effective at promoting toys on television, and its catalogs highlighted items promoted on TV (see the illustration opposite).

Crammed into one-action-packed-minute color TV commercial in the 1960s were series such as the one shown on the preceding page, Fort Apache Fighters, which had proven retail success. The illustration displays fully articulated figures that were packed along with accessories in a lithographed full-color box.

Even though Louis Marx & Company was still the industry leader in the early 1960s — the world's largest toy manufacturer — its influence began to wane. Newer, younger companies increased their market share with each passing month. Although the Marx company's reputation for quality and value still turned decent profits for the company, and the major toy buyers still came directly to Marx to place their orders, Mattel, Remco, and Topper were growing. Ideal Toys, even older than Marx, was able to pass from generation to generation. However, Louis was not entirely willing or able to pass this company on to a new generation.

Marx's past policy regarding the hiring of salespeople was eventually somewhat modernized, however. During the 1960s, the Marx company also changed its policy regarding outside distributors. It opened the door to jobbers, including the New York firm of S. N. Horowitz & Son, Inc. (the author's grandfather and father). Marx developed a few little-known distributors in Texas, California, and New England. These independent companies were started by relatives and known internally as "captive jobbers." It has even been speculated that an off-shoot of one of these companies became Kay-Bee Distributors, a very large and successful toy retail chain today.

Some industry analysts have concluded that Louis Marx & Company simply lost its momentum in the

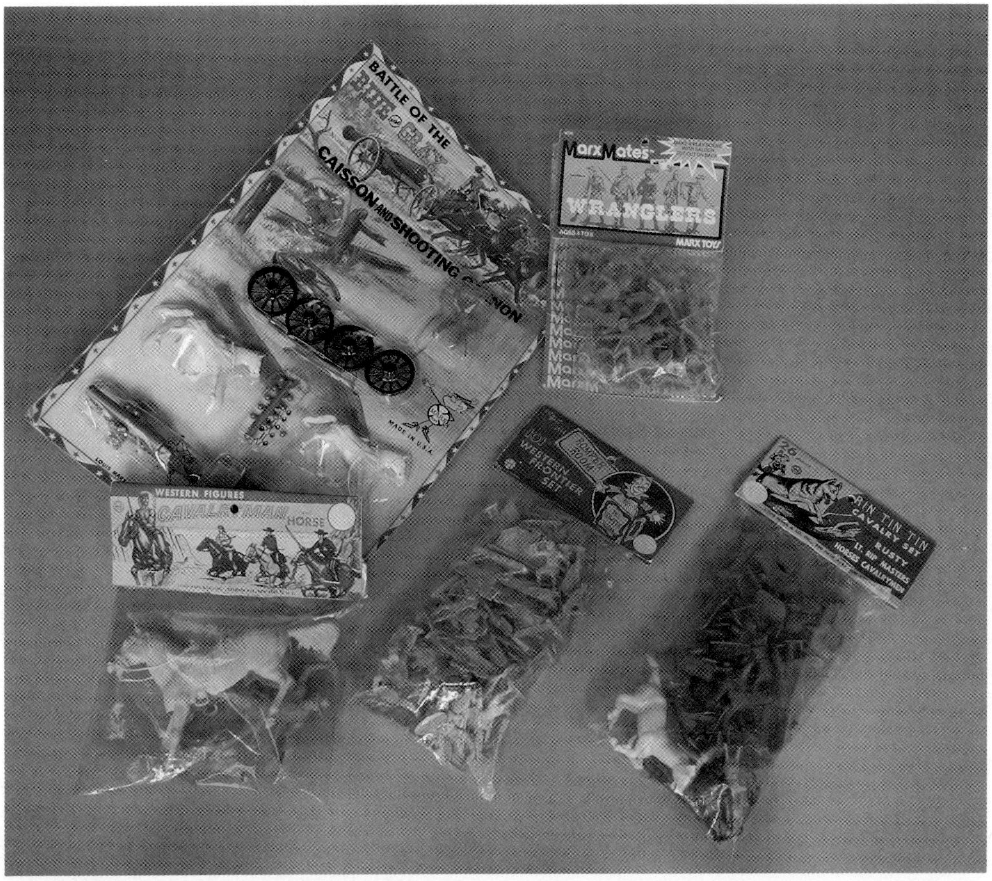

At the heart of the Marx product line were the finely crafted figures that were offered in a variety of boxed and bagged sets. Above, Gary J. Linden Collection; below, Don Faruolo Collection.

1960s. Others joked that aging, burned-out Marx officials attended toy shows only to copy the products they had seen. It seemed to many as though the company had lost its innovation, was slow to computerize, and moved too slowly in getting into television advertising, thereby missing an opportunity to secure a new identity that was cohesive with its established position.[9] Children of the 1960s and 1970s who grew up with television could easily blurt out names like Mattel and Kenner when asked about toys.

Marx never lost sales, nor did it become unprofitable. It simply stood still. The younger companies slowly eroded Marx's market share. In 1967 Mattel topped the $100 million sales mark, surpassing Marx to become the world's largest toy manufacturer in terms of dollars. Then the Big Wheel rolled in!

At age seventy-one, Louis sensed the dangers of the changing times: Mattel had been mortgaged and overextended in order to attain its position, setting the trend for a new and precarious era in the toy industry. In 1971 Louis commented that the published financial statements of a certain rival company could not possibly be accurate. Although everyone believed that he knew the business better than anyone else alive, many felt that the old man was consumed with jealousy due to the rival's advancing position. But sure enough, as the public record shows, company officers of Louis's rival — Mattel — were indicted a few years later for fraud, proving once again that Louis really did know the business.[10] Again, this old man's uncanny vision foresaw the plague of the 1970s and 1980s, where financially strong and well-established toy companies would begin to disappear, falling victim to a new era of big-time financial wheeling and dealing.

Although David and Louis attempted other types of business ventures, such as forming the Charmore cosmetic company, or manufacturing and distributing early ballpoint pens and plastic housewares, they always came back to what they knew best: toys.

THE PRODUCT LINE

Developing new and better toys was not only a challenge, but a high-priced risk. The cost of developing a new toy in the 1940s was as much as $100,000 to $150,000, which meant that poor decisions were costly. The Marx company would get ideas for new products from (1) facsimiles of real-life items; (2) competitors' successes; (3) old items they could redo, renew, redesign, and improve; (4) a few outside inventors; and (5) many employee suggestions. As mentioned earlier, an additional important source of ideas was Marx customers. This is apparent in the creation of playsets, which were often designed around the suggestions and requests of specific store chains. We will see documentation of this in Chapter Four; here we touch upon a few other toy lines significant in the history of Louis Marx & Company.

The Yo-Yo

Louis's vision enabled him to modify existing toys into new toys. He always asserted that there were no new ideas, only new twists on old toys. One of the most noteworthy such adaptations came in 1928, while observing Philippine children at play. Louis watched them whittle a block of wood into a hand-carved wooden disk. Closer inspection revealed that it was actually made of two carved wooden disks joined in the center by a wooden dowel. By wrapping a string around the dowel, the children twirled the wooden disks. The crude wooden toy impressed Louis. Eventually, he refined the concept and his company introduced the "Yo-Yo." It was a smash hit, eventually selling over 100 million units world-wide. *Time* magazine touted it as "the greatest idea in toydom's history."[11] Since that time, the Marx company always demonstrated an instinct for fad successes, although the brothers differed on this matter.

The argument between fast-and-furious hit products versus staple standard products often became a test of strength between Louis and David. Louis was always more in favor of fads. David preferred the staples. Playsets eventually came to be Marx staples; in the company's earlier years mechanical vehicles, trucks, guns, play kitchens, and even roller skates were among its staples. Louis said that a hit product could sell more in one year than the staple could in a lifetime. When successful, one hit product could provide greater profitability than a company's entire line. But, as David pointed out, risking the venture of an unsuccessful toy could jeopardize the very existence of a toy company. The annals of toy history are full of stories about companies who have either made their mark by the fortunes or been wiped out by the failures of a single product.

Although there is certainly merit to both Louis's and David's sides of the argument, this author believes the Marx company actually achieved the optimum situation: the lion's share of the Marx budget was devoted to offering a full range of standard, staple products such as playsets, which comprised most of the line and produced a conservative annual assurance of covering overhead as well as providing a reasonable return. A small percentage of the annual budget was set aside to develop and market the novelty hit (or miss) product. In the worst case, even if the promoted products were flops, the loss was measured and budgeted. However, a hit such as the Big Wheel would mean jackpot profits.

Throughout Louis's career, the Marx company was never at financial risk. The firm had already established a strong staple sales base before it considered investing in risky promotional products. Moreover, it minimized the risk by keeping its investments in fad-type products down.

It has been reported that, contrary to popular belief, Louis did not think of himself as imaginative; the company simply knew how to get extra mileage out of each product. Toys that flopped were face-lifted to toy history, as "last year's submarine became next year's rocket ship. . . . After a 25¢ truck had saturated the market in the mid-30s, Marx loaded it with plastic ice cubes (then a new product) and called it an ice truck."[12] The result — of an employee's suggestion — was another winner.

Another concept Marx used to get more mileage out of each product was to bring back or reintroduce old successful favorites after an absence from the market. After Louis Marx & Company's 1928 Yo-Yo fad had run its course, the company successfully reintroduced the Yo-Yo about every seven years. Louis discovered that each new generation of children would find it a novelty. The Marx company used this marketing recycling technique many times throughout the half-century it manufactured and marketed toys.

Big Wheel

In 1969 Marx's "Big Wheel" tricycle changed the course of toy history. Designed by Ray Lohr in Erie, it was the hit of the industry and carried the Marx company into and through the 1970s. The wheel-good business was never the same: the Big Wheel still sells out its inventory every year. Twenty-three years after its introduction, the Big Wheel remains the backbone of Empire Toys, which acquired the rights from Marx over twelve years ago as well as from American Plastic Equipment. The Big Wheel is now a staple and is counted among the ranks of the Cabbage Patch doll, Barbie, and the Hula Hoop as a classic.

Over the years, some of the most notable Marx toys, in addition to the Big Wheel, were Johnny West, Crazy Car, Marvel the Mustang, Tony the Pony, Rock-em Sock-em Robots, Big Bruiser, playsets such as Battleground and Fort Apache, dollhouses, service stations, trains, guns, the arcade shooting gallery, Magic Shot, a large line of plastic bagatelle games, the Za-Zoom motor, and of course the Yo-Yo!

Marx Trains

The history of toy lines other than the playsets is told in *Greenberg's Guide to Marx Toys,* volumes I and II (a third is forthcoming), and in *Greenberg's Guide to Marx Trains,* volumes I, II, and III. Let us share one memory of a former Marx employee here.

As mentioned earlier, George Dessler joined the Marx machine to handle sales. An enthusiastic, energetic man who loved toys, he took many of the daily demands off Louis's shoulders and personally helped develop many of the Marx products, especially trains. It was work he enjoyed, and it showed. Every year, George would don an engineer's cap and appear in the showroom, bearing miles of track, an assortment of the different stock cars, locomotives, various accessories, and a trainload of ideas. He would then spend weeks creating layouts, assembling unique components, designing new accessories, setting up and tearing down until he found just the right balance between product and price. If a product was selling well, he would leave it alone. If not, he would try to change it: add some figures, rearrange pieces, try new colors or graphics, maybe add a new name. Presto, a new item! Sometimes the challenge was to provide a specific customer with a new product at a designated target cost.

One Monday morning, Dessler came in with a set from the previous year's line. His mission was to modify it to create a new set, maintaining a certain price point. He took his seat, put on his engineer's cap, blew his train whistle, and proceeded to tear the layout apart — adding new components, removing other parts, and trading still others. He changed, deleted, embellished, and compressed. Every time he tried a new combination, the price came in too high or the product was flawed. He worked all week, stayed late each night, and continued through the weekend. As employees arrived at work the following Monday morning, they found a tired but triumphant George operating the new layout, wearing his cap, blowing his whistle, and behaving as boyishly enthusiastic as his waning energy level permitted. The ensuing conversation went something like this:

"What's up, George?" they asked.

"I got it!" he beamed. "The set is ready!"

"Good. Let's see."

The rest of the office proceeded to view George's masterpiece. He demonstrated the set in great detail. They watched with pleasure. He finished and looked up anxiously for the verdict of the jury.

Amidst the congratulatory comments came a question from one observant person: "George, what's the difference between this model and the one from last year?" They awaited his response.

"Well, eh, ah, well," he stammered . . . and then the reality hit him. After a week of exhausting work, he had completely disassembled the old product and, without realizing it, laboriously recreated the exact same set! It was the only time it ever happened, but they never let him forget it.

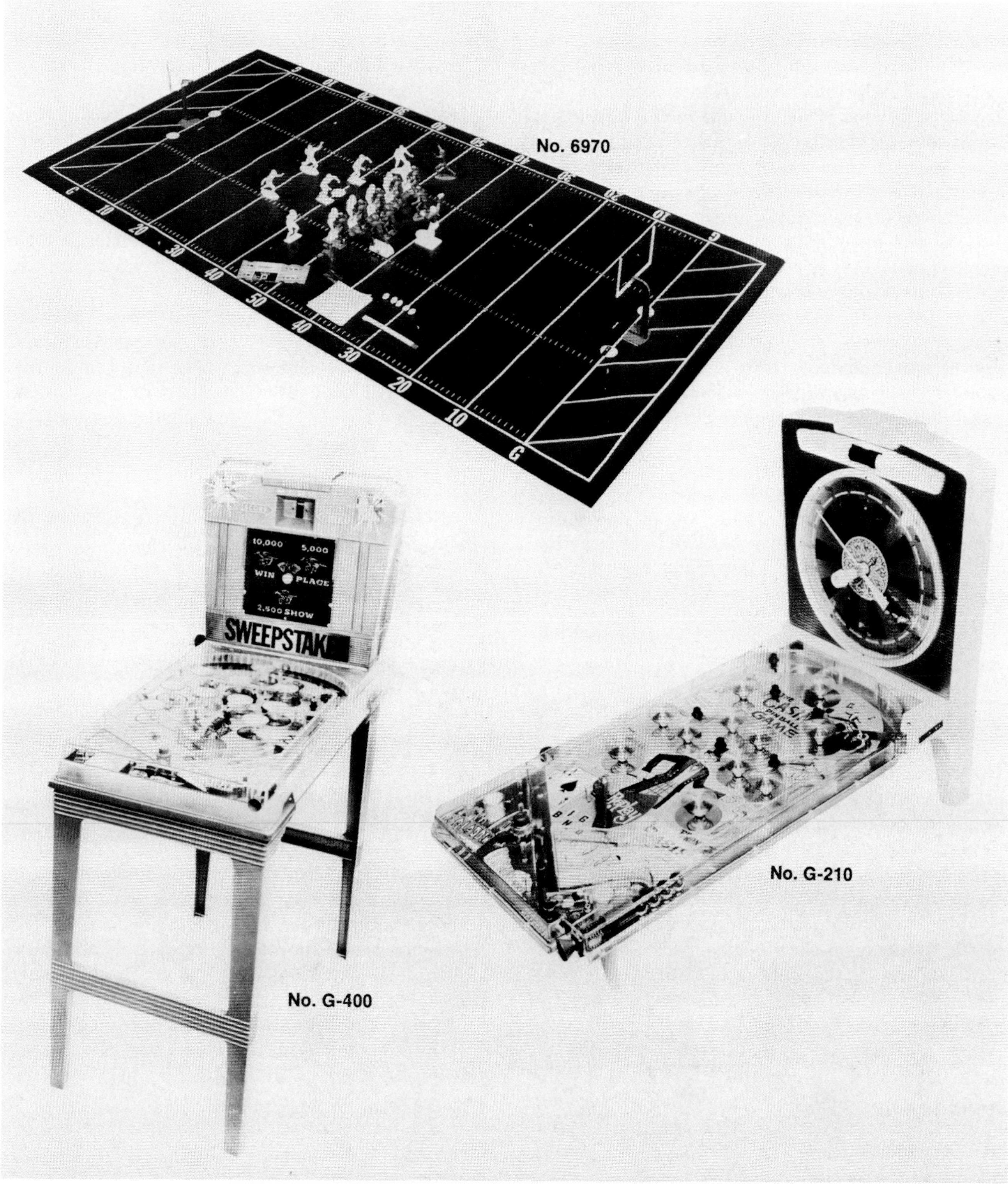

Looking through the archival copies of Louis Marx & Company catalogs gives an idea of the many products, such as bagatelle games, that were successful but not destined to survive the new management of the 1970s.

The Presidential Series

Certain products, such as the Presidents of the United States set of the 1950s, did not attain financial success despite the Marx touch. The set consisted of thirty-six plastic figures, each about two and a half inches tall. The Marx company even published a book in conjunction with this set entitled "American Presidents in Miniature," detailing the history of all the presidents up to Eisenhower. The series, presented within boxes, even included a miniature replica of the White House made out of plastic. Apparently, America's youth never found presidents as inspiring as cowboys and Indians. It is to Louis Marx's credit that although the presidential series never caught on, he maintained the tradition of creating new presidential figures because of his patriotism. People marveled at how Marx was always ready: shortly after the election results, the new president's likeness was already being delivered to retail outlets across the country. The world saw just how fast Marx worked! Actually, there is no substitute for preparation, whether in a toy factory, a lawsuit, or a movie. The Marx company made the cavities of both candidates in advance, ready for either outcome. As soon as a winner was determined, production and delivery of the new presidential figure commenced. The losing cavity was then destroyed.

Louis Marx & Company also commemorated Churchill and great generals, producing molded figurines of each, as it did Jesus, Moses, and many notables, including Jackie Gleason! Not to be forgotten among the parade of celebrities, Marx even made a plastic figure of himself, complete with his ever-present cigar.

WARTIME PRODUCTION

World War II briefly interrupted toy production at the Marx company. Considering Louis and David's circle of friends in the military, one could imagine that Louis Marx & Company would patriotically support the war effort. During World War II, Marx changed from production of consumer toys to production of munitions. The public knew little of the specifics of this activity, since the conversions were made under the tightest military security. In the Marx archives are files formerly labeled "Top Secret" which contain some of the drawings and blue prints of products produced by Marx for the War Department.

This production is certainly testimony to the company's patriotism, technical excellence, precision tooling, and fail-safe security — not to mention the prestige at having been chosen for this honor. For its contributions to the war effort, Louis Marx & Company earned many "E" awards, given by the United States government to suppliers for production "Excellence."

Because of its wartime work, Marx factories were all geared up to resume their normal toy production as soldiers jubilantly returned to the girls who anxiously awaited them. "Swing" was in; love and marriage filled the country. Burns and Allen spoke to the world on radio, and the comic Milton Berle made the country laugh on a new picture box called "television." Economics and babies boomed, providing the demand for new homes, baby carriages, and even more toys.

At Eisenhower's request, Louis visited Germany following World War II to survey the state of the factories. Eisenhower was relying upon Louis's assessment of whether or not the factories were capable of producing munitions. All that Louis was personally willing to reveal to the public was that during his five-week stay in Germany he visited 171 factories and lost eleven pounds. Although Louis understood German, he always awaited the translator and conducted his meetings in English. This gave him an edge.

He learned that the Germans had been making certain metal toys up until their surrender, a fact that surprised Louis. He concluded that the continued manufacture was probably done to boost wartime morale, in addition to foreign exchange reasons.[13]

Fortune reported: "He believes the U. S. should have permitted the making of at least a few metal toys, especially velocipedes, during the war. 'A man that gets cut down on his smoking in wartime can make it up afterward,' he reasons. 'A kid that passes through the velocipede age without a chance to own one can't make it up.' Marx himself, whose war record is excellent for both production and profits, does not happen to make velocipedes, so this can hardly be construed as what lawyers call 'a self-serving declaration.' "[14] [Author's note: a velocipede is a tricycle.]

ENTERING NEW TERRITORY: PLASTICS

As the firm entered its postwar Golden Years, everything was in place for peak production. Here was a mature, high-quality manufacturing company that clearly dominated the market; a creatively prolific, well-known chief executive who was the envy of the toy manufacturing world; a strong customer base; a powerful financial position; thirty years of equity and goodwill; and a solid reputation for know-how, dependability, and service. Timing, the key to catapulting an unemployed young man into a career that would make him a multi-millionaire by his late twenties, again favored Louis Marx & Company. The firm entered its halcyon years, as the victorious and patriotic postwar era created a prosperous and prolific market, hungry for the products of American initiative and ingenuity.

In the face of such unlimited potential, it was a time for new toys and new production techniques. Again, Marx proved to be the leader. At a time when Louis could have retired to enjoy a new life with his new wife, he expanded his company into new markets with a vehemence surpassing even the energy with which he first started the company.

this line of toys without carefully regarding the consequences. At a time when Quaker increased Marx overhead, it cut out a stable and profitable source of income. Had those constant sales figures been replaced by another product, it may not have been as detrimental. Nonetheless, the official version was that Marx's toy gun line was eliminated because it did not fit the wholesome Quaker image.[16]

Beside the military guns, rifles, and other so-called violent toys, Quaker discontinued *entire lines of profitable products,* including trains, dollhouses, bagatelles, speedways, and typewriters. The Big Wheel dominated the residual line. Certainly, it was one of the greatest products in history, but one item alone was not enough to carry a giant company.

In 1980 the *Wall Street Journal* reported: "Another problem was that, with the exception of the Big Wheel, Marx has had few spectacular products in recent years. It missed the boat on space dolls and failed to capitalize on the electronic games craze. In the mid-1970s, a new Safari group of hunters, animals and jungle accessories just didn't catch on with youngsters."[17] (It is interesting to note that ten years later, American Plastic used some of these molds to simulate the jungle scene for Rambo under lease to Coleco.)

Quaker raised the selling prices of Marx toys as it did with Fisher-Price products, which negated one of Marx's key selling advantages: more toy for less money (high value).

When Quaker was finally able to computerize Marx, it interrupted business and added to the confusion. The new high-tech systems caused the company to lose its personal touch. The computer filled orders in alphabetical order, and did not take into account the priority needed for specific clients. For example, Art's Corner Toy Store (at the beginning of the alphabet) would get preference over Woolworth's (near the end of the alphabet). Anyone could see that Woolworth's or Zayre's was not getting the care it deserved. Louis Marx & Company always gave its customers individual attention and customized orders. Quaker's Marx did not strive to give special attention.

Another problem occurred when Quaker centralized purchasing. This cut off business relationships that had been built over many years. It proved a critical error during the 1973 oil shortage when plastic molding companies had their material supplies put on allocation. The new Marx could not get delivery because it had cut off and lost its old long-term local sources.

Within a year of Quaker taking over, the Marx company lost money for the first time in fifty-two years. Some people say that Quaker was embarrassed by the obvious losses, and that this may have motivated them to sell the gun molds to Kusan to reflect additional sales that would help counterbalance the losses. According to the uncorroborated story, the sale was a one-time paper profit of income received for molds that were already written off. The sale of the molds, which may have netted $3 million, apparently improved the bottom line of that particular fiscal year, reversing an operational loss to an overall profit by adding a one-time recovery. However, the sale of the molds may also have eliminated tens of millions of dollars in future sales and millions in earnings. Guns were in and out of style at times due to the whims of the market and public opinion. An example would be when the Rambo craze hit in the 1980s and toy guns became highly profitable again. Louis would never have sold molds. His practice of updating old favorites into new amusements prevented that. This was obvious through the fact that when American Plastic purchased the Marx assets, the molds were all accounted for — from mold #1 on.

Quaker blamed circumstances such as the oil shortage, Watergate, the 1975 recession, and rising industry overhead for the failure of Marx Toys — all circumstances outside of its control.

In 1975 Quaker closed the Erie plant. The first and oldest of the Marx factories, its close was symbolic of the demise of Marx. Being the elder sister, Erie had many of the earlier integrated processes on site. Wire forming was one of these. As Glendale developed its equipment in steel stamping and later injection molding, and Girard developed model trains and speedway road racing, there was no need to duplicate the wire forming. Because the parts were small enough to be easily transported, Erie had been supplying the wire parts to the other plants. With the close of the Erie plant, a new source was needed to continue supplying the wire components for the remaining Glendale and Girard plants. The Erisco Wire Co., a small, independent firm, leased Marx's Erie plant and equipment to fill the void. Many of the workers at the Erie plant then went to work at the Girard facility, which was only twenty miles away. Some joined Erisco. Late in 1976 The Erisco Wire Co., acting much as Louis Marx would have, purchased the plant and the equipment that it had previously leased from Marx.

Meanwhile, Marx's Mexico operation was at its peak. Therefore, Quaker retained the Mexican operation, putting it under Fisher-Price's authority. Plastimarx slowly deteriorated, and by the late 1980s it entered into "Congelacion de Pagos," a situation similar to Chapter 11 under the United States Bankruptcy Code. In 1988 American Plastic actively negotiated for the purchase of Plastimarx. When it finally appeared to have reached an agreement with the Diaz-Barreiros, certain international complications set in. A Mexican group received preference and purchased the company. Plastimarx never went back into the toy business, and, as stated earlier, was completely liquidated by 1991. Thus ended the Quaker years in the history of Marx.

Dunbee-Combex

By 1975 all Marx operations other than Mexico were losing money. In April 1976 Quaker Oats sold Marx to Dunbee-Combex Ltd. for approximately one-third of the price it originally paid. Quaker took a $23.2 million pretax write-off, and Dunbee-Combex gained the Marx enterprises at well below their book value.[18]

In 1976 *The Economist* reported that since Quaker Oats purchased Louis Marx & Co., Inc. for "$51 million (of which $14 million was for working capital), it has seen profits from toys shrink from a peak $32m to only $3½m. Now it is flogging off Louis Marx (minus its Mexican interests) to the British Dunbee-Combex-Marx group for only $15m (plus $3m for working capital) — a huge loss on the investment, however you measure it."[19] Quaker Oats did everything it could to sweeten the deal for potential Marx Toys buyer Dunbee-Combex. Even before the deal was signed, Quaker invited Dunbee as its guest at the New York Toy Fair.

Dunbee-Combex's purchase of Marx Toys, which was completed just as the country was pulling out of a recession, raised general confidence levels. Many plant workers at the Marx sites considered the departure of Quaker Oats a godsend. Spirits were high. "It's turn-around time at Marx!" was the vibration felt by many employees and the industry in general.

The Economist, too, was optimistic and printed the following: "Why should Dunbee succeed where Quaker failed? Well, it has a good track record . . . It hopes to break even this year (1976), after making sure that Quaker bears the losses to date, and to be on peak form by 1977 . . . It will do this, it says, by cutting red tape and restoring dynamic management. . . . If it works it would be an excellent deal for Dunbee."[20]

The Economist further reported that Dunbee-Combex-Marx (DCM) had announced that Marx Toys was operating from a wasteful thirty-two locations in 1975, of which fewer than a third were necessary. DCM's priority was to reduce by half the number of primary factories and sell the surplus properties.[21]

The principal in DCM was Richard Beecham, an entrepreneurial executive with a strong background in the toy business and prior involvement with the Marx operation in England. His solution was to try to systematically remove the Quaker "improvements" and return to the original, profitable Louis and David Marx ways. Never mind that history has proven that, in the face of progress and a continually changing market, one can never really turn back the clock in business.

The first Quaker action Beecham reversed was the name: "Louis Marx & Company" was restored! Beecham cut unnecessary expense and bureaucracy, and appointed Larry Passick to try to sell any assets not necessary for the ongoing operation, including antiques to collectors through Sotheby's auction house. Next, he brought back the toy guns. He used the British Marx molds because the American molds had been sold. Apparently, Beecham had the right idea. Unfortunately, it was too little, too late. The new Louis Marx & Company lacked a star product. It tried several ideas but did not hit on the right one. The Big Wheel was ten years old, and although it still returned a nice profit, it was not enough to carry the company. Passing the control of development and tooling to English engineers was a mistake, resulting in poor quality and huge losses from returns of two expensive new toys in 1978.

The Bankruptcy

1978 was the last year of full production. In 1979 Marx did participate at the New York Toy Show, but the positive attitude was gone and they did not know whether or not they would be able to ship the goods. Dunbee-Combex-Marx of England, no longer able to meet its obligations related to Marx Toys, lost control. In 1980 bankruptcy was filed in the Federal Court, Southern District of New York. Production had ceased. Assets were frozen and finally were awarded in 1982 to the Chemical Bank of New York as its preferred creditor through its L. F. Dommerich Factoring Division.

Even in bankruptcy, Marx retained its pioneer spirit. The creative financial arrangements of the sale may have worked, had the market and/or economy cooperated. (The company's approach seems to be a forerunner to the many bankruptcy situations afflicting our economy in the early 1990s through failing banks, airlines, major department stores, and other companies that might be healthy if it were not for junk bonds and leveraged buyouts.)

The Girard and Glendale plants closed in January 1980. When a group of creditors filed a bankruptcy petition against DCM on February 1, 1980, the company attempted to pay its debts, operating under the protection of the courts. DCM's situation quickly deteriorated. The final blow came on February 23rd, when DCM went into receivership in England.

Once clear of the legalities, two years later, the Chemical Bank proceeded to liquidate the many valuable Marx assets in order to recover cash. Ironically, the same bank that had once invited David Marx to sit on its advisory board was now to foreclose on the remnants of his company. Even more ironic, almost seventy years after Louis Marx entered the toy arena under Ferdinand Strauss, the court appointed David Strauss & Company (no known relation to Ferdinand), to act as final liquidators of Louis Marx & Company. Ashes to ashes, dust to dust, Strauss to Strauss. It was through Strauss that American Plastic purchased the assets of Marx, including the molds used to make the playsets.

Admirers and historians of Marx have noted that under the leadership of Louis and David the company was financially strong, efficient, and profitable during each of the fifty-two years they controlled it, including (and especially during) the Depression. Immediately upon relinquishing the reins to others, the "same" company lost money in operations, and continued to increase its rate of loss dramatically as the old grand momentum dissipated, until the downward course terminated in bankruptcy. If nothing else, this reality presents a powerful statement in favor of the two boys from Brooklyn.

EPILOGUE

And so the story of Marx continues. What began as a fledgling enterprise in 1919 evolved through several owners and name-changes to become a possible toy staple of the 1990s. Louis and David Marx, men of vision and business savvy, established the groundwork for a name that refuses to be squelched. Read on to find out more about the production of Marx playsets, from inception to renaissance.

NOTES

1. "Louis Marx: Toy King," *Fortune*, January 1946, p.127.
2. Ibid. p. 163.
3. "The Little King," *Time*, December 12, 1955, p. 94.
4. Ibid., p. 93.
5. Ibid., p. 96.
6. Ibid., p. 92. (Author's note: Although not noted therein, Hong Kong was important. Furthermore, Marx exported to other foreign markets.)
7. Ibid.
8. "Louis Marx: Toy King," p. 123.
9. Cynthia Saltzman, "Successors Couldn't Match His Genius, So Louis Marx's Toy Empire Crumbled," *Wall Street Journal*, February 8, 1980.
10. Sydney Ladensohn Stern and Ted Schoenhaus, *Toyland: The High Stakes Games of the Toy Industry* (Chicago: Contemporary Books, 1990, pp. 72-75).
11. "The Little King," p. 94.
12. Ibid.
13. "Louis Marx: Toy King," p. 125.
14. Ibid.
15. Saltzman, *Wall Street Journal*.
16. Ibid.
17. Ibid.
18. Ibid.
19. Quaker Oats/Dunbee, "Dialectical yo-yo," *The Economist*, April 24, 1976, p. 108.
20. Ibid., p. 111.
21. Ibid., p. 108.

CHAPTER THREE

HOW TO MANUFACTURE A PLAYSET

Undoubtedly, one of Louis Marx & Company's greatest contributions to the delight of children as well as collectors was its exhaustive development of the playset. This chapter brings you behind the scenes, into the midst of the complex set of processes behind the creation and production of a plaything — specifically, the Marx playset.

The playset consists of miniatures in plastic or other material, usually produced to a relative scale, depicting a certain theme, and including environmental settings, human and/or animal figures, vehicles, buildings, and accessories. Marx produced five main categories of playsets: the Western, Military, Farm, Space, and Theme sets (such as those created around a popular television series). Western playsets date from at least 1952, the same year a Sears catalog offered the Mineral City and Roy Rogers Double Bar Ranch sets. There have been over 250 standard variations of Marx Western playsets — including favorites such as Daniel Boone, Roy Rogers, Johnny West, and Fort Apache. The number of Military playsets exceeds even this. In all, it is safe to estimate that well over 10 million playsets were produced and sold by Marx from 1950 to 1975.

THE CREATIVE PROCESS

As explained by Frank Rice, who was most directly involved with playsets during his long tenure at Louis Marx & Company, the playset line *evolved* — rather than being something deliberately planned. Rice feels that playsets were the outgrowth of the original #3540 Service Station, which was designed specifically to compete with an item produced by T. Cohn, at specific buyers' requests. Marx developed a toy superior in quality and play value at a much lower price ($2.98 vs. $4.98). And then came the #4050 Dollhouse, complete with furniture for $3.98 retail, which was introduced around 1950, after Louis Marx convinced Ed Hjelte to join the firm. As we know from the discussion of this segment of Marx company history in Chapter Two, the success of the dollhouse paved the way for a whole new line of mail-order merchandise, with playsets in the spotlight.

The history of Marx playsets begins with a Happi-Time (a Sears exclusive name) Farm Set, which the buyer of boys' toys for Sears, Lothar Kiesow, promoted with great success to his store's typical customer. Ed Hjelte and Frank Rice listened to the buyers' suggestions, and this eventually led to a Western set. Westerns were highly popular at the start of the 1950s, as can be seen by the popularity of early television programs about heroes such as Hopalong Cassidy, Gene Autry, and, of course, Roy Rogers.

With the full support of Louis Marx, Hjelte pushed hard to get the new line going. Archie Marcus quickly recognized the advantages in terms of cost and competition and embraced the concept. The bottom line and the

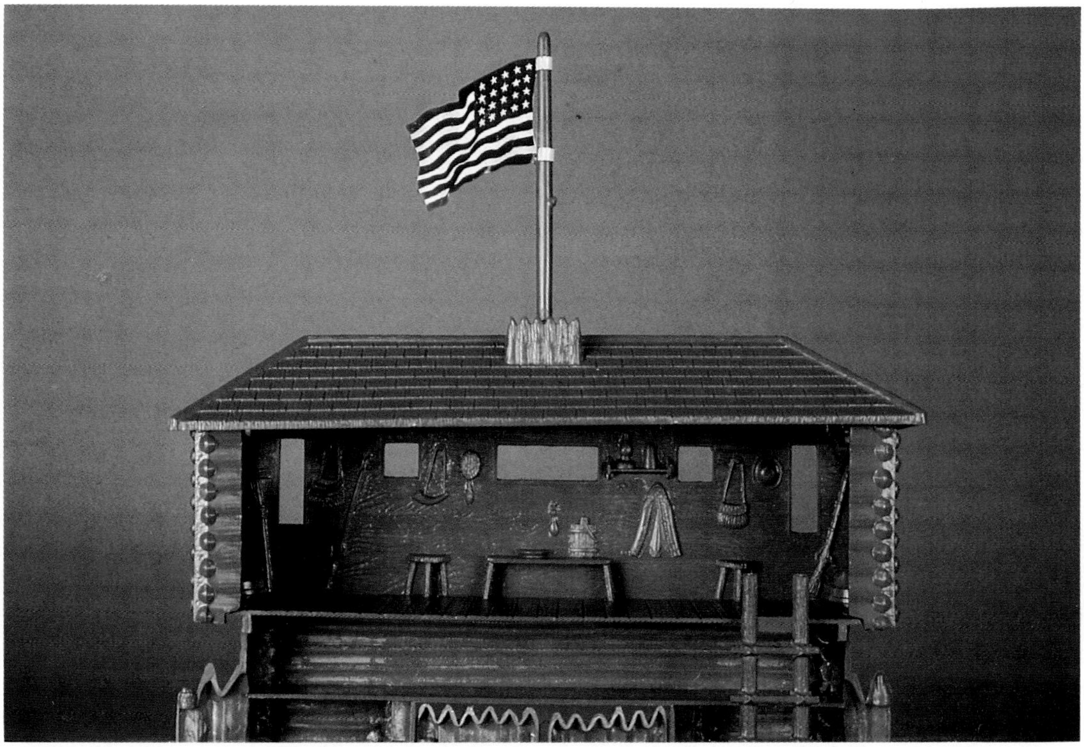

The detailing, inside and out, of Marx playsets contribute to their enduring appeal.

enduring popularity of the playsets proved the wisdom of this move.

Harmer Cox's work with plastic molding made the whole thing possible at minimum cost and short time development. The documentation in this chapter and elsewhere notes molds coming from a supplier named Ferriot. Wally Gryce introduced Marx to Joseph Ferriot of Ferriot Brothers, Akron, Ohio, toolmakers, who also was, in the words of Frank Rice:

> . . . one of the best sculptors and modelmakers from a plastic molding standpoint that this industry ever had. Joe could see in his mind's eye and in his hands the essence of the action and detail in a figure or accessory, and this actually trapped the realism of the situation in a moment. He worked well with Wally, Don Lemoine, our plastic production manager, and myself — together we contributed probably the quintessential charm of the Marx playset.
>
> Hjelte and I did a lot of masterminding in the late night meetings we had at 200 Fifth Avenue and directed the path that the next year's line would follow. Our model shop at Glendale, headed by Walter Nisperly, worked with us almost religiously and gave us improvements and alternatives. But it was Wally Gryce, Ferriot, Don Lemoine, and a very capable Bucky Livingston who made it all happen. Jay Darglitz, Gene Liden, Harry Quinn, Roy Burkett (our staff artist), and Clayton Reece of Graphic Arts in Toledo, Ohio, handled the metal dies and lithography of the buildings in each playset — as well as the service stations and dollhouses, which continued along for years.
>
> It almost got to a point where our horizons were unlimited and there was not anything we would not attempt — from prehistoric times to advanced space exploration. We felt we could pull it off!

A specific playset, like every new product, begins with an *imaginative idea* that is expected to produce consumer interest and demand. In the toy world, it may be a new invention altogether, such as the Hula Hoop; a miniature version of an adult object, like a toy truck, telephone, or typewriter; or a new design of an existing concept, like the Big Wheel tricycle. It may even be the redesign or playful reapplication of a practical device, such as a dollhouse. Sometimes the idea simply involves combining and adding to existing units — as was often the case with Western playsets.

Many toymakers have found that no matter how good an idea may seem, ingenuity alone will not ensure success. For every good toy idea, there are hundreds, even thousands, of ideas that fail because of the vagaries of timing, place, or price; many fall short in terms of the engineering, marketing, and distribution capabilities. All of these elements are prerequisites for a product to turn a profit and be considered successful. No wonder the failure rate is so high.

Once a new product achieves rare "hit" status in the market, success is so sweet that it motivates a manufacturer to keep looking for hits for months, even years!

One successful product can offset the expense of a string of failures. The whole process must begin again with a first step — a good idea.

THE MANUFACTURING PROCESS

After a good playset idea has been identified, the manufacturing process begins. Drawings or sketches are made. The next step is the development of a *prototype*. Through illustration and sculpture, a model of the new playset is fashioned; it may include existing and new components — such as cowboys, horses, bulls, calves, fences, and corrals. The model is then studied, tested and reworked, then tested and reworked again, before it is scrutinized by executives, who in turn show it to prospective buyers, spouses, friends and other influential parties to obtain marketing feedback. Marx often used the children of employees to test their toys.

Then the prototype is improved as much as possible. At this stage, any changes are made easily and inexpensively; these same changes, if made later, would be costly in time and money, and may be so extreme as to cause the discontinuation of the product's development. Once the prototype is approved, the process continues. As you will see in the next chapter, prototypes do not always lead to mass production, however.

The next step in the process is the *engineering*, where a product design which appears clear and simple on the outside is modified and complicated with inner details, often beyond comprehension. Engineers redesign the product to meet tooling, manufacturing, assembly, and packaging standards — all within cost parameters. *Tooling* consists of all those special pieces of equipment designed and built for no other reason than to make that particular product. (Of course, once made it sometimes can be used in the manufacture of another product.) It includes all molds for injection or blow molding of plastic pieces, metal dies for stamping or casting, jigs, dies, and assembly fixtures, decorating equipment, packaging, and quality control apparatus. Tooling does not include standard machinery and equipment designed for general industrial use — machinery such as molding machines (injection, blow, and die-cast), stamping machinery, assembly belts, packaging (blister, shrink, skin), packing, decorating, etc.

The Marx company excelled in getting mileage out of its tools. Usually, Marx chose to reuse tooling from its classic models. The company utilized the highest quality, design, material, and construction in its tooling, which was built to last "forever." As an example, Marx used its #174 fence mold to produce many different products. Originally built in 1950, it has been used in dollhouses, and in Western, Military, and Theme playsets. Another example is the small horse mold used in a variety of Western and Military playsets, in conjunction with animal transport vehicles, trains, and farm sets. The mold sheet for PL-532, Buckboard Horse, contains notations that this item was used in

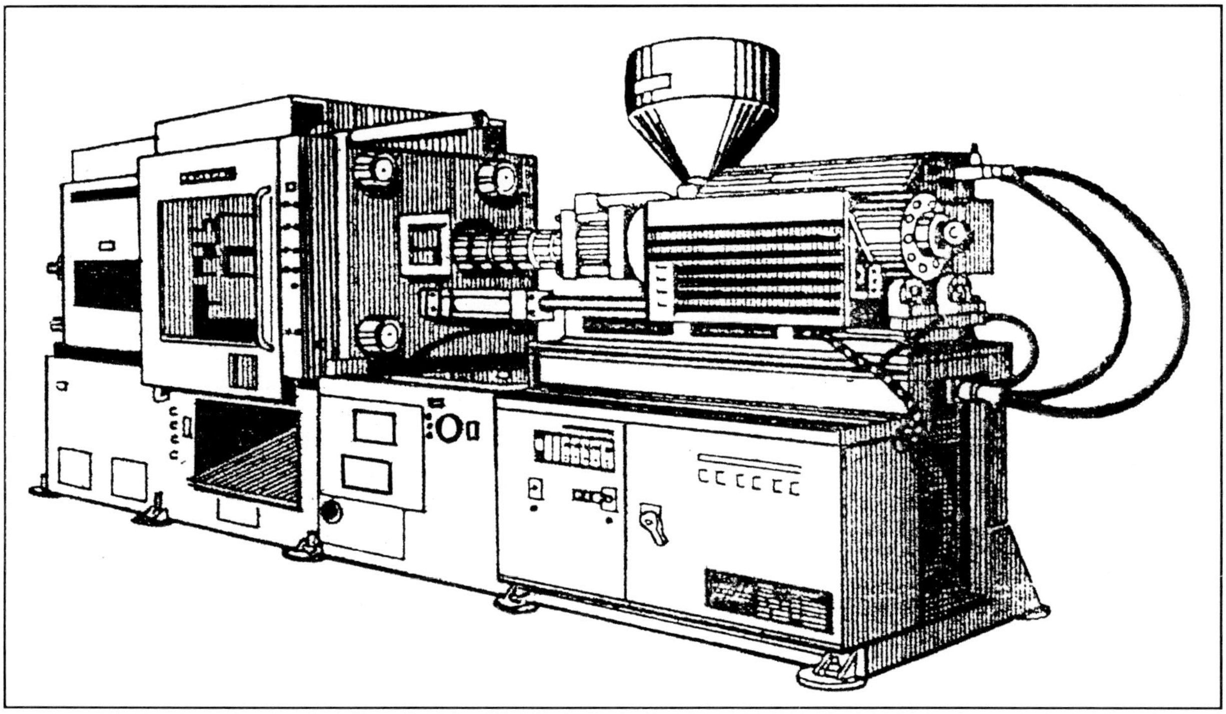

An injection molding machine.

Left, the gold mine mold, PL-1057, used in several playsets. Below, this partial view of the Vintage Collections Gold Rush playset shows on far right, the structures and track made by the mold. Right, a partial view of the American Plastic mold warehouse.

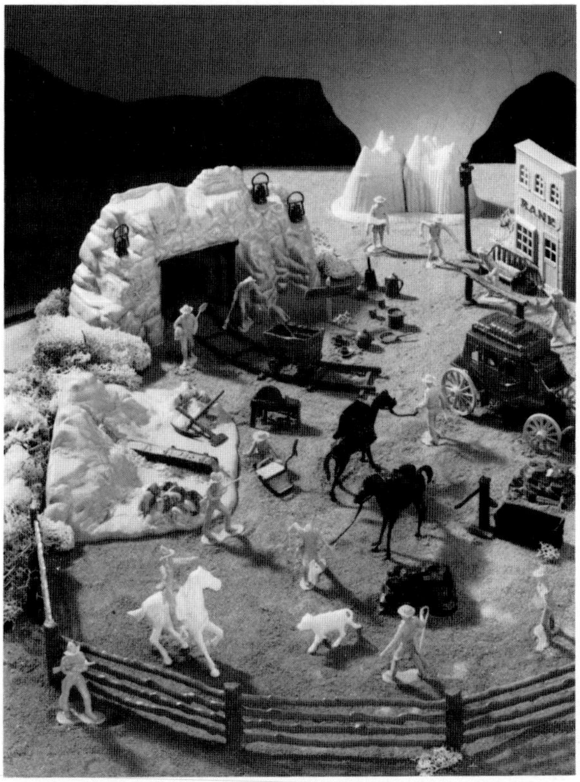

Fort Apache #3609 and in Cowboy and Indian sets #3940 and 3950. (See the photos and mold sheets from the Marx archives reproduced in this chapter.)

Design engineers who evaluate tooling are concerned with *wall thickness* for cooling, which governs weight and cycle time and in turn cost. The *weight of the part* is one of the prime cost considerations. The engineers also determine molding procedures such as the *ease of ejection* (the way the part will be released or "knocked out" of the mold). *Shrinkage* must be planned for and calculated in advance. Of major concern is, of course, the anticipated or desired *productivity*. The higher the desired productivity, the higher the cost of building the appropriate tooling. Often, the higher the tooling cost, the lower the unit manufacturing cost. Hence, higher start-up tooling cost is intended to be recovered by long runs.

The increased productivity should outweigh the start-up cost after reaching a certain break-even point. In a long-term successful product, the savings will repeat year after year. By the same token, a strong-selling product would require a multi-cavity, high-production set of tools. The level of investment in a tool or set of tools is based on what marketing feels they can sell. Therefore, engineering designs the tooling based on marketing projections and financial appropriations.

After all the executive decisions have been made, each plastic part of the playset is designed and drawn in detail to scale. Material finishing and tolerances are indicated. These are known as *part drawings*. The

tooling is now studied and designed in *concept*. After redesigns, drawings are made for blueprints and materials are chosen. Shrinkage is calculated. Then the toolmakers, applying many hours of crafting skill, build the molds and dies. After what seems like an eternity of delays and unforeseen events — often overdue and over budget — the final *testing* begins, and the tooling is perfected. For example, air could be trapped in a cavity, which prevents the plastic from completely filling the space of the cavity. Vents may be added opposite the gate where the piece did not fill to allow for the exit of the trapped air. Once tooled, assembly jigs and fixtures are built. Time and motion studies are carried out to design the *assembly* and *packaging* processes, and *purchased parts are then designed or contracted.*

It is easy to understand why it may be quicker, easier, and less expensive to build a house than a toy mold. The original molds for a complete set of Western playset molds may have cost $132,000 in the 1950s. The replacement price for these molds today would be at least $1 million. The reproduction on page 58 of an Operations Sheet found in the Marx archives shows the processes involved in modification of a die — namely one used in the Battle of the Blue & Gray.

With an eye to the final product, one of the most important ingredients in the success of a playset that is sold in retail outlets is undoubtedly the *packaging*. Since the 1960s, and increasingly so each year, the packaging sometimes may be more of a sales factor than the product itself, and constitute a large portion of product costs.

In the years when the bulk of Marx playsets sales was through the large mail order firms such as Sears, attractive boxes were not as important as impressive numbers of pieces and other features that could be promoted in catalog advertising. Frank Rice recalls that in the first five to ten years of the playset, packaging was the lowest cost, simplest box available — corrugated with one-color rubber-plate printing. Marx relied on the special "demonstrator" versions of playsets — prepared by Cliff Freelander in the New York office

On the following pages reproductions of documents from the Marx archives reveal the progression of a mold numbered PL-342, the Fort Apache gate, illustrated by an archive snapshot. The Marx mold sheet for stockade gate and fence PL-342B indicates it was used in Fort Apache set numbers 3606, 3607, 3609, 3610, and 3612. Whatever the version, this mold produces one set of three parts each time, and early records indicate that on average 130 sets can be produced in an hour. Note the mold sheets also reproduced here for Alamo Frontiersmen, PL-745, and for the miniature Civil War accessories, PL-908: the latter mold accommodated four sets of 35 individual pieces, for a total of 140 cavities.

3-18-65

PL- 342

Item: STOCKADE GATE AND FRAME

Model No.

No. of Cavities: 3

No. of Sets: 1

Cost: $3650.00

Made By: Newark

Date Ordered: 11/14/50

Delivery Date: 4/18/51

Date Received:

Machine: 4 - 6 Oz.

Average Per Hour: 130

Gross Per Day:

Weights: Per Shot-

Per Piece-

Per M-

Mold Contains: One Archway w/Fort Apache
One Right Side Gate
One Left Side Gate

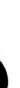

PL - 500

PL-342-A

Item: STOCKADE GATE AND FRAME

Model No.

No. of Cavities: 3

No. of Sets: 1

Cost:

Made By:

Date Ordered:

Delivery Date:

Date Received:

Machine:

Average Per Hour:

Gross Per Day:

Weights: Per Shot-

Per Piece-

Per M-

Mold Contains: Remove Name "Fort Apache"
Put in Flat Insert
One Archway without name
One Right Side Gate
One Left Side Gate

3694-Fort Commanche 342B
for 72

PL - 500

PL- 745

Item:	**Alamo Frontiersmen**
Model No.	**2436**
No. of Cavities:	**10**
No. of Sets:	**1**
Cost:	**$4350.00**
Made By:	**Ferriot**
Date Ordered:	7/22/55
Delivery Date:	9/3/55
Date Received:	9/6/55
Machine:	**8 oz.**
Average Per Hour:	**120**
Gross Per Day:	
P. E. Weights: Per Shot-	**50.6**
Per Piece-	**39.8**
Per M-	**87.7**
Mold Contains:	

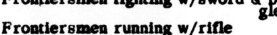

TAN

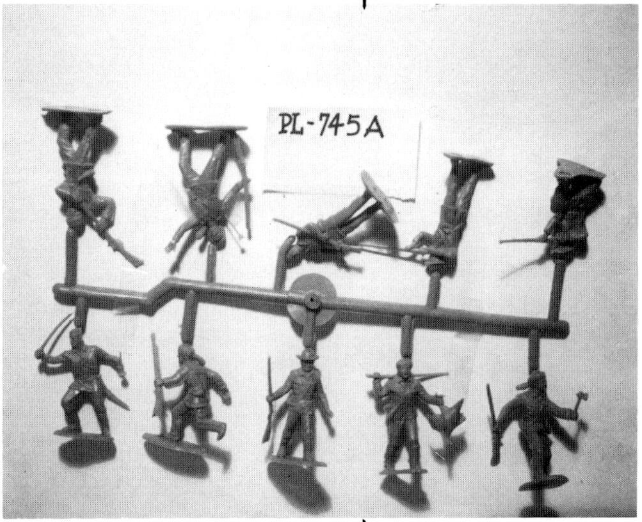

Frontiersmen swinging rifle
Frontiersmen running w/rifle
Frontiersmen w/goose
Frontiersmen walking w/rifle
Frontiersmen standing shooting
Frontiersmen fighting w/sword & bugle
Frontiersmen running w/rifle
Frontiersmen kneeling w/rifle
2 Cavalry Riders.

11/5/64 — 10/21/64 REB 69
PL 745A 10 Frontier figures
Replacing 2 new figures in place of the 2 riders (NO riders)

PL - 500

PL- 908

Item: **Miniature Civil War Acc's**

Model No.

No. of Cavities: **140**

No. of Sets: **4**

Cost: **$8725.00**

Made By: **Ferriot**

Date Ordered: **7/18/57**

Delivery Date: **10/26/57**

Date Received: **11/23/57**

Machine: **12-16**

Average Per Hour: **360**

Gross Per Day:

P. E.

Weights: Per Shot- **75.6**

Per Piece- **16.8**

Per M- **36.9**

Mold Contains: **- per set**

5 swords
2 Cavalry Type Bugles
3 Belts w/cavalry type holsters
5 Cavalry Type Revolver & Pistols
3 Cavalry Type Carbines
3 Belts w/Scabbards
1 Cavalry type Guidon
1 pr. folded Cav. gloves to fit over belt
2 wooden confederate type Canteens
1 camp Fire 1 Coffee Pot 1 Frying Pan
1 Dish w/Cup 2 pr. field Glasses 2 Dispatch Cases

PL - 500

5-1-58

DIE NO.	#4746 Battle of the Blue & Gray #4759 Battle of The Blue & Gray	STEEL	DIE SHUT HGT.	MIN. PRESS	STROKE
PT-1467	B Blk Front & Sides	30 Ga. Litho.	9-1/2	8 HAM	7
	C Form "		9-3/4	A4-1/2	4
	D Curl "		7-7/8	A4-1/2	4

Litho: Red Brick w/Plain White Coat inside.

DIE CHANGES

Blk: Remove 2 Punch end sections w/lugs, 4 End Die sections w/lugs,
2 Stripper end inserts & 2 K.O. pad inserts marked #3992
Remove Door Opening punch
Install 2 Punch plates marked #4759
Install 2 Punch end sections w/o lugs, 4 End Die sections w/o lugs,
2 Stripper inserts & 2 K.O. pad inserts marked #3630

Form: Remove 2 Punch & 2 Die blocks w/gages marked #3992
Remove Pad inserts marked #3992
Remove Door opening forming punch.
Install 2 Punch & 2 Die blocks marked #3630
Install pad inserts marked #3630

Curl: Remove 2 Punch end, 2 Side blocks & Pad marked #3992
Remove Spring gages marked #3992
Remove Door opening Curling blocks
Install 2 Punch end, 2 Side blocks & pad marked #3630
Install 2 Die end & 2 Side blocks w/gages marked #3630

PT-1037	B Blk #3510 Roof - Red w/Black	30 Ga. Litho.	11-1/4	A4-1/2	4
~~SE-997~~	C Form "		~~9-1/4~~	4	3-1/2
PT-~~997~~ 495	D Curl & Pierce #4759 Roof		7-3/8	7	3-1/2

DIE CHANGES

Blk: Remove 2 Stove Pipe, 3 Chimney & 5 Back punches marked #3992

Curl: Install 4 Punch plates (10 punches) marked #4759

PT-1092	B Blk #4759 Chimney -(2 Req'd.)- Red Brick	30 Ga. Litho.	7-1/2	5	3
	C Form "		6-3/4	4	2-1/2

PT-1054	B Blk Flag - 36 Star Union	30 Ga. Litho.	6-1/4	4	2
	B Blk Flag - Confederate				

Form Flags in Rough Assembly

All other parts are Plastic
Model #2557-A

— to sell the product at the retail level and the catalog photo to do the job for mail-order selling. Catalog house sales were the "financial fuel" for the creation and production of playsets with large numbers of figures, accessories, and structures. As more attention was paid to the retail market in the later years of Marx, more money had to go into colorful packaging, and thus the number of pieces included had to be reduced.

Nowadays, it is often the package rather than the content which the buyer sees. The product itself may not be visible until long after it is purchased, as it is brought home, gift-wrapped, given, and opened in front of the Christmas tree. Finally, the bare product is viewed by the user — who is often not the purchaser.

It is sometimes said that good packaging can sell anything — even a rock (remember the Pet Rock?). Therefore, manufacturers invest considerable time and money in packaging, including design, illustration, photography, graphics, type, color separations, printing, die-cutting, gluing, and assembly.

Not until all of the previous steps are taken does production begin. The plastic parts are molded; the metal parts are lithographed and/or stamped; the purchased parts are brought in; the package is printed, die-cut, and glued; the pre- and sub-assemblies are prepared. Then everything is brought to the assembly department.

ALONG THE ASSEMBLY LINE

A typical *assembly line* is composed of a moving conveyor belt, carrying work in progress in measured units to operators along the way, each one of whom completes a simple, non-decision making, repetitive action in the process. Timing is fundamental. The Marx people continuously studied and improved their assembly. Records show that several different time and motion studies were conducted for each toy product. A typical playset could receive a box from one person, a corral from another, and figures from another. Component after component is added until, finally, the assembly is complete. Customer assembly instructions are enclosed at the end of the process.

Any decoration, such as silk screening, hot-stamping, and labeling, may also be done at the assembly line. Decals may be applied in the mold during the molding cycle. Today, however, manufacturers often opt to supply the consumer with pressure-sensitive labels that may be applied after purchase, saving the manufacturer the cost of additional labor. This is also done with certain toy parts, thereby often passing the task on to the unsuspecting parent.

At the end of the assembly process, when the product is finished but not yet packaged, it is tested for proper

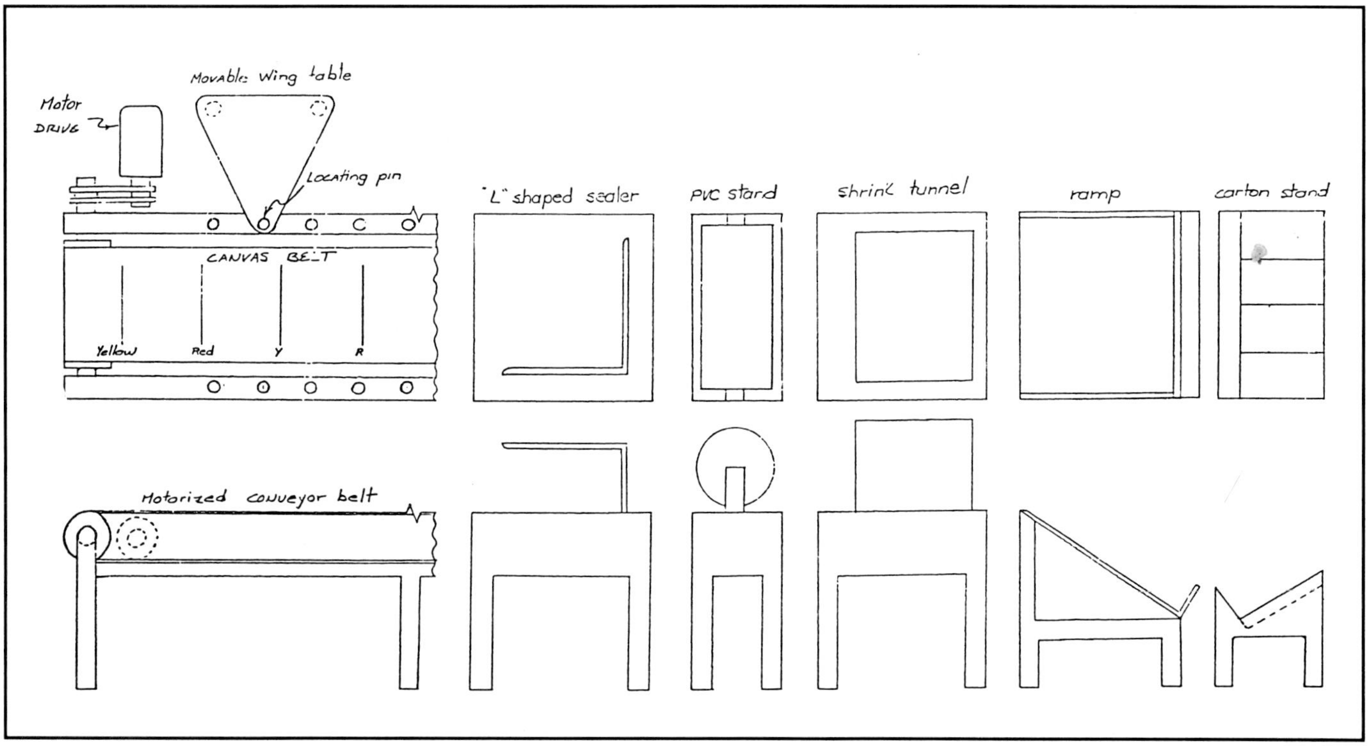

Assembly line layout

Marx figure molds enjoy new life in the Marx Vintage Collector Series Gold Rush Playset.

assembly and operation. Quality control measures take place all along the way.

The man in the best position to know — Frank Rice — comments that tree molds, fence, cactus, and accessory molds occasionally were used beyond their capacity to accommodate the piece-count which was so important to mail-order operations, advertising programs, and price justification. Temporary substitutions of pieces therefore were sometimes made to meet customer deadlines.

And at the very end of the assembly line, the product is slipped into the package, which is checked for having all its listed contents. The package is sealed. A standard number (often six or twelve) are loaded into a master shipping carton, and several of these are stacked, loaded, and warehoused or shipped.

Naturally, the success of the playset still depends largely on advertising, sales, distribution, management, and financing. This book's scope does not cover those steps specifically; suffice it to say that marketing and sales can represent a significant percentage of the product's final cost.

And so now you, too, know how to manufacture a playset. Go out and make one — or if you are not quite ready to actually apply your new knowledge, at least what you now know should give you an increased appreciation of the Western playsets that are described in the following chapter.

GLOSSARY OF PLASTIC MANUFACTURING TERMS

A & B Plates: Metal plates used to hold the cores and cavities onto the mold base.

Assembly: The process of putting sets of objects together to form a single unit (also see **Assembly Line**, **Pre-Assembly**, and **Sub-Assembly**).

Assembly Line: A group of operators placed along a moving conveyor belt in order of their tasks. The belt helps to keep the pace of the work steady at a specific predetermined rate.

Assembly Jig (or Fixture): Small machine or apparatus designed especially to join certain parts or perform other tasks on a uniform and repeated basis.

Bill of Materials: The detailed list of materials and their quantities used in a product.

Blow Mold: A form, usually made of aluminum, housing the shape of a part to be made under the blow-molding process. The part is always hollow.

Blow Molding: The process of forming a hollow part out of plastic material by using heat and air pressure within a mold. The initial stage is extrusion, in which the hot pliable plastic tube known as "parison" is vertically extruded. A hollow mold closes around the parison, and air is injected or blown in through a needle into the center of the parison. The air forces the material to take the shape and texture of the inner surface of the mold. After a cooling period, the mold opens to eject the part and the cycle begins again. Typically speaking, the parts are hollow and will not stack or nest.

Cavity: (a) That area in the mold that shapes the plastic into the desired part. (b) The female side of the molding area, as opposed to the core.

Compression Molding: The process of forming a part under pressure. The material used is thermoset. This is not used to make Playsets.

Core: The male side of the molding area.

Curing Time: The time it takes for the plastic material to harden into its final shape and dimensions. It occurs in stages, for example: 60 seconds to cure 90%, 1 hour to cure another 5%, 2 hours for another 3%, 24 hours for another 1%, and 48 hours for another 1%.

Cycle Time: The period of time it takes to complete the molding process, typically 15 to 60 seconds. It is also expressed in cycles per hour, such as 120/h.

Die: See **Extrusion Die** and **Metal Stamping Die**.

Die-Cast: The process of forming metal parts in a press and mold similar to and preceding injection molding.

Die Cut: The process of cutting, folding, and scoring cardboard parts.

Drawings: Refers to mechanical drawings or blueprints.

Ejection: Process which releases, removes, blows, or "knocks out" the molded part from the mold.

Ejector Pins: Rods used to remove plastic parts from a mold.

Extrusion: The process by which plastic material is forced through a two-dimensional die to form a continuous part. The resin is loaded via a hopper into a "screw" within a barrel. The material melts under heat from solid to liquid as the "screw" turns, moving the material forward under controlled heat from the outer heater bands. The melted material is then forced through a nozzle at the forward end of the barrel into a tubular or other continuous profile form, such as a garden hose or PVC pipe. Injection and blow molding processes also begin with extrusion. After this initial process there is some sort of secondary "take off" process to cut, store, and/or further treat the material.

Extrusion Die: A two-dimensional form placed after the nozzle of an extruder. This die shapes the profile of the plastic extrusion. The slide that fits into the Play-Doh Fun Factory is an example of such a die.

Family Mold: A mold designed with several parts used together in a set. The parts may all fit together to form one unit. For example, the mold which makes the block house for Fort Apache makes the four walls (in two sections) and the roof in one shot.

Figures: Miniature forms such as of people or animals, generally made in plastic.

Gate: Small area that connects or leads the runner into the cavity. The size and shape of the gate is of utmost importance to control the pressure and flow of the plastic.

Hot Runner: A sophisticated heating system that keeps the plastic material liquid to save time and regrinding.

Injection Mold: A form, usually made of a steel base, that houses the cavities (cores and cavities) used to shape the plastic parts into their final form, under the injection molding process.

Injection Molding: The process by which plastic material is shaped under heat and pressure into a three- dimensional part or parts. The initial stage is similar to extrusion; however, once the material has moved forward in the barrel, a torpedo head on the screw (or plunger) forces the molten material through the nozzle out of the machine and into the sprue bushing, leading into a mold that is being held closed in the clamp end of the machine. Within the mold, the material flows into the runner system and cavities. After a time during which the material "freezes" back into the solid state, the mold opens and the parts are ejected. The mold closes and the cycle begins again.

Knock Out: Used synonymously with "eject."

Lithography: The process of printing on paper, cardboard, or metal sheets, usually offset.

Metal Stamping Die: A steel form, with a male and female component, mounted on a base with posts to guide it; used to press a steel sheet into a desired shape. It may cut, fold, or perforate the sheet in one or more stages.

Mold: A metal form used to shape the plastic material into the cured plastic part. The most common type used in manufacturing the products described in this book are injection molds (also see **Blow Mold**, **Family Mold**, **Injection Mold**, and **Multi-Cavity Mold**).

Mold Base: The parts of a mold used to house the cavities.

Molded Part: The piece of molded and cured plastic as it comes out of the mold before it is assembed or decorated.

Molding: The process by which plastic material is shaped into a part, generally under controlled time, heat, and pressure (see **Blow Molding** and **Injection Molding**).

Multi-Cavity Mold: An injection, or even a blow, mold with the same part repeated, (e.g., an injection mold designed to make wheels with twenty-four identical cavities).

Parison: The hot, pliable plastic tube that is extruded from the head of a blow molding machine and which is covered within the blow mold.

Plastic: The main material used in the playset. For our purpose, it is the organic material that can be shaped or formed under controlled heat and pressure. We will deal only with thermoplastic (as opposed to thermoset). Those materials chiefly used in the manufacture of toys are high-impact polystyrene (HIS) which is rigid, crystal clear polystyrene (GP, which stands for General Purpose), high density polyethylene (HDPE), low density polyethylene (LDPE) which is flexible, and polypropylene (PPL). The two materials mostly used in the 1950s Playsets were the HIS (rigid) and the LDPE (flexible). Collectors often distinguish between these types as "hard" and "soft" plastic.

Playset: As used in this book, a product consisting of miniatures in plastic and other material, usually made to relative scale, depicting a certain theme and including an environmental setting, figures, vehicles, and accessories. Those sets covered in this book usually have human figures of approximately 2" to 2¾" high.

Pre-Assembly: Those parts or components prepared for assembly before arriving at the line.

Primary Runner: That runner which departs from the sprue itself.

Processes: See **Blow Molding**, **Extrusion**, **Injection Molding**, and **Rotational Molding**.

Prototype: The original, experimental model, usually made by hand, that serves to illustrate the typical physical qualities of a product.

Rotational Molding: The process by which a hollow product is made by centrifugal force. Usually a series of hollow molds are spun in a circular motion. The plastic material is loaded in measured doses in each mold and, due to the centrifugal force, coats the inner surface of the mold to take on that shape. The material may need to be pliable or flexible in order to remove the part from the opening in the mold without having the mold open. A typical example is polysol, used to make the heads of dolls. Spring-mounted horses are also made by rotational molding, but these molds are larger and may be hinged to open.

QC: Abbreviation for **Q**uality **C**ontrol.

Quality Control: A checking and inspection system to ensure that the product is being made in accordance with specific standards.

Resin: The granular form of plastic raw material.

Runner: The tubular-, round-, half-round-, square-, or trapezoidal-shaped plastic channel used to transport the plastic material from the sprue to the gate of the cavities. There are several types of runner systems (i.e., hot runners, with controlled heating elements, and insulated runners, which allow the material to freeze on its perimeter, while running liquid through the center and conventional runners). When a runner is cut, a hollow core may be found through the center (also see **Hot Runner**, **Primary Runner**, and **Secondary Runner**).

Runner System: The entire set of runners, from sprue to gate. In order to maintain pressure, the sum of the cross-section of all of the tributary runners leading off from the runner of a prior step must be less than the cross-section of the prior runner. The runner system must be well-balanced. The term "sprue" is often used incorrectly by collectors to describe the runner system (see **Sprue**).

Scale: The proportion of the height or length of the toy to the real-life object, such as 1:24 or 1:32. For practical reasons, playset parts, although generally in scale with themselves, sometimes are not necessarily in scale with each other. For example, a prehistoric Dinosaur Playset might have a figure of a Tyrannosaurus, representing a monster 120 feet high, and a figure representing a prehistoric reptile 2 feet high. In order to include both toys in the same scale, one would have to be sixty times the height of the other. It would not be practical to have one at 2 inches and the other at 120 inches. Playset makers have always taken the poetic license to mix the products scales as necessary.

Secondary Runner: A runner that is a tributary from the primary one.

Shot: (a) The completely cooled plastic that has been removed from the injection mold, usually consisting of the sprue, runners, gates, and parts. (b) Shot also describes the molding cycle. (c) A third application of shot describes the size or weight of injection.

Silk Screen: Type of printing used to decorate a surface.

Specification Sheet: A detailed list of the part numbers, the required quantities, qualities (material and color), and often the sources of parts. The actual paperwork may vary from manufacturer to manufacturer.

Sprue: That conical-shaped plastic part of the shot that leads from the nozzle of the injection molding machine, through the plates, into the molding area between the A & B plates. The sprue is the only part of the runner system designed with increasing diameter, which must lose pressure in order to eject the sprue with the entire shot. This is the term that collectors often confuse with the runner system.

Sprue Bushing: The steel conical part that transports the molten plastic material from the nozzle of the machine to the molding area. This is what forms the sprue.

Sub-Assembly: Components prepared simultaneously with their assembly on line. They are prepared off to one side and fed into the main assembly line on a timed basis.

Thermoplastic: Material that can be shaped or formed under heat and pressure. It can be reprocessed.

Thermoset: Material formed under pressure; this cannot be reprocessed (except as filler).

Tooling: The apparatus, machinery, or equipment designed and made especially for a specific purpose in order to manufacture a particular product, such as molds, dies, assembly fixtures, and spray masks.

WIP: Abbreviation for **W**ork **I**n **P**rocess.

Year Shown: The Roman numerals engraved on the cores that indicate the first year of the mold's use as a later issue.

CHAPTER FOUR

THE WESTERN PLAYSET PARADE

1

From Alamo to Zorro, Marx Western playsets have meant enduring entertainment. Photo 1 is the Official Walt Disney version of the Alamo, #3534; collectors Ed Bielcik and Don Faruolo point out that the Mexicans are 54mm, the defenders 45mm. Another Disney production inspired the Zorro set shown in Photo 2. Both sets were issued before tin buildings were outlawed on the grounds of child safety. Mike Poko Collection.

2

3

One of the earliest versions (Photo 3) of Fort Apache shows a variety of color and the eventually banned tin building, while the Rin-Tin-Tin set (Photo 4, below) shows a few modifications. Photo 5 is #4202, a 1977 revision of much earlier sets. Don Faruolo Collection.

4

5

6

Fort Dearborn (Photos 6 and 7) was created as fresh use of Fort Apache components: notice that the building is the same as the earliest Fort Apache pictured here. Don Faruolo Collection.

7

3416—COMANCHE PASS PLAYSET

(NEW—TV)

Comanche Pass, the new vertical mountain playset is like a visit to the Old West with an authentic replica of a typical mountain pass and all the figures from the historic old frontier. Imagine the action as Indians defend the pass when the wagon tries to get through. Mountain set consists of 2 mountains, 2 connecting land bridges, falling boulder and 1 connecting roadway; all of high impact styrene. Set rests on printed "terrain" poly sheet 32" x 36." 120 accessories including cavalry & frontier figures, cavalry horses, Indians, totem poles, cavalry equipment, cactus plants, cannon. 19¾" high, 18" deep, 18" wide.
PACKED: 3, wgt. 24 lbs., cube 6.89

3416
COMANCHE PASS WILL BE ON TV. COMPLETE WITH FALLING BRIDGE, BOULDER, CAVALRY, INDIANS, ETCETERA, ETCETERA.

9

10

As shown in Photo 8 (a catalog sheet), the entire Comanche Pass playset rested on a 32 x 36-inch poly sheet printed with terrain detail. Photo 9, Cattle Drive, is described under Western Towns; Photo 10 is the catalog photo of the wagon-train theme Red River Playset. The 1970s saw the release of a series of lower-priced playsets, such as the 50-piece Cowboy playset, shown in the catalog sheet in Photo 11.

11

12

Gunsmoke is recaptured in the playset shown above and on the front cover. Gary J. Linden Collection. In true Marx Toys tradition, the recent issue of the Gold Rush Playset (Photo 13) uses the mine mold and other Western playset components in combination with new additions.

13

14

The Lone Ranger (Photo 14) and *The Rifleman* (Photo 15) were among the television series inspiring Marx playsets. Don Faruolo Collection.

15

16

17

Roy Rogers was featured in the very first Marx Western playsets and went on to inspire a large number of variations.

Photos 17 and 18 are interiors of the buildings shown in Photo 16. Photo 21 shows the Music Hall version of the Jail House building in Photo 18.

18

19

20

Photos 19 and 20 feature the steel ranch house.
Photos 16-21: Don Faruolo and Ed Bielcik Collections.

21

22

23

None of the specifications listings in the Marx archive factory documents exactly match the contents of the basic Western Town with its one-story building and a tepee that is shown in Photos 22 and 23 (from the collection of Don Faruolo). The picture of Magic Marxie on the box cover rules it out as one of the very earliest variations.

The popularity of the Western Towns made it a natural for production in the smaller scale as well. Photo 24 is the miniature set; Photo 25 is an O-scale ranch designed for use with Marx trains. Gary J. Linden Collection.

24

25

26

Photo 26 is the not-often-seen HO-scale Alamo ("Border Battle"), probably incomplete as shown here. The Blue and Gray Armies received detailing in the HO-scale set pictured in Photo 27. Gary J. Linden Collection.

27

The whole gang for the large-scale Johnny West Adventure promotion. See text for identification of the individual figures.

1864C
5072C
2072C
2071C
2061C
1863C
1861C
2085C
1865C
1866C
2057C
2063C

HOTEL
BANK
SALOON
THE READY GANG™
Here come the Ready Gang all set to fight it out in this authentically recreated Western setting.
Four 9½" fully poseable Western figures •
Sturdy construction •
Realistic outfits include holster or bandolier, pistols, rifle or shot gun, knife, canteen •
Fully articulated horses come complete with saddle, saddlebag, bridle, reins and rifle-sheath •
Three dimensional authentic Old West Town •

29

Unique among Marx Western playsets is The Ready Gang, with figures 9½ inches high, shown in the catalog photo reproduced as Photo 29.

Closeups of Marx figures reveal much about their artistry, production, and collectibility. In Photo 30 we see the reverse color Confederate soldiers, cast in blue to serve as the 7th Cavalry in the Custer's Last Stand Playset (the standard bearer is missing his flag in this set). Gary J. Linden Collection.

30

Warriors of the World (Photo 31) are 60mm hard plastic, hand-painted figures individually packaged in a box that contained a brief history of the subject. Gary J. Linden Collection.

Photo 32 is a hard-to-find cowgirl, generally referred to as the "Annie Oakley" pose. A 6-inch cavalry officer and a frontiersman are pictured in Photo 33, and Photo 34 shows the Marx Indians climbing over still another type of packaging, the "polka-dot" box. Gary J. Linden Collection.

31

32

33

34

35

The dramatic, desirable, and thus very rare fallen horse and rider, cast in both gray (found in Civil War sets) and in cream (for both Civil War and some Fort Apache playsets). Gary J. Linden Collection.

Completing the Marx Western playset parade, a line of figures in the range of scales: left to right, 11-inch General Custer from the Johnny West series, 9-inch Sundance Kid from the Ready Gang, 6-inch cowboy, 4-inch Roy Rogers, 3-inch cowboy, 60mm cowboy, 54mm miner, 40mm cowboy, and HO-scale 7th Cavalryman. Gary J. Linden Collection.

36

CHAPTER OVERVIEW

What follows — a guide for collectors of Marx Western playsets — is based on official Marx company documentation, which is here being made available to the public for the first time. This chapter consists of three elements:

1. An introduction looks at the kinds of information, produced through careful investigation of the Marx archives, which have been used to reconstruct the past in order to compile the comprehensive listings of Marx Western playsets; it then surveys the present and future of Marx playsets.
2. An index serves as a summary of the Western playsets we can document. This provides an overview of the detailed listings.
3. More detailed descriptions of the individual playsets and variations, illustrated, give collectors the fullest information available.

HOW TO USE THIS CHAPTER

How the Listings Are Organized

As indicated in the Index of Marx Western Playsets on pages 86 and 87, we have classified the playsets according to scale and crossover themes: "Standard Playsets" refers to the normal 2- to 2½-inch-high figures, as contrasted to "Larger-scale Playsets," generally 11-inch-high figures, or the miniature or HO-scale sets, with 1-inch-high figures. You will note that the factory records always speak of size in terms of inches; collectors today use millimeter measurements, with 54mm and 60mm being the sizes usually found in our "Standard Playsets."

As for theme: It has seemed most sensible to have the Civil War theme sets in a separate category, since they represent both the Military and the Western themes. One category is set aside for the "crossover" playsets designed to complement Marx train sets. Note that the focus of this volume is Marx *playsets*; the following listings do not include the smaller sets of theme-related figures.

The standard playset listings begin with the incomparable Fort Apache™ — in a class by itself — and are thereafter run alphabetically. You will note that sometimes you will be referred to other, more comprehensive categories of playsets; for example, Rin-Tin-Tin is, logically, grouped with Fort Apache. Especially in view of the Marx approach of reusing molds and borrowing from several playsets to create a new one, there are sometimes a number of categories into which a given playset might go. We have selected the most useful basic categories and liberally cross-referenced, so that you can find a specific playset by consulting the alphabetical index that precedes the detailed listings of Western playsets.

This book, in working toward its goal of providing for the first time absolutely reliable information, reflects what can be learned by examination of the Marx archives (as available from the U. S. records; this does not include products manufactured in Hong Kong or Japan, for example). If any reader has a significant variation of a Western playset that can be identified as a Marx playset but finds it missing from this guide, he or she is invited to pass along information including playset number, any dating information, playset name, and contents to the author, c/o Greenberg Publishing Company, Inc., 7566 Main Street, Sykesville, Maryland 21784. Readers are also invited to help us identify the numbers used by the various retail chains for their exclusive playsets. Do you have, for example, a Sears set that matches one of the Marx-numbered sets?

Each entry in the detailed listings of Western playsets includes:

- **product number(s) or "Item No."**; on the reproductions of the factory documentation you will note at the top both "Item No." and "Model No." — the former is the playset number and is thus the one cited throughout this book;
- **name of variation** (using the names on the archive documentation);
- **known year(s) of production** (using the dates appearing on the documentation that was found in the Marx archives; clearly, documentation setting up production of a playset would predate its availability on the retail market).

You will note that some factory specification sheets include products designated "D," "SD," or "Demonstrator." As mentioned in Chapter Three, these are playsets specially made for store display or marketing purposes. The designation "MO" indicates it was produced for a mail-order customer, such as Sears.

What the Listings Show

The listings include notations — taken from the wording of original catalogs and factory documents — of significant differences between one variation and another. It is important to note that the playsets are listed in this book in the order of their official numbers — and that these numbers do *not* reflect the chronological order of the introduction of the playsets (the Marx company apparently did not follow one sequence of numbers year after year). However, a listing's notation of a modification from one set to another refers to change from one year to another (again using the dates indicated on the documentation that was found in the Marx archives). In comparing playsets we include the numbers of the sets involved, to be as clear as possible.

Within each category of playset at least one variation has been selected to be featured in further detail: for this variation we reproduce original factory documentation instead of creating a detailed listing. When many variations were produced, we selected one or more playsets to be featured on the basis of its scope and/or its broad interest to collectors. We strove to represent a range of styles and hope we have featured one of your favorites.

In any event, you will see one or more representative playsets in detail and gain a sense of how playsets evolved across the years. Furthermore, the reproduced factory specification sheets, bills of materials, and/or catalog sheets, as well as original promotional photographs and other illustrations, will aid you in determining exactly which set you have, when it was manufactured, whether it was produced for a particular retail chain, what the set was supposed to include, as well as other specific information.

What the Documentation Shows

The format of the various documentation described in the Preface — specification sheets, bills of material, etc. — varied from year to year. We have selected that portion of each document that contains the most useful information. Note that in some cases a document runs to two pages.

Frank Rice, in charge of playsets at Marx, recounts that Bob Lee, who reported to Archie Marcus, was responsible for preparing all the product information sheets: "Bob was very anxious to be accurate and precise, but he was overburdened at times with other duties, such as scheduling production, placing orders for manufacture, serving as traffic manager at all three plants, and, as an effective salesman, handling certain accounts." Rice puts this multidimensional role in Marx perspective: "Like most everybody at Marx, his job was not limited to one specific area — we all were somehow responsible for making sure that whatever was necessary for success really happened. As L. M. used to say, 'we are all part of the family!' No titles, no big salaries, no special offices, no percs . . . you were just part of the team and you did what was expected and necessary and most times you were rewarded."

In the reproductions of archive documents you will often see notations such as "1 Set Outside Accessories," accompanied by a mold number. In order to help you identify more precisely the intended contents of any one playset, we are providing lists of the items produced by the molds for accessories most commonly used in Western playsets. In addition to those listed below, our search of Marx archives uncovered a number of other mold sheets for sets of accessories used occasionally, such as those for Chuck Wagon Accessories (PL-1047), or Pack Horses and Accessories (PL-1099), as well as many Civil War accessories (which we reproduce under that section). Bear in mind that just as Marx typically put together components from various existing playsets to create a new playset, the standard contents of an accessory set may have been modified for a specific new playset (often this is noted on the reproduced documentation), and molds of figures or accessories were revised and given new product numbers as time went by. A discussion of the use of molds and illustrations of mold sheets and documentary photos are found in Chapter Three.

■

WESTERN ACCESSORY SETS

Cowboy Accessories (PL-891 when combined with Indian Accessories; PL-891 B when molded separately)

2 Coiled lariats
2 Canteens
2 Carbines (short cavalry rifles)
2 Shotguns
1 Camp fire
1 Plate with cup
1 Frying pan
1 Coffee pot
1 Guitar
2 Bull whips
2 Branding irons
4 Holster belts
10 Pistols
2 Bags of gold dust
2 Cow skulls

Indian Accessories (PL-891 when combined with Cowboy Accessories; PL-891 A when molded separately)

2 Cow skulls
2 Peace pipes
2 Spears with feathers
2 Quivers with sling
10 Arrows
2 Bows
2 War clubs
2 Shields
4 Tomahawks
2 Knives
2 Knife belt with scabbard
2 Tom toms
2 Bear-claw necklaces

Stockade Accessories (PL-351)

1 Chopping block
1 Anvil
2 Powder kegs
1 Churn
1 Pile of logs
1 Well base
1 Arm with bucket
1 Fireplace
1 Arm with pots

Outside Accessories, Ranch House (PL-130)

1 Forge
1 Hitching rail
1 Grinding stone
1 Chopping block with ax
1 Pile of logs
1 Anvil
1 Rain barrel
1 Pump with pail
1 Well base
1 Well top
1 Well crossarm
1 Well pail

Small Western Wagon and Accessories (PL-1030)

1 Wagon body
1 Front swivel axle
1 Seat
1 Wagon tongue
2 Front wheels
2 Rear wheels
1 Tool box
1 Water barrel
1 Bucket
1 Tub
1 Lantern

Western Town Outside Furniture / Outside Accessories (PL-388)

1 Log-type hitching rail
1 Square-type hitching rail
1 Lamppost
1 Garden-tool rack
1 Broom-and-mop rack
1 Bench with back rest
1 Watering trough
2 Boardwalk signs
3 Lanterns
1 Peddle-type grindstone
1 Bench with arm rest
1 Tavern chair
1 Crate with rifles
1 Barrel
1 Feed sack
3 Cuspidors

Western Town Inside Furniture (PL-386: 21 items)

1 Bed
1 Dresser
1 Washstand with basin
1 Rocking chair
1 Bar
1 Round table
2 Tavern chairs
1 Table lamp
2 Swinging doors
2 Benches with back and arm rest
2 Hall trees
1 Table with books
1 Carpet bag
1 Teller cage
1 Slanted-top desk
1 Desk (sheriff)
1 Chair
1 Barber chair base
1 Barber chair seat
1 Dry goods counter
1 Cider barrel with spigot
1 Flour sack
1 Feed sack

Western Town Inside Furniture (PL-387: 22 items)

1 Dry goods counter
1 Cider barrel with spigot
1 Barrel
1 Feed sack
1 Flour sack
2 Crates
1 Display rack with tools
1 Counter with nail bins, etc.
1 Display rack withguns
1 Counter scales
1 Spool barbed wire
2 Roll-top desks
1 Type cabinet
1 Chair
1 Printing press
1 Sheriff's armchair
1 Table with books
1 Bench
1 Cot
1 Washstand with pail and wash basin

Gold Mine Accessories (PL-1057)

Hill and sluice
Hill and entrance
Track
1 Ore car
2 Wheels and axle
1 Barrel-type rocker on sluice
1 Sign post "Velendi"

Tracking the Past

The Western playsets described in this chapter are known to have been produced as early as 1954. The records in the Marx archives provide reliable information on Western playsets produced from 1954 to 1978, but concrete, specific data on the few sets made before 1954 have not been located. The early records we do have show that the Roy Rogers Double Bar Ranch and Mineral City playsets were offered by Sears in 1952. And the famous Fort Apache playset, with metal log cabin and shell-shooting cannon, first appeared in the 1953 Sears catalog. Therefore, we can conclude that Marx definitely made playsets earlier than 1954.

Further, there is evidence that the first Western playset was made after June of 1950 and most likely was the one advertised in the 1952 Sears catalog. The dating of the Western playsets has been aided by the fact that the Marx archives reveal that the first molds built by Marx to be used in playsets were the following:

#79 Fence: Received (at the Marx factory) June 28, 1949; first used in the Playground Set and the Service Station Set.

#127 Ranch House Furniture: Received May 8, 1950.

#128 Ranch Animals: Received March 3, 1950.

#129 Cowboys: Received April 27, 1950.

#130 Outside Accessories–Ranch House: Received March 8, 1950.

#131 Trees: Received March 3, 1950.

In Chapter Three we saw that the Marx Western playset had its origins in a Happi-Time Farm Set, with its realistic accessories: toy buyers' suggestions guided Marx toward the great heroes of the American West. As Frank Rice puts it: "The basic philosophy of a successful playset was the good guys against the bad guys, with a base of some sort — log cabin, fort, castle, etc., usually metal lithography in the early days."

Of course, technologies, customer preferences, child-safety concerns, and the standards of Marx led to various modifications as time went by. Documents for the playsets listed below sometimes note the need for a new mold for a particular playset. This might have been dictated by customer needs, or simply by the capacity of existing molds. Colors were changed from time to time, and an important change in the plastics used occurred. Western ranch figures were originally molded in a soft vinyl unbreakable plastic (previously most toy figures were die-cast or hard polystyrene and thus susceptible to breakage). But vinyl took a "set," as Rice explains, and often did not stand properly:

> This infuriated L. M., and Walter Gryce and L. M. had many confrontations, which eventually led to polyethylene material. L. M. demanded that no matter what, the figures must stand. At first Wally, realist that he was, tried to balance the figure by pose and weight distribution, but the vagaries of plastic shrinkage and material variations were impossible to control — hence in many instances, especially in the early cowboy and Indian molds, platforms were added to the cavities to satisfy the Boss, even after the molds were actually in production.

Marx would always economize where appropriate — for example, reprocessing plastic for use in Fort Apache stockade manufacture — but the artistry and play value of the playsets would not be compromised. In fact, each of these features was steadily enhanced by Marx craftsmen and the moldmakers they engaged. The crude animals of the Happi-Time Farm Set or the first depictions of Western people were eventually replaced by markedly finer figures. Before turning to the descriptions of the sets themselves, we pause to update the story of Marx Toys.

MARX WESTERN PLAYSETS RIDE AGAIN!

The enduring quality, classic design, and play value of the Marx playsets have enabled them to thrive and survive the turmoils of the various companies that took ownership and/or possession of the molds. Here we pick up the saga of Louis Marx & Co., Inc. as we left it in Chapter Two.

Toward the end of its Marx toy production and sales, Dunbee-Combex-Marx (DCM), still striving for survival, put certain Marx assets up for sale to raise cash to meet obligations. Richard Beecham, director of DCM, personally chose Lawrence Passick, a long-term, loyal, and knowledgeable Marx employee, to lease or sell certain products or product line molds to specific companies. The Marx line was so extensive that an entire company could operate with a partial line or even a single product. Several deals were struck, the most notable being the sale around 1980 of the best-selling "Big Wheel" and other ride-on toys to Empire of Carolina. The strength of the Big Wheel product is illustrated not only by its continuing sales pattern, but also by the numerous copies of it — particularly in the United States, but also throughout the world.

American Plastic Equipment, Inc. has played a major role in the continuation of the Marx saga. It was incorporated in 1978 in Tallahassee, Florida, as a supplier of product-tooling and rights to companies, especially those outside the United States. As opportunity arose, American Plastic purchased molds, first on a product-by-product basis, later on a full product line, and eventually entire company assets. The company purchased Marx assets, including the Marx molds, from the Chemical Bank of New York in 1982. But it was only after long and complicated negotiations that American Plastic was able to secure the rights to the Marx name and all other rights through a separate transaction in 1988. Among other projects, American Plastic has built a toy factory in mainland China, using Marx toy truck molds and Ideal Toy machinery (after purchasing the plant in 1985 from CBS).

Many companies were interested in Marx molds. The molds for Marx's popular line of typewriters was sold to a Japanese company. Combi, a new company, purchased the molds for certain ride-on toys. And in 1980, Marx sold approximately $1.5 million worth of its playset molds and rights to Mego Toys of New York. The sale included the most famous of all Marx playsets, Fort Apache. Also included was the Guns of Navarone playset, which turned a standard two-dimensional playset into three dimensions by adding the vertical mountain. A newer, less well-known Undersea Set and the perennial Prehistoric Monsters were also sold.

Mego was one of the highfliers of the toy industry in the early 1980s. Its success came to an abrupt crash when unusual circumstances strangled the company by 1983, causing the sale of the molds of the Marx playsets to Packaging and Assembly Corporation (PAC). Until then, PAC had been a custom manufacturer and assembler of toy products for other toy companies in the greater New York area. The company's principal was Joseph Ruzzi, a knowledgeable and talented man. Like other suppliers and custom manufacturers before him, Ruzzi had concluded that if his firm could make the goods for others to sell, why not make and sell them for itself? Therefore, in 1983 PAC came out with a consumer toy line that included the playsets. PAC also purchased the molds for the Rock 'em Sock 'em Robots from American Plastic. The products were exhibited at the New York Toy Show in February 1984.

Unfortunately, PAC ran into difficulties that forced it out of business. Once again, American Plastic Equipment, Inc. enters the picture. In 1986 it purchased all of PAC's and Mego's molds, including the Marx molds from The Bank Leumi, through liquidators. Thus, the absent playset molds were finally reunited with the rest of the Marx playset molds (that American Plastic had purchased in 1982 from the Chemical Bank). That was fortunate indeed, as Mego had naturally chosen the Western and Military as two of the most important and lucrative lines.

In 1986 American Plastic licensed the rights to manufacture and distribute the Military and Prehistoric playsets to the Superior Toy Company of Chicago, headed by Michael Landsman. Four years later, Superior Toy, after almost a half-century of operations, filed for protection under Chapter 11 of the Bankruptcy Code, and its contract expired. Therefore, in 1990, the playset molds and rights reverted back to American Plastic.

Just prior to the 87th annual American Toy Fair held in New York City, February 1990, American Plastic licensed a new company, Toy Street of West Caldwell, New Jersey, to manufacture and market certain Marx Western playsets updated for the 1990s. Toy Street's philosophy, like that of Louis Marx & Company's, is quality and value at a realistic price. Like Louis and David Marx, the experienced and energetic owner, Ray Wharrie, has built his rapidly growing company on the re-use of unique, high-quality tooling to avoid the prohibitive cost of development described in Chapter Two. Wharrie is able to couple low start-up costs with low overhead, running the no-frills business by himself. Toy Street has set about to prove that a small, well-run toy company with a good product can succeed financially even today, in a market dominated by billion-dollar companies.

The firm chose the legendary Fort Apache name under which to market the expanded set (the original Fort Apache playsets date back to the early 1950s). Immediately, important retailers such as Toys "R" Us and Jamesway have purchased the new Fort Apache for their stores. In the Marx tradition, Toy Street has also made an economical, scaled-down version of the Fort Apache playset for cost-conscious consumers. Since that time, Toy Street has added Military, Prehistoric, Pirates, and Medieval playsets.

Charles Marx, son of David, has been instrumental to the rebirth of Marx itself as a mass-producing toy manufacturer. Thanks in part to Charles's commitment, Western playsets are again becoming available to the public under the Marx Toys brand.

Aware of avid collector interest, American Plastic has reinstated Louis Marx & Company. It provides consumers with authentic Marx toy products, adhering to the policies, traditions, and standards that made Marx number one in the industry. The Gold Rush playset, Louis Marx & Company's first issue in its Vintage Collector Series, represents the first new Marx product in over a decade. It sold out after its issue. Other playsets have followed — including a new Fort Apache — and more are in the works.

What else does the future hold for playsets fans? We can only wait and see, as Marx history continues to be written and the Marx Western playsets ride again!

INDEX OF MARX WESTERN PLAYSETS

Name	Number of Variations	First and Last Years of Known Documentation	Page
Western Town. *See* **Western Towns** and **HO-scale Playsets**.			
Western Towns			
Old Western Town Set	1	1954	153
Silver City	4	1954–1956	153
Tales of Wells Fargo Western Town with Dale Robertson	4	1958–1959	153
Western Cattle Drive	1	1972	153
Western Mining Town	4	1960	153
Western Town	1	1964	153
Western Town. *See* **HO-scale Playsets**.			
Wyatt Earp Dodge City	3	1957–1958	153
Wild West Ranch Set. *See* **Western Ranches**.			
Wyatt Earp Dodge City. *See* **Western Towns**.			
Zorro	1	1966	162
Civil War Playsets			
The Blue and the Gray	24	1956–1975	165
Figures	2	1955	166
See also **HO-scale Playsets**.			
Crossover Items: Trains and Playsets			
Old-Fashioned B. & O. Train — Wild West Set	1	1959	173
Wells Fargo Wild West Town	2	1959	173
HO-scale Playsets			175
Blue and Gray Armies	1		
Border Battle (Alamo)	1		
Covered Wagon Attack	1		
Custer's Last Stand	1		
Fort Apache	3		
Miniature Masterpieces: Confederate Soldiers; Union Soldiers			
Western Town	1		
Larger-scale Playsets			
Covered Wagon Set. *See* **Western Stagecoach and Wagon Sets**.			
Daniel Boone Frontier Set. *See* **Western Stagecoach and Wagon Sets.**			
Johnny West and the Best of the West	34 basic items	1966–1976	176
The Ready Gang	1	1977	181
Western Stagecoach and Wagon Sets	5	1965–1972	183
Western Action Figure Sets			
Western Playset	1	1976	187
Marx Vintage Collector Series			
Fort Apache	1	1992	189
Gold Rush Playset	1	1990	189

STANDARD SETS

FORT APACHE and RIN-TIN-TIN

History has proven Fort Apache to be the staple of all the Western playsets. It was, along with two Roy Rogers sets, an early entry into the Western playset market: the Sears Christmas catalog of 1953 introduces the seventy-five-piece Fort Apache with shell-shooting cannon. The original cost of the playset production molds, in 1950, was $185,273. At the time of this writing the replacement cost would be in excess of $1,200,000.

Although it has evolved through changes such as metal buildings becoming plastic, the basic set always had a fort as its environment and two types of figures — cavalry and Indian. The standard set could easily be customized by adding or deleting parts for a specific customer and, indeed, variations designed for Sears Roebuck, Montgomery Ward, or W. T. Grant abound. Some customers even offered more than one variation; the 1967 Sears catalog, for example, advertises both a 101-piece and a 330-piece Battle of Fort Apache. There were at least forty-five different variations. Featured on the following pages are playsets numbered 3675, 3678, 3680, 3681, and 3686.

Furthermore, when a particular Western setting became popular due to a movie or television show, the set could be adapted in response. Rin-Tin-Tin is a perfect example of adding a simple six-cavity figure mold, PL-781, containing two Rin-Tin-Tins, two Rustys, and two Lieutenant Rip Masters; one set of the trio adapted the Fort Apache playset to a then-popular theme.

The long-lasting popularity of Fort Apache is no doubt due to its containing all the elements of a good playset, especially the diversity of figures and the drama of opposing forces. And since the action took place in an historic setting, it could never have a "dated" look but remained classic and timeless.

See also **HO-scale Playsets** for three additional variations. See Color Photos 3, 4, and 5.

1870SD Fort Apache and Johnny West Demonstrator (1955, 1967)

(See **Larger-scale Playsets**)

1875 Fort Apache (1967)

(See **Larger-scale Playsets**)

2049D Best of the West and Fort Apache Fighters Display (1968)

(See **Larger-scale Playsets**)

3616, 3616D Fort Apache Stockade with Famous Americans (1955)

Stockade complete with two blockhouses, log cabin (steel, lithographed inside and out), tepee, and outside accessories; and twelve cavalrymen, fourteen Indians and horses of flexible plastic; featuring authentic miniatures of five famous Americans of frontier history (Buffalo Bill, Sitting Bull, Daniel Boone, Kit Carson, Gen. George Custer). Completely equipped, both inside and out, to accurately reproduce a walled frontier fort with an adjoining Indian camp. Stockade walls consist of eleven interlocking log-type plastic sections, each measuring 5¾" long, 4⅜" high, plus a log-type archway with two gates that swing open or snap closed. Molded of sturdy plastic in tan or brown.

3627, 3627SD, 3628, 3628SD Rin-Tin-Tin Fort Apache (1956)

Virtually the same as #3616 but Rin-Tin-Tin, Rusty, and Lt. Rip Masters replace the five famous historical figures, and instead of #3616's use of two different molds for a total of fourteen Indian figures in a variety of poses, #3627 uses one set of PL-310 and #3628 uses two sets.

3630 Fort Apache Stockade with Famous Historical Americans (1956)

In this playset the miniature historic figures are General Custer and Sitting Bull, and there are thirty Indians and thirty frontier figures.

3657 "Rin-Tin-Tin" Fort Apache Set (1957)

Factory specification sheet indicates "Extra small lithographed log cabin" (this was same one used in #3997, 3998; see **Rifleman**), two sets of cavalry figures for a total of twenty, a different set of fifteen Indians and one totem pole, the new blockhouse style introduced that year, and three character figures.

3660, 3660MO Fort Apache Stockade (1957, 1958)

Stockade walls here are ten interlocking straight log-type fence sections with two new corner sections to permit a recessed location for the archway with its two swinging gates; includes two tepees; tree added. Such modifications were typical of Marx efforts to boost and/or customize value for mail-order customers.

3675, 3675SD Fort Apache Playset (1957)

See reproduced documentation for description of this featured playset.

3676, 3676D Large Fort Apache (1957)

Factory records indicate this set featured a new cavalry headquarters building, new lithographed roof sign for building (as used on the Alamo playset), new corner wall sections and blockhouses, four cavalry horses, two Indian horses, a harness horse, and a dead horse.

3677, 3677SD Fort Apache Playset (1958)
This replaces item #3657 (see above).

3678, 3678SD "Fort Apache" Playset (1958)
Featured set; see reproduced documentation.

3680, 3680MO "Fort Apache" Playset (1959, 1962)
Featured set; see reproduced documentation from 1962. Factory records from 1959 indicate certain items were produced in colors different from those listed in 1962; the tepee was light gray, the stockade and blockhouses were brown. #3680MO, produced for Montgomery Ward in 1962, added a fallen horse and rider in gray.

3681, 3681A, 3681AF Fort Apache Playset (1964, 1972, 1975)
#3681 is a featured set; see reproduced documentation. Note that cavalry accessories had been added in 1964 but these do not appear by 1972. The "F" in the product number designation "3681AF" indicates the addition of a bilingual instruction sheet.

3682, 3682D Fort Apache Playset with New Gate and Blockhouse (Sears) (1959)
Factory documents indicate that a "new" stockade gate, with its own 9¾"-long overhead blockhouse emblazoned with the "Fort Apache" name, has a roof flagpole with a twenty-star U. S. flag. Two additional blockhouses, with ladders, serve as watchtowers at either end of the fort. It was a Sears mail-order item in 1959 and replaced #3660MO (1958).

3683 Fort Apache (Sears) (1968)
Similar to #3681 but with fewer pieces.

3684 Fort Apache Set (1965, 1972)
The 1965 playset, produced for Montgomery Ward, and the "Sears Heritage Set," documented in 1972, are similar and each has a thirty-six-star flag, but there are numerous differences, such as six tepees reduced to one, a hospital wagon and covered wagon being dropped, and two cannons becoming one in the 1972 version.

3685, 3685SD "Rin-Tin-Tin" Fort Apache Set (1958, 1966: Sears)
The 1958 documentation indicates this playset replaced #3675. The Sears set is identical with #3681 except that a small Western wagon, a wagon cover and wagon accessories, and two harness horses have been added.

3686, 3686SD, R-3686 "Rin-Tin-Tin" Fort Apache Playset (1958)
#3686 is a featured set; see reproduced documentation. Compare with that for #3680.

3686 Fort Apache (Sears) (1975)
Similar to #3686 above (also shown in reproduced documentation), but had fewer figures (only twelve cavalrymen, sixteen Indian figures and totem poles), only two tepees — and no Rin-Tin-Tin.

3690 Happi-Time Fort Apache Playset (1961)
Includes cavalry building without roof sign, new Fort Apache building porch, shooting cannon with shells and shooting pistol with bullets. Factory documentation notates customer's desire for more reddish-brown fencing.

3692 Fort Apache Set (Sears) (1962)
Larger number of Indians, three tepees, two cannons, covered wagon, hospital wagon, pack horses, fallen horse and rider (see Color Photo 35), and two sets of cavalry accessories included in this version.

3694 Fort Apache (Sears) (1964, 1965)
Similar to #3692 (above); also includes bows and arrows.

3698 Fort Apache Set (Sears) (1964, 1965)
Trees as well as bows and arrows included.

4202 Fort Apache Playset (1977)
Documentation indicates this was a revision of #3681, 3681A, 3681AF (above); updated packaging.

4500 Fort Apache (1992)
(See **Marx Vintage Collection Series**)

4681, 4681MO Fort Apache Play Case Set (1967)
Metal case measures 19" x 4¼" x 12¾". See photo.

4685, 4685MO Action Carryall Fort Apache (1970)
Similar to #4681 (above), but lithography inside building has been revised; cannon and shells added, standing cavalry figures increased from ten to sixteen, and horses reduced from eleven to nine.

4688D Carryall Action Display Demonstrator (1970)
Consists of one saleable Fort Apache set (#4685) in a metal case and one cardboard display unit.

4689D Carryall Action Display Unit (1968)
Same as above.

On this and the next two pages appear original glossy photos for Marx catalogs: #3680, #3681, #3692, #3698, and #4681; examination of the first four reveals clearly the modifications across the years in terms of additions of tepees, blockhouses, etc.

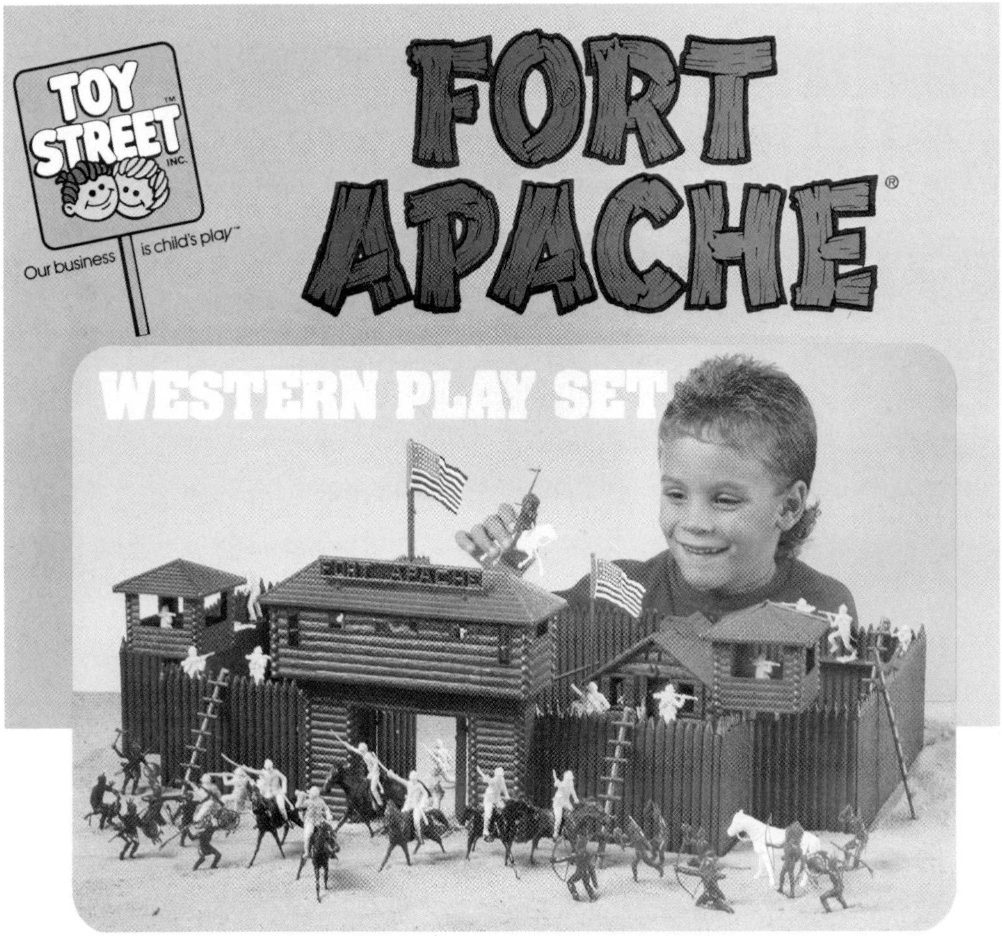

Toy Street has used Fort Apache as the keynote of its new playset promotion.

LOUIS MARX & CO.
200 Fifth Ave., New York

GLENDALE DIVISION
5/23/57

NO. 3675 FORT APACHE PLAY SET

Fort Apache, outpost of the west, features the U. S. Cavalry, and Indian Village and an assortment of equipment that will keep youngsters active and happy for hours.

The U. S. Cavalry Headquarters measures 13-1/4" long, 6-3/4" high, 4-1/2" wide. It is a lithographed building sturdily constructed of steel. Featuring log cabin style plastic pegs and a roof sign lithographed, "U.S.Cavalry Headquarters", the building houses the Commandants office and the cavalry stabled.

Fort Apache is a stockade fort and it is built with 12 sections of 4-1/2" high stockade fence and a Fort Apache sign and gatepost. Four blockhouses provide observation towers. Blockhouses ladders are constructed of plastic.

A nearby Indian Village includes three Tepees, two Totem Poles, and a Canoe. There are 30 Indian Figures and two Indian Horses. The figures are handsomely detailed and carry bows and arrows, tomahawks, shields and war standards.

Twenty U. S. Cavalrymen see duty at Fort Apache. Durably constructed of plastic the figures carry rifles, sabres and game. There are four cavalry horses with integral saddles and one dead horse.

Two large cannons are supplied with shells which really shoot. Other accessories include:

Tree	Powder Kegs	Ladders	Woodpile	Well with Bucket
Chopping block with axe		Churn	Anvil	

PACKED: Each in a box, 1/4 dozen to shipping carton
Weight per carton - 15 lbs.

NO. 3675SD SPECIAL DEMONSTRATOR W/SILK SCREEN LAYOUT

Entire set securely mounted to board for display purposes.
PACKED: Each in a shipper, Weight per carton - 15 lbs.

FACTORY SPECIFICATIONS:
Model No. 6352X

1 - Model 6091X-1	New Cavalry Headquarters Building
1 - PL-727	Set Plastic ladders and pins
1 -	Lithographed roof sign for building (as used on Alamo Set)
4 - PL-840	Sections Stockade fence without platform
8 - PL-341	Sections Stockade fence w/platform
1 - PL-342	Stockade gate
2 - PL-884	New Corner wall sections
4 - PL-854	New Blockhouses w/ladders
1 - PL-351	Set outside accessories
2 - PL-745	Sets Cavalry Figures (20 pieces)
2 - PL-787	Sets Indians & Totem Pole (total 30 figures - 2 totem poles)
3 - Model 6222X	PL-684 Indian Tepees
4 - PL-779	Cavalry Horses
2 - PL-692	Indian Horses
2 - PL-411	Cannons w/shells
1 - PL-346	Flagpole w/base
1 -	Lithographed Flag (Early American)
1 - PL-850	Lying down Horse
1 - PL-763	Canoe
1 - PL-524	Trees

5000 SERIES

LOUIS MARX & CO.
200 Fifth Ave., New York

GLENDALE DIVISION
2/28/58

NO. 3678 "FORT APACHE" PLAY SET

The Fort is enclosed in 12 sections of brown stockade fence, includes two special setback sections and a Stockade gate with Fort Apache gate sign. Two blockhouses serve as watchtowers at either end of the Fort.

Cavalry Headquarters measures 12" long, 7-1/4" high overall and 4-1/2" wide, is a "Log Cabin" constructed of lithographed steel but with real "log" ends. The Commandant's office and the stable are both represented. There is also a "U.S. CAVALRY HEADQUARTERS" roof sign.

Manning the Fort are 20 Cavalry men in live action poses. A nearby Indian Village supplies a war party of 15 Braves. There are also 3 Cavalry Horses and an Indian Horse. All figures are molded in plastic.

A shell shooting cannon that shoots shells, a 20-star U.S. Flag with pole, a well with Pie and bucket, a churn, anvil, cooking pot over campfire, 2 powder kegs, and a woodpile, and a chopping block with axe, complete Fort Apache's equipment.

The Indian Village includes a Totem Pole, Tepee, and a 35-pcs. set of equipment featuring tom-toms, tomahawks, bows, arrows, etc.

PACKED: Each in a box, 1/4 dozen to shipping carton,
Weight per carton - 16 lbs.

NO. 3678SD DEMONSTRATOR

The above item completely set up for demonstration purposes.

PACKED: Each in a shipping carton, Weight per carton - 20 lbs.

FACTORY SPECIFICATIONS:

This item replaces 3658

1 -		Cavalry Headquarters Building - as used last year on 3658.
1 -		Lithographed Sign U.S. Cavalry Headquarters.
1 -	PL-727	Set Pins and ladders
6 -	PL-890	Stockade fence w/out ramp
4 -	PL-341	Stockade fence w/ramp
2 -	PL-884	Stockade fence corner sections
1 -	PL-342	Stockade gate & frame
2 -	PL-854	New blockhouses w/ladders
1 -	PL-351	Set outside stockade accessories
2 -	PL-745	Sets Cavalry figures (20 pcs.)
1 -	PL-~~781~~ 787	Set Indian figures (15 Indians & 1 Totem Pole)
1 -	PL-864	Tepee (molded in polyehtylene)
3 -	PL-779	Cavalry Horses
1 -	PL-692	Indian Horses
1 -	P-	Instruction sheet
1 -	PL-411	Cannon w/shells
1 -	PL-346	Flagpole
1 -		Lithographed Flag - 20-stars
1 -	PL-891	Set Indian accessories on runner

Note: This item contains no Rin-Tin-Tin

1000 Series

LOUIS MARX & CO.

200 FIFTH AVE. NEW YORK

GLENDALE DIVISION

5/22/62

NO. 3680 "FORT APACHE" PLAY SET

Relive the exciting days of the Indian Wars with "fort apache", a rough and ready action play set.

Build a real stockade of 12 sections of stockade fence (some with interior ramp, 2 special setback sections (and the "Fort Apache" swinging gate with sign. A big plus: two corner block-houses with ladders. Each stockade section measures 4-1/2" high, 5-3/4" wide, is molded in high impact plastic.

Cavalry Headquarters , a lithographed steel building that measures 11" long, 6" wide, 5" high, includes a stovepipe chimney.

Join the 20 Cavalry men in the Fort. Ride the three Cavalry Horses. You'll find Fort equipment including two Shell-Shooting Cannons with shells, two powder kegs, a churn, anvil, log pile, chopping block, well with pole and bucket and 20 Star lithographed steel American Flag on pole.

You'll ride against a war party of 15 braves, watch the nearby Indian Village with its Tepee and Totem Pole.

You'll even find a 35 piece set of Cavalry gear including swords, bugles, field glasses, pistols, carbines, dispatch cases- and more.

All this in "Fort Apache", the rough and ready action play set.

PACKED: Each in a box,
1/4 dozen to a shipping carton
Weight per carton- 15-1/2 lbs.

NO. 3680D SETUP DEMONSTRATOR

The above item completely setup with all items securely affixed to board for counter display purposes.

PACKED: Each in a box,
Weight per carton- 17 lbs.

Acknowledged By:________________ Date:________

Replaces sheet dated 2/18/59

Date 5/22/62

Item Number 3680

How Packed EACH IN DIE CUT CORRUGATED BOX

Quantity Packed 1/4 dozen   Demo 1 only

Wgt. per Shipping Ctn. 15-1/2 lbs.   17 lbs.

		L.	W.	D.
Carton Dimensions		16	15	24-3/4
	Demo	40-1/2	24-3/4	13

Frt. Classification Cartons, Games or Toys, N.O.I.B.N., Iron or Steel, 20 ga. or thicker, or any gauge, KDF

Net Wgt. 9-1/2   12   Gross Wgt. 15-1/2   17

Tare Wgt. 6   5   Legal Wgt. 13-1/4   15

FACTORY SPECIFICATIONS

1-Regular size Log Cabin Building - 11" long w/Stovepipe & Chimney- Glendale's No. 9
6-PL-890 Stockade Fence Sections w/o Ramp- Red- Brown
4-PL-341 Stockade Fence Sections w/ Ramp- Red- Brown
2-PL-884 Stockade Corner Fence Sections- Red-Brown
1-PL-342 Stockade Gate- Red- Brown
2-PL-854 Blockhouse w/Ladders- Red-Brown
2-Sets (20) Cavalry Figures- PL-745- Blue
1-Set PL-787 Indians (15 Indians & 1 Totem Pole) - Yellow & Copper
3-Cavalry Horses- PL-779- Ivory & Brown
1-Indian Horse- PL-692- Ivory
1-Flag Pole - PL-346- Gray
1-Litho American Flag - 20 Stars
1-Set PL-351 Outside Accessories- Brownish Tan & Light Gray
1-PL-864 Tepee- Beige
2-PL-411 Cannons- Black
1-Set PL-908 Cavalry Accessories on runner- Silver Metallic
[illegible]
1-P- Inst sheet
1093

ITEM NO. 3681
Date 5/28/64
Customer No.
Replaces Sheet 2/14/64

GLEN DALE DIVISION
SPECIFICATION SHEET

Model No.
Cost No. CO 3026

Item FORT APACHE PLAY SET

Quantity	Part No.	Description		Color
1	PT-1145	#11A Cavalry Building	3304 70 / 2153 07 / 1600 39 / 541.12	
1		#4100 Litho Flag - 36 Star		
1 set	PL-854	Blockhouses (2) w/Ladders (4)	3700	Reddish Brown
1	PL-864	Tepee	3150 00	Beige
1 set	PL-1112	Building Porch & Acc.	5825 00	Reddish Brown
2 pcs	PL-341	Fence w/Ramp	4250 00	Reddish Brown
1 set	PL-342	Stockade Gate	3650.00	Reddish Brown
1 set	PL-351	Outside Accessories	7450.00	Dark Brown
1 set	PL-411	Cannon	5630 00	Black
2 pcs	PL-884	Corner Sections	4900 00	Reddish Brown
6 pcs	PL-890	Fence w/o Ramp	2750 00	Reddish Brown
1 set	PL-908	Cavalry Acc. on runner	~~8725 00~~	Black
3 sets	PL-745	Cavalry Figures (30)	4350.00	Blue
1 set	PL-787	Indians (15) & Totem Pole (1)	5225.00	Copper & Yellow
1 set	PL-779	Cavalry Horses (6)	2800.00	Brown & Black
1	PL-692	Indian Pony	2500.00	Ivory
1	P-1500	Caution Notice		
1	P	Instruction Sheet		
			72804.28	

Length
Width
Height
Dia.

Replaces 2/17/67
Date 6/26/72

LOUIS MARX & CO.
GLEN DALE W. VA.

Item No. #3681
Model No. #7784X
File No.
Authorized

SPECIFICATIONS FOR " Fort Apache Play Set" Page 1 of 2

PART NO.	PCS.	PART NAME	MATERIAL	COLORS
PT-1054	1	#4100 Flag - (36 Star)	Metal - Litho.	
PT-1145	1	#11A Cavalry Building	Metal - Litho. 3304 2153 1600	
PL-341	2	Fence w/Ramp	Plastic (Sty.)	Reddish Brown
PL-342	1Set	Stockade Gate - (3 pcs.)	Plastic (Sty.)	Reddish Brown
PL-351	1Set	Outside Acc. (10 pcs.)	Plastic (Sty.)	Gray, Brown, & Tan
PL-411	1	Cannon	Plastic (Sty.)	Black
PL-692	1	Indian Pony	Plastic (Poly.)	Ivory
PL-745	2Sets	Cavalry Figs. - (20 pcs.)	Plastic (Poly.)	Blue
PL-779	1Set	Cavalry Horses - (6 pcs.)	Plastic (Poly.)	Brown & Black
PL-787	1Set	Indians - (16 pcs.)	Plastic (Poly.)	Coppertone
PL-854	1Set	Blockhouses & Ladders-(6 pcs.)	Plastic (Sty.)	Reddish Brown
PL-864	1	Tepee	Plastic (Poly.)	Beige
PL-884	2	Corner Sections	Plastic (Sty.)	Reddish Brown
PL-890	6	Fence w/o Ramp	Plastic (Sty.)	Reddish Brown
PL-1112	1Set	Building Porch & Acc. (7 pcs.)	Plastic (Sty.)	Reddish Brown
S-84	1	Spring - (PL-411 Cannon)	Wire	
P-1500R	1	Caution Notice	Paper	Printed
P-1570	1	Inst. Sheet		Printed
P-2090	1	Label - (Satin Finish)	P/S - 2-7/8" Dia.	Printed
		IND. CARTON - EACH IN A D/C CARTON w/4 COLOR LABELS.		
		Inside Size: 23-7/8" X15-5/8" X 3-3/4"		
		Outside Size: 24-1/2" X 15-3/4" X 4"		
		Diag: 29"		
		Wt:		

LOUIS MARX & CO.
200 Fifth Ave,, New York

GLENDALE DIVISION
2/28/58

. Dargitz

NO. 3686 "RIN-TIN-TIN" FORT APACHE PLAY SET

Rin-Tin-Tin Fort Apache, a rough and ~~rough~~ ready action set features Rin-Tin-Tin, Rusty, and Lt. Rip Masters and a wealth of frontier equipment.

Thr Fort is enclosed in 14 sections of brown stockade fence that includes two special setback sections. A new stockade gate has its own 10" long blockhouse with a roof flagpole and 20 Star U. S. Flag. Two additional blockhouses serve as watchtowers at either end of the Fort.

Cavalry Headquarters is a log cabin that measures 11" long, 6" wide and 6" high and is constructed of lithographed steel.

Manning the Fort are 20 Cavalry Men, Lt. Rip Masters, Rusty, and Rinny. There are also ~~xx~~ 4 Cavalry Horses. Fort equipment includes a tree, two shell shooting cannons, ladders, two powder kegs, an anvil, a well with ple and bucket, a chopping block, woodpile, a cooking pot over campfire and a churn. There is also a 35 pcs. set of Military equipment such as carbines, pistols, lariots, etc.

A nearby Indian Village supplies a war party of 30 Braves and two horses. The Indian Village includes 3 tepees, 2 totem poles, a canoe, and a 35 pcs. set of accessories such as tom-toms, tomahawks, bows, arrows, and others.

PACKED: Each in a box, 1/4 dozen to shipping carton,
Weight per carton - 19-1/2 lbs.

NO. 3686SD DEMONSTRATOR

The above item completely set up for counter display purposes.

PACKED: Each in a shipper Weight per carton - 15 lbs.

FACTORY SPECIFICATIONS:

1 -		Log Cabin w/out base, w/new wire support (reg. size) w/stove pipe chimney
4 -	PL-341	Sections stockade fence w/ramp
2 -	PL-884	Sections stockade fence corner sections
8 -	PL-890	Sections stockade fence ~~w/ramp~~ w/out ramp
1 -	#6569X-1	New blockhouse - gate unit w/flagpole
1 -	PL-351	Set outside accessories
2 -	PL-854	New blockhouses w/ladders
2 -	PL-692	Indian Horses
2 -	PL-779	Cavalry Horses
2 -	PL-745	Sets Cavalry figures (20 pcs.)
2 -	PL-787	Sets Indians (consisting of 30 Indians & 2 Totem Poles)
3 -	PL-864	Indian Tepees
2 -	PL-411	Cannons w/shells
1 -	PL-763	Canoe
1 -	PL-524	Tree
1 -		Lithographed American Flag - 20 stars
1 -	PL-891	Indian accessory set on runner (35 pcs.)
1 -	PL-908	Cavalry accessory set on runner
3 -	PL-781	Rin-Tin-Tin figures (Rin-Tin-Tin, Rusty, & Lt. Rip Masters)
1 -	P-	Instruction sheet

5000 Series

ALAMO and DAVY CROCKETT

The Alamo playsets feature a prime example of using standard Marx Western molds and adding a mold with a likeness of Davy Crockett to take advantage of a theme popularized by a major motion picture. The mold sheet and photo of the figures that constitute Alamo Frontiersmen (PL-745) are reproduced in Chapter Three. Marx created two different sets of frontiersmen, one 60mm hard polystyrene, also used in the Famous Americans series, and one 40mm in the softer polyethylene.

Note that there are Davy Crockett playsets that are not strictly Alamo sets. Also, study Color Photo 26 in the Album of Playsets for information about the HO-scale version of the Alamo (see **HO-scale Playsets**).

0710 34-Piece Texas Frontier Set (1956)

Bagged assorted group including one unofficial Davy Crockett figure, twenty frontier figures in beige and silver, ten blue Mexican soldiers, and three horses.

0948, 0948D Davy Crockett and Frontier Figures (1955)

The six famous Americans (see photo). Each figure had his birth date written on the back. Originally all made in tan, the figures appeared in a mixture of tan, yellow, and gray for 0948D as of May 1955.

2707, 2707D Bagged Alamo Playset (1957)

The first time, according to the original catalog sheet, that Marx presented a complete playset in a sturdy sales and storage bag (with cardboard header). The twenty-seven pieces include a replica of the famous fort in lithographed steel (the archway without gates features the word "Alamo") three sections of fence, one shell-shooting cannon, ten Mexican soldiers, ten frontiersmen, and two horses.

3518 Davy Crockett Alamo Figure Set (1955)

Six frontiersmen, ten Mexican soldiers, official Davy Crockett figure, tree, cactus, four sections of fence. The specifications were for Mexican soldiers, and the archives produced mold sheets notating that PL-674, the mold for Mexican War Soldiers, was received at the factory 3/9/55, and PL-726, Davy Crockett & Soldiers, was received 6/3/55. However some collectors report that their early Alamo set included Indians. The original promotional photograph of #3546 and the photo taken for this book of #3534 (see below) both show Mexican soldiers in action.

3520 Official Davy Crockett Frontier Set (1955)

Features an L-shaped plastic ranch house, in yellow and brown, enclosed by four sections of white slat-type fence. Davy is joined here by ten silver cavalrymen and twelve Indians. Factory specification sheet indicates photo of Davy Crockett used in #3534 had been eliminated June 17, 1955.

3530, 3530D Davy Crockett Alamo Set (1956)

Featured set; see reproduced documentation.

3534 Official Walt Disney Davy Crockett Alamo Set (1955)

Featured set; see reproduced documentation. Note that this is distinguished by authentic Davy Crockett figure, as portrayed by Fess Parker on the Disney TV show and in the movies, and photo. This appears to be the earliest full Alamo playset for which Mexicans were listed on the factory specification sheet (they appear in #3518 also). See Color Photo 1.

3539, 3539D Alamo Set (1956)

Eight lithographed steel interlocking wall sections surround the Alamo; pins are to be inserted around the Alamo fence for catwalk platforms for post defenders. The metal walls used the Fort Dearborn dies, with new lithography. Fifteen frontier accessories include the official Alamo flag; also includes Davy Crockett figure, twenty cavalry figures, and ten Mexican soldiers.

3540, 3540D Alamo Set (1956)

Similar to above, except six horses instead of four, plus two cactus, two trees.

3542 Alamo Playset (Sears) (1968)

Distinguished by nine horses, twenty Mexican soldiers, twenty cavalry figures, sixteen Mexicans.

3543, 3543D Alamo Playset (1960)

This is a featured set; see reproduced documentation. Note that due to a typographical error, "#2543" appears on the factory specification sheet, instead of #3543.

3546 Alamo Playset (1967)

See photo on catalog sheet. Similar to #3542 but includes two shooting cannon and here the flagpole was specified as brown, not gray. Arch and gate made of molded plastic (used again in #3548).

3548 "Sears Heritage Set" Alamo (1972)

Includes twenty each of Mexican soldiers, Alamo figures, and Mexican figures as well as a booklet about the history of the Alamo.

NO. 3546 ALAMO PLAYSET

The famous battle in the fight for Texas Independence is brought to life in this realistic lithographed metal fortress playset. Fierce Mexican Troops and horses for the attack, Stalwart Texans for the defense; number more then sixty pieces. Two shooting Cannon, flagpole and flag, hitching post and many other accessories included. PACKED: Each set in a box, 1/4 dozen to shipping carton, Wgt. per carton - 15 lbs. F.O.B. Glendale, W. Va.

LOUIS MARX & CO., INC. 200 FIFTH AVE., NEW YORK

Although faded now, this original glossy catalog photograph from the archives is important documentation and illustrates the proper Mexican soldiers.

Six famous Americans, 60mm: Kit Carson, Buffalo Bill, General Custer, Sitting Bull, Daniel Boone, and Davy Crockett. Gary J. Linden Collection

LOUIS MARX & CO.
200 Fifth Ave., New York

GLENDALE DIVISION
10/15/56

NO. 3530 DAVY CROCKETT ALAMO SET

A realistic and authentic, official Davy Crockett at the Alamo Set.

Set consists of the Alamo Fort building, made of steel and realistically lithographed in color and design.

Four lithographed wall sections are included, made of steel, and interlocking, each measuring 8-1/2" long, 3-3/8" high.

The Gate section has two door panels which form the entrance to the fort.

House and fence are supplied knocked down, but easy to assemble without the use of tools. All edges and windows turned, and double rolled for extra strength.

All of the figures supplied are authentic and official replicas and include Frontier figures in fighting poses, ten Cavalry Soldiers, twelve Indians, and six life-like action horses with saddles, and the authentic and official figure of Davy Crockett. An 8-1/2" x 11" photo of Davy Crockett is included.

PACKED: Each set in a box,
1/2 dozen sets to shipping carton,
Weight per carton - 19-1/2 lbs.

NO. 3530D DAVY CROCKETT ALAMO SET DEMONSTRATOR

This is the above item, completely set up and mounted on a display board, for demonstration purposes.

PACKED: Each in a shipping carton,
Weight per carton - 10-1/4 lbs.

FACTORY SPECIFICATIONS:

1 - Metal lithographed Alamo Fort w/out Tower (Space Academy) Model No. 5806
1 - Metal Sign on top of building - Model 5806X
4 - Sections interlocking metal lithographed fence without platform
1 - Archway and set of gates (2) - Lithographed metal

1 - Set	PL-351	Stockade Accessories	Brown, Tan, Gray, Assorted
1 -	PL-411	Shell Shooting Cannon	Black, GH-1
1 - Set	PL-442	Cavalry Figures (10 pcs.)	Silver GP-11B
1 - Set	PL-443	Indians (12 pcs.)	Yellow GP-13 & Copper GP-21 asst'd.
6 -	PL-444	Horses	Ivory, Gray, Brown, assorted
1 -	PL-726A	Official D. Crockett Fig.	Tan - GH-20

Include 8-1/2" x 11" photo of Davy Crockett - P-665
Packing box 2 print design (yellow and blue)

LOUIS MARX & CO.
200 Fifth Ave., New York

GLENDALE DIVISION
6/10/55

NO. 3534 OFFICIAL WALT DISNEY DAVY CROCKETT ALAMO SET

Authentic Davy Crockett Figure, as portrayed by Fess Parker on the Disneyland TV Show and in the movies.

Realistic Alamo Fort building of colorful lithographed steel measures 12" long, 4" wide, 7" high overall.

Six wall sections, each measuring 8-1/2" long, 3--3/8" high, will surround the Alamo Building in appropriate lithographed design. Two sections are supplied with fighting platforms. Gate section with Alamo insignia and two swinging gates.

Ten stalwart frontier figures in fighting pose, to defend the Alamo.

Fifteen attacking Mexican Soldiers in regulation uniform.

Six life-like Action Horses with integral saddles.

Two shooting Cannons with miniature shells.

Eleven Frontier Accessories, including Flagpole with the official Alamo Flag, Anvil, Assault Ladders, Well, Powder Keg, etc.

Entire set, over 50 pieces, shipped knocked down..........exceptionally easy to set up for play. An 8-1/2" x 11" Davy Crockett photo is included.

PACKED: Each set in a box,
1/2 dozen sets to shipping carton
Weight per carton - 22 lbs.

FACTORY SPECIFICATIONS:

Special for Sears, Roebuck - 1955
1 - Alamo Building
1 - Alamo Sign or Rampart for top of building
6 - Wall sections (2 have Cat Walks)
1 - Gate section w/2 Gates
1 - PL-351 Stockade Accessories - GH-5 Gray - GH-15 - Tan - GH-17 - Brown
6 - PL-610 Horses GP17E Brown GP-6 Ivory - GP-5 - Gray
2 - PL-411 Shell Shooting Cannon w/Shells - GH-1 - Black
1 - PL-442 Set of Cavalry Figures (10-pcs.) - GP-11 - Silver
1-1/2 - PL-726 Sets of Mexican Soldiers (15 pcs.) GP-2C Blue metallic
1 - PL-726A Davy Crockett Figure GH-20 - Tan
1 - PL-727 Ladders and Pins GH-17 - Brown
Include 8-1/2" x 11" Davy Crockett photo.

Date 2/24/60

PACKING INFORMATION

Item No. 2543 ALAMO PLAYSET
How Packed EACH IN DIE CUT CORRUGATED BOX
Quantity Packed 1/4 DOZEN
Wgt. Per Shipping Ctn.
Carton Dimensions L. W. D.

Cartons, Games or Toys, NOIBN, Iron or Steel, 20 ga or thicker or any gauge KDF
Frt. Classification
Net Wgt.
Tare Wgt.
Gross Wgt.
Legal Wgt.

FACTORY SPECIFICATIONS

Sears exclusive 1960- Mail Order & Retail
1 - Lithographed alamo Building (Note: No Disney copyright markings att all)
1 --Pediment Lithogaph for Building
8 - Sections of Alamo Fence (as before)
2 - Catwalks for Fence- lithographed
1 - Set PL-727 Ladders & Pins- Brown Polyethylene
1 - Plastic Archway & Gate w/Ladders, Model No. 5806 X-4 PL-1054
1 - PL-346 Flag Pole- Light Gray
1 - Lithographed Alamo Flag
1 - Set PL-130 Outside Accessories- Astd. Colors- Brown, Gray & Beige
2 - PL-148 Cactus- Light GreenPolyethylene
3 - PL-411 Cannon- Black
3 - Sets PL-745 Frontiersmen (20 pcs.)- 1 Set Sivler, 1 Set Beige, 1 Set Lt. Gray
2 - Sets PL-726 Mexican Saldiers (30 pcs.) - Pastel Blue
1 - Set PL-970 Mexican Soldiers (16 pcs.) -Pastel Blue
9 - PL-610 Horses- 3 Brown, 3 Ivory, 3 Bege
2 -PL-524 Trees- Light Green Polyethylene
1 - P-1237 Instruction Sheet

Changes F. X. R. memo of 3/10 cc to W

CAVALRY SETS

Studying the mold sheets for cavalry figures reveals how Marx modified basic groups of figures from time to time, keeping the line competitive with the likes of Ideal, Multiple, and Pyro manufacturing companies. In 1964 the mold of eighteen cavities for riding cavalry figures produced two standard bearers, two buglers, two officers, two sergeants, and ten troopers. In 1967 a new mold converted the two sergeants to two additional troopers (but the original mold was kept for future use). See archive photo of mold for PL-1212. Note that under **Cowboys and Indians**, below, the Indian Warfare set also has a cavalry theme and that the cavalry enters the picture in several other sets (Custer's Last Stand, Fort Apache, etc). Because of the appearance of the cavalry in many Marx Western sets, we are including below those sets which are, because of the lack of a "base (fort)," not strictly playsets. (See also **Fort Apache and Rin-Tin-Tin.**)

54/1 33-Piece Cavalry Figure Set (1957)

Three sets of cavalry soldiers, three horses.

54/2 30-Piece Cavalry Figure Set (1957)

Two sets of cavalrymen, one set of Indians.

55/2 Cavalry Soldier Set (1956)

Eighteen-piece set including two cavalry horses, four miniature Western guns, and one set of the basic twelve cavalry soldiers (mold PL-693):

2 Standing, dueling with sword
2 Standing, shooting rifle
2 Kneeling, with pistol
1 Rider with sword
1 Kneeling, shooting rifle
1 Rider with pistol
1 Bugler with pistol
2 Standing officers with sword and pistol

55/13 Cavalry Set with Horses (1956)

Cavalrymen joined by frontiersmen in twenty-seven-piece set.

0709 26-Piece Rin-Tin-Tin Cavalry Set (1956)

In this bagged set Rin-Tin-Tin, Rusty, and Lt. Rip Masters are joined by six assorted action Indians and twelve cavalry figures in various poses, two horses, and three miniature guns.

1695 Cavalry Set (1957)

Bagged ninety-five-piece set includes twenty-four cavalry figures, one cavalry horse, thirty-five-piece set of cowboy accessories on runner, thirty-five-piece set of Indian accessories on runner.

3682 Indian & Cavalry Set (Montgomery Ward) (1969)

Featured set; see reproduced documentation. Compare with Sears version.

3687 Cavalry Set (Sears) (1968)

Featured set; see reproduced documentation. Compare with Montgomery Ward version.

The photo is from the Marx archives and shows the output of mold PL-1212: two standard bearers, two buglers, two officers, two sergeants, and ten troopers. Note the closeup of the cavalry officer, shown with a frontiersman, in the color section; the fine detailing of Marx figures is evident.

ITEM NO. 3682
Date March 17, 1969
Customer No.
Replaces Sheet

GLEN DALE DIVISION
SPECIFICATION SHEET

Model No.
Cost No. CO 3291

Item Indian & Cavalry Set (Ward's)

Quantity	Part No.	Description	Color
1	PT-1145	#11A Cavalry Bldg	
1	PT-1054	Litho Flag - 36 Star	
1	PL-1112	Porch & Acc.	
2	PL-341	Sects. Stockade Fence	
1	PL-342	Stockade Gate	
1	PL-351	Set Outside Acc. (10)	
1	PL-411	Cannon	
1	PL-854	Set (2) Blockhouses & (4) ladders	
2	PL-884	Sects. Corner Fence	
6	PL-890	Sects. Stockade Fence w/o catwalk	
1	PL-692	Indian Pony	
9	PL-779	Cavalry Horses	
1	PL-787	Set Indians (16)	
1	PL-1212A	Set Cav. Figures (9)	
1	PL-1449	Set Cav. Figures (32)	
1	P-1500R	Caution Notice	
~~1~~	~~P~~	~~Instruction Sheet~~	

REMARKS:—

DEMONSTRATOR DATA:

SHIPPING CARTON Size— L W H Gross Tare Net Legal

SHIPPING CARTON INFORMATION:—

Individual Carton:—L (approx.) 24¼ W 15½ H 4 Diagonal Girth Weight

Description Each in a die cut box w/ 2 prints

Master Carton Size—L 16 W 12-3/4 H 24-3/4 Diagonal Girth Weight

Quantity Packed Per Shipping Carton 3 pieces

Freight Classification

Net Weight Gross Weight Tare Weight Legal Weight

Acknowledged by Date

ITEM NO. 3687
Date February 19, 1968
Customer No.
Replaces Sheet

GLEN DALE DIVISION
SPECIFICATION SHEET

Model No. 8361 X
Cost No.

Item Cavalry Set - Sears

Quantity	Part No.	Description	Color
1	PT-1145	#11A Cavalry Bldg.	
2	PT-1054	Flag	
4	PL-341	Stockade Fence	Rust Red
1	PL-351	Set Outside Accessories	Assorted
1	PL-411	Cannon	Black
2	PL-532	Harness Horses	Brown
2	PL-692	Indian Pony	Ivory
9	PL-779	Cavalry Horses	Assorted
1	PL-787	Set Indians (32)	Coppertone
2	PL-854	Set Blockhouses & Ladders	Rust Red
1	PL-864	Tepee	Beige
8	PL-890	Stockade Fence	Rust Red
1	PL-903	Set Bow & Arrows	Brown
1	PL-908	Set Cavalry Accessories	Black
1	PL-947	Set Blockhouse & Gate	Rust Red
1	PL-1030	Covered Wagon	Dk. Brown
1	PL-1084	Wagon Cover	Beige
1	PL-1112	Set Porch & Bldg. Accessories	Dk. Brown
1	PL-1212	Set Riding Figures (9)	Cavalry Blue
2	PL-1449	Set Figures (32)	Cavalry Blue
1	J-45	Pistol - Die Cast	
1	P-1500R	Caution Notice	
1		Instruction Sheet	

REMARKS:—

DEMONSTRATOR DATA:

SHIPPING CARTON Size— L ... W ... H ... Gross ... Tare ... Net ... Legal ...

SHIPPING CARTON INFORMATION:—

Individual Carton:—L ... W ... H ... Diagonal ... Girth ... Weight ...

Description ... Ind. Corr. Die Cut printed Sears overall print.

Master Carton Size—L ... W ... H ... Diagonal ... Girth ... Weight ...

Quantity Packed Per Shipping Carton ... 1/4 dozen (3) per case

Freight Classification ...

Net Weight ... Gross Weight ... Tare Weight ... Legal Weight ...

Acknowledged by ... Date ...

RETURNED FR. N.Y. -
NOT SIGNED

COMANCHE PASS

Both versions of this playset were produced after the sale of Louis Marx & Co., Inc. Quaker followed the Marx approach of reusing molds: the mountain appears in military and prehistoric sets as well. The Comanche set is pictured during playtime in Color Photo 8.

3416, 3416F Comanche Pass (1974)
See reproduced documentation; see also color photo.

3423 Ambush at Falling Rock (1975)
Apart from the name change, this set has fewer figures, no cannon, wagon, cactus, nor cavalry accessories.

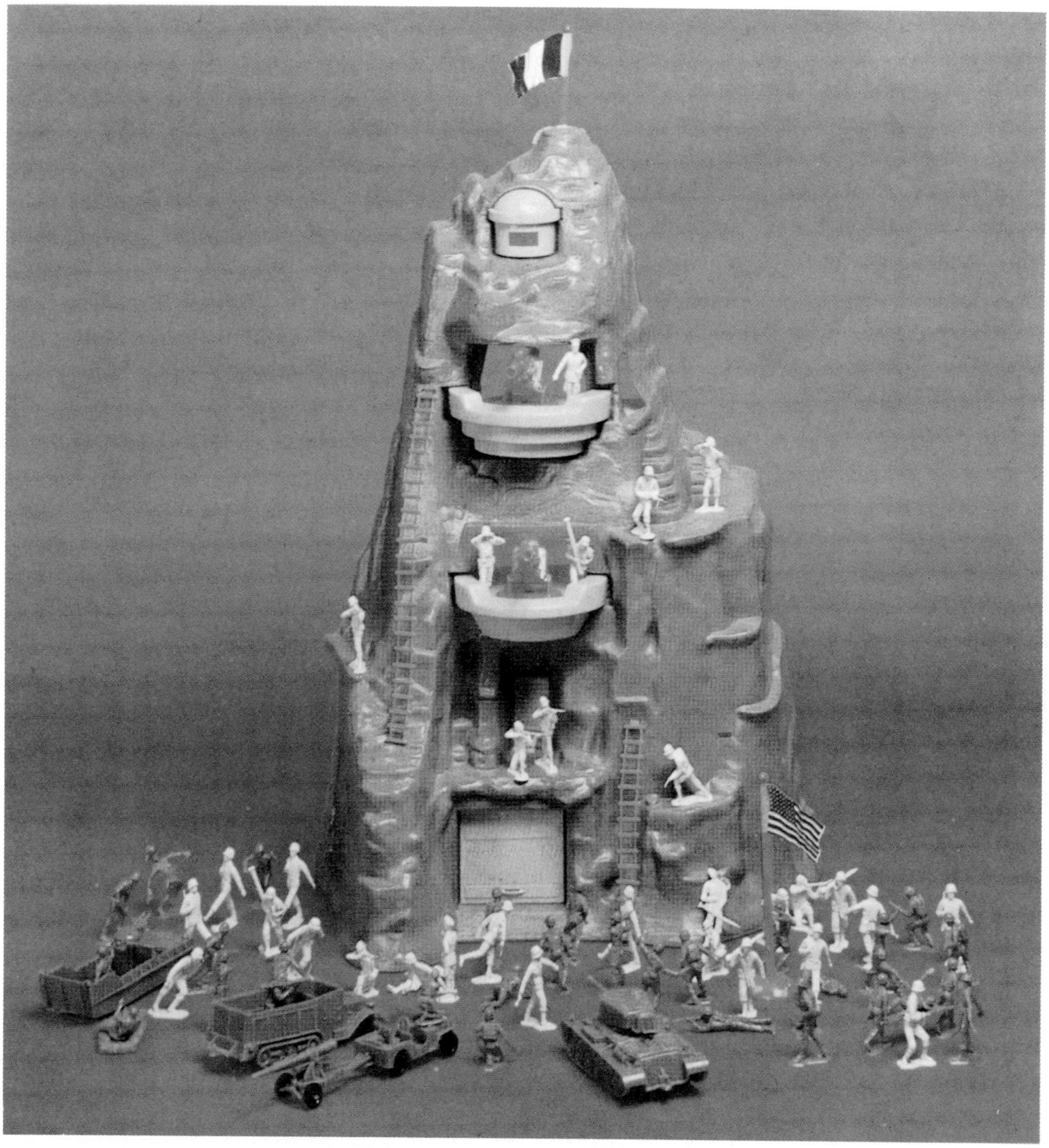

The World War II battle scene of the Navarone™ playset shows one of the several uses of the mountain mold.

BILL OF MATERIALS

PART NO.	LEVEL & QTY. 1	2	3	4	5	6	PURC	DRAWING NO.	PART NAME	MATERIAL OR SIZE	COLOR NO.	REMARKS
7897	1/3						P		Master Carton			
7898		1					P		Individual Box			
7906 8550			1				P		Insert			B
												(E) D
PL-10512			1					8-1299	Front Mountain	F.H.I. Styrene	PMS-142 Tan	
PL-10513			1					8-1300	Rear Mountain	F.H.I. Styrene	PMS-142 Tan	
PL-10514			1					8-1301	Base	F.H.I. Styrene	PMS-142 Tan	
PL-10515			1					6-1846	Upper Bridge	F.H.I. Styrene	PMS-142 Tan	
PL-10517			1					B-1009	Falling Bridge	F.H.I. Styrene	PMS-142 Tan	
ASY-120			1						Rock Assy.			
PL-10510				1				6-1845	Rock Top	F.H.I. Styrene	PMS-142 Tan	
PL-10511				1				6-1845	Rock Bottom	F.H.I. Styrene	PMS-142 Tan	
PL-1449			1 set						Cavalry Figures	Polyethylene in Poly. Bag	PMS-300 Blue	(Glendale) 32 pcs.
PL-787			1 set						Indian Figures	Polyethylene in Poly. Bag	PMS-471 Brown	(Glendale) 32 pcs.
PL-745			1 set						Frontier Figures	Polyethylene in Poly. Bag	PMS-391 Green	(Glendale) 10 pcs.
PL-692			½ set						Indian Pony	Polyethylene in Poly. Bag	PMS-175 Brown	(Glendale) 2 pc.
PL-411 A			½ set						Cannon	H.I. Styrene in Poly. Bag	GP-225 Black	(Glendale) 3 pcs.
#8275			1				P		Instruction Sheet	Bilingual - Printed		C

REV	NO.	CHANGE DESCRIPTION	BY	DATE	REV.	NO.	CHANGE DESCRIPTION	BY	DATE
A	176	Name change	RK	3/14	(E)	669	Deleted #E-1747 Poly Bag for hardware.	RK	6/23/6
B	185	Insert was Paper; Delete Material & Size;	RK	3/19					
C	278	Added Cat. No. & Instr. Sheet;	JL	5/15					
D	339	Added poly bag;	RK	8/4					

MARX TOYS
ERIE GIRARD GLEN DALE
CAT. # 3416/3416F * G * See Note | MODEL # Y-4735
TOY NAME Commanche Pass A
ISS'D BY RK | APPR. BY
DATE 11-4-74 | PAGE 1 OF 2

BILL OF MATERIALS

PART NO.	LEVEL & QTY. 1	2	3	4	5	6	PURC	DRAWING NO.	PART NAME	MATERIAL OR SIZE	COLOR NO.	REMARKS
PL-779			½ set						Horses	Polyethylene in Poly. Bag	50% Black 50% Brown	(Glendale) 2 pcs.
PL-864			½ set						Tee Pee	Polyethylene in Poly. Bag	PMS-475 Tan	(Glendale) 2 pcs.
PL-1030B			½ set						Wagon	Polyethylene in Poly. Bag PMS-475 Tan	Remove Seat	(Glendale) 12 pcs. CH
PL-1084			½ set						Wagon Cover	Polyethylene in Poly. Bag PMS-475 Tan	Seat included w/cover mold	(Glendale) 9 pcs. C
PL-532			½ set						Horses	Polyethylene in Poly. Bag	Ivory PMS-439 Brown	(Glendale) 2 pcs.
PL-908			¼ set						Cavalry Acc. Runner	Polyethylene in Poly. Bag	Black	(Glendale) 35 pcs.
PL-148			½ set						Cactus	Polyethylene in Poly. Bag	PMS-356 Green	(Glendale) 3 pcs.
9184			1				P		Poly Bag w/Hardware			J
E-5192				5			P		Screw	Machine Screw #6-32 X ½" Round Head		In Poly Bag J
E-1951				5			P		Nut	Hex #6-32		In Poly Bag J
7903			1				P		Ground Sheet	Printed Polyethylene 32" X 36", .0025 thk.	PMS-142 Tan	AD
7905				12			P		Poly Bag	6-3/4 X 8½ .002 thk w/1" lip		E
P-2247			1				P		Brochure	Printed		
PL-971			½ set						Wagon Driver	Polyethylene	PMS-391 Green	(Glendale) 1 pc.
8114			1				P		Instruction Sheet -	Printed		B
						X	P		Paint (Accent)		PMS-154A	
						X	P			Styrene Cement		
PL-10999			2					B-1297	Wagon Axles	Polyethylene	PMS-475 Tan	Added to Glen Dale Mold PL-1030 I
								*NOTE: Item No. for Canadian Sales, "F" Designates Bilingual Instruction Sheet				G

REV	NO.	CHANGE DESCRIPTION	BY	DATE	REV.	NO.	CHANGE DESCRIPTION	BY	DATE
A	--	Size change was .003 thk.	RK	1/28	E	137	.002 thk. was .0015 mil	RK	3/5
					F	176	Name change	RK	3/14
					G	278	Added Note & Cat. No.;	JL	5/15
B	70	Added instruction sheet	RK	2/12	H	339	PL-1030B was PL-1030; 12 pcs. was 13 pcs.	RK	8/4
C	97	Mold arrangement	RK	2/19	I	352	Added PL-10999 & B-1297, Polyethylene was B.B.W. Added Color Tan;	RK	8/11
D	122	PMS-142 Tan was PMS-152	RK	2/27					
					(J)	669	Added #9184 Poly Bag; Added	RK	6/23/6

MARX TOYS
ERIE GIRARD GLEN DALE
CAT. # 3416/3416F * G * See Note | MODEL # Y-4735
TOY NAME Commanche Pass F
ISS'D BY RK | APPR. BY
DATE 11-4-74 | PAGE 2 OF 2

COWBOYS AND INDIANS

Under this large category we group various larger (more than fifty pieces) sets that were primarily figures and accessories; the figures appear on the Lone Prairie, awaiting imaginative placement and encounters with one another. (Two of these sets do include small dwelling structures, however.) Exciting, well done, always good sellers. Through the years Marx packaged individual figures and small groups in numerous ways; for example, there were several series of smaller figure sets in 1956-1958, including the 1957 sets packaged in the red and white polka dot boxes. The listings below do not cover every single type of Western item. See also **HO-scale Playsets** and the color plates in the Album of Marx Western Playsets.

RR-9, 9MO, and 9MO-D 101-Piece Western Frontier Figures & Equipment (1956, 1958)

Catalog sheet describes "over 101 pieces, consisting of various groups of items such as cowboys, Indians, frontiersmen, wigwams, covered wagons, canoes, etc. Each item stands on its own platform, and may be used in many and varied effects." The mailer carton of 1956 became a clear poly bag with header in 1958.

54/103 69-Piece Indian Figure Set (1958)

See reproduced documentation and note the conversion of a 1957 thirty-four-piece set.

54/109 73-Piece Cowboy Figure Set (1958)

Thirty-six assorted cowboys, two horses, set of cowboy accessories (PL-891; see page 82). This also was a conversion of an earlier set through the addition of accessories.

1692 95-Piece Cowboy Set (1957)

Bagged set of fourteen cowboys plus two rifles, eight rodeo cowboys, one horse with integral saddle, two sets of cowboy accessories on runner (seventy pieces).

1693 95-Piece Indian Set (1957)

Bagged set of eight Indian warriors, sixteen other Indians, one Indian horse, two sets of Indian accessories on runner (seventy pieces).

1704 100-Piece Cowboys & Horses Set (1957)

Featured set; see reproduced documentation.

1708 102-Piece Indian Set with Accessories (1957)

See page 82 for the standard Indian accessories.

2257 Cowboys Set (also known as Cattle Rustling) (1975)

Over fifty pieces of cowboys, rustlers, cattle, and cowboy equipment on vinyl terrain sheet, in snap-top storage box (see Color Photo 11). It was also distributed as part of a low-end-of-market playset assortment.

4778 Indian Warfare Set (Montgomery Ward) (1957)

Featured set; see reproduced documentation.

This is the archive documentary photo of the output of mold PL-610, "Western Horses with Saddles." Made by Ferriot in early 1954 at a cost of $5100, the mold could produce hourly 200 sets of six horses with saddle, two without.

The mold sheet documentary photo from the archives and the photos of the Indian and cowboy figures (Gary J. Linden Collection) all attest to the skill of Marx artists.

Put-To-Gether Cowboys & Horses Set: Each cowboy was composed of six or more interchangeable parts to be put together. Don Faruolo Collection.

LOUIS MARX & CO.
200 Fifth Ave., New York

GLENDALE DIVISION
5/12/58

Mr. Dargitz

NO. 54/103 69-PIECE INDIAN FIGURE SET

Set consists of:

30-Indian Figures in assorted poses
1-Indian Horse
1-Canoe
2-Totem Poles
35-Indian Accessories

PACKED: Each set in 2-piece mailing carton,
3 dozen sets to master carton,
Weight per carton - 15 lbs.

FACTORY SPECIFICATIONS:

Sears - 1958

Convert any inventory of the 54/3, add contents to equal as follows:

1 - PL-692 Horse ok
1 - PL-763 Canoe ok
2 - PL-787 Sets Indians (32 pcs.) no
*1 - PL-891 Accessories on runner (35 pieces) ok

* Can convert 54/3 by adding PL-891.

LOUIS MARX & CO.
200 Fifth Ave., New York

GLENDALE DIVISION
5/21/57

NO. 1704 100-PC. COWBOYS & HORSES SET

100 Pieces of Cowboy Figures and Cowboy equipment make this set a vital accessory to rodeo or western town games.

Handsomely packaged in a sturdy vinyl bag with a colorful car enclosure, our Cowboy & Horses Set features 22 Cowboy Figures, 2 Horses, 2 detachable Saddles and 2 detachable bridles. All figures are constructed of durable polyethylene.

Accessories included

2 - Rifles	2 - Coffee Pots
4 - Coiled Lariots	2 - Guitars
4 - Canteens	4 - Bullwhips
4 - Carbines	4 - Branding Irons
4 - Shot Guns	8 - Belts w/Holsters
2 - Campfires	20 - Pistols
2 - Plates w/cups	4 --Bags of Gold Dust
2 - Frying Pans	4 - Cow Skulls

PACKED: Each set in transparent bag w/cardboard closure,
1 dozen sets to shipping carton,
Weight per carton -

FACTORY SPECIFICATIONS:

1 - PL-389	Set Cowboys (14 figures and 2 rifles)	
8 - PL-463	Set Rodeo Cowboys	
2 - PL-865	Horses	
2 - PL-326	Saddles & Bridles (4 pcs.)	
2 - PL-891	Sets Cowboy Accessories on runner (total 70 pcs.)	

1 - P-864 Card Closure.

LOUIS MARX & CO.
200 Fifth Ave., New York

GLENDALE DIVISION
3/15/57

NO. 4778 INDIAN WARFARE SET

FACTORY SPECIFICATIONS:

Montgomery Ward - 1957.

1 - Model 6324X-1	Small Log Cabin Building w/pierced out door
3 - Model 6222X	Tepees
3 - PL-524	Trees
1 - NO. 2454	Set General Custer Accessories
2 - PL-336	Buckboards
2 - PL-345	Buckboard Harness
1 - PL-407	Covered Wagon Accessories
2 - PL-865	Horses without saddles
4 - PL-610	Horses w/saddles
2 - PL-705	Dead Horses
2 - PL-692	Indian Horses
10- PL-369	Sections Small fence - brown
30- PL-787	Indians & Two Totem Poles
20- PL-745	Cavalry figures
2 - PL-337	Buckboard wheels
2 - PL-148	Cactus

CUSTER'S LAST STAND

This category includes listings of the Little Big Horn playset and Sitting Bull and Indian figures. All variations used the basic Western playset environmental accessories and figures and added special historic figures to highlight a theme. Some sets include a personage modeled after Wayne Maunder, the actor who played Custer in the shortlived television series. See also **HO-scale Playsets** and **Indian Warfare** (for a more complete set).

3135MO Sitting Bull and Indian Figure Set (1955)

A tan Sitting Bull is accompanied by eight Indian warriors (copper, yellow, tan) in the following poses: charging with rifle, charging with tomahawk, crawling with dagger and tomahawk, crouching with dagger, kneeling shooting bow and arrow, kneeling shot by arrow, riding with spear, dancing with spear; one horse included.

4670 "Custer's Last Stand" (Sears) (1963)

Featured set; see reproduced documentation. Note the use of the PL-848 mold for the Confederate soldiers as cavalry officers, as shown in Color Photo 30.

4679MO Little Big Horn Set (J C Penney) (1972)

Has number of pieces in common with #4670 and #4780, our featured sets; distinguishing characteristics include two sets of Indians and totem poles (as did #4780), nine cavalry horses, four brown and ivory Indian ponies, and yellow Indian accessories. The instruction sheet (reproduced on page 116) reflects the lack of fence sections on the factory specification sheet. This J C Penney set included a 36" x 72" printed plastic layout sheet.

4779 General Custer's Last Stand (1957)

Similar to #4780, the featured set listed below, this one is somewhat smaller, with less fencing and fewer horses, but it does have a set of PL-891 Indian accessories.

4780 General Custer's Last Stand (1957)

Featured set; see reproduced documentation. The small cabin and O-gauge fence referred to are probably those shown in Color Photo 25 (see also **Crossover Items: Trains and Playsets**).

LOUIS MARX & CO.
200 Fifth Ave., New York

GLENDALE DIVISION
2/15/57

NO. 4780 GENERAL CUSTER'S LAST STAND

FACTORY SPECIFICATIONS:

1 -		Extra small Log Cabin Bldg. Model No. 6324X-1
2		Indian Tepees - No. 6222X
3 -	PL-524	Trees
1		Set Gen Custer Access. Model No. 2454, as costed 12/27/56
2 -	PL-336	Buckboards (no integral hitching shaft)
1 -	PL-[illegible]	Covered Wagon Parts
2 -	PL-345	Buckboard harness
2 -	PL-865	Horses for buckboards
2 -	PL-705	Dead Horses
10 -	PL-369	Sections small '0' gauge fence in brown
2 -	PL-787	Sets Indians & Totem Pole (total 30 Ind. & 2 totem poles)
2 -	PL-745	Sets Cavalry figures
1 -	PL-687	Gen.Custer figure & 1 - sitting Bull figure
2 -	PL-337	Extra buckboard wheels
2 -	PL-148	Cactus
4 -	PL-610	Horses
2 -	PL-692	Indian Horses

Date April 1, 1963

Item Number 4670 "Custer's Last Stand"

How Packed Each packed in die cut corrugated box

Quantity Packed 1/4 dozen

Wgt. per Shipping Ctn. 15 lbs.

Carton Dimensions L. W. D.

INDV. BOX:
TYPE BOX:
DIAGONAL:
GIRTH:
WGT.:

Frt. Classification

Net Wgt. Gross Wgt.

Tare Wgt. Legal Wgt.

FACTORY SPECIFICATIONS

Exclusive Sears 1963.

Consists of:

1-Set (10) Cavalry Figures-PL-442-Blue
1-Set (16) Cavalry Figures-PL-848-Blue
1-Set (16) Cavalry Figures & 1 Stretcher-PL-1093--Blue
1-Fallen Horse & Rider-PL-1153---Ivory
2-Drivers-PL-971---Blue
1-Set Pack Train-PL-1099 ---Brown
1-Die-Cast Miniature Pistol - JW-5253
1-Set (15) Indians & 1 Totem Pole-PL-787--Copper (M.R.Lee 5/10)
2-Sets (30) Indians & 2 Totem Poles-PL-919--Copper
1-Set Bow & Arrow-PL-903-Beige (styrene)
5-Cavalry Horses-PL-779---Brown & Black
3-Indian Horses-PL-692---Ivory
3-Units (6) Trees-PL-1145-A ---Green
1-Tree-PL-524---Green
2-Tepees-PL-864---Beige
1-Set Rock Formations-3 pcs. - PL-1018-A---Brown Mottle
5-Sections Split Rail Fence-PL-1092-Dark Brown
4-Wagons-PL-1030---Beige
1-Wagon Top-PL-1031---Light Blue
1-Hospital Wagon Top w/Accessories-PL-1084-A----Light Blue
6-Horses for Wagons-PL-532---Brown & Ivory
2-Dead Horses-PL-850----Brown
1-Set Indian Accessories on Runner-PL-891---Copper
1-P---Instruction Sheet
This item to be packed in a Sears' overall print box.

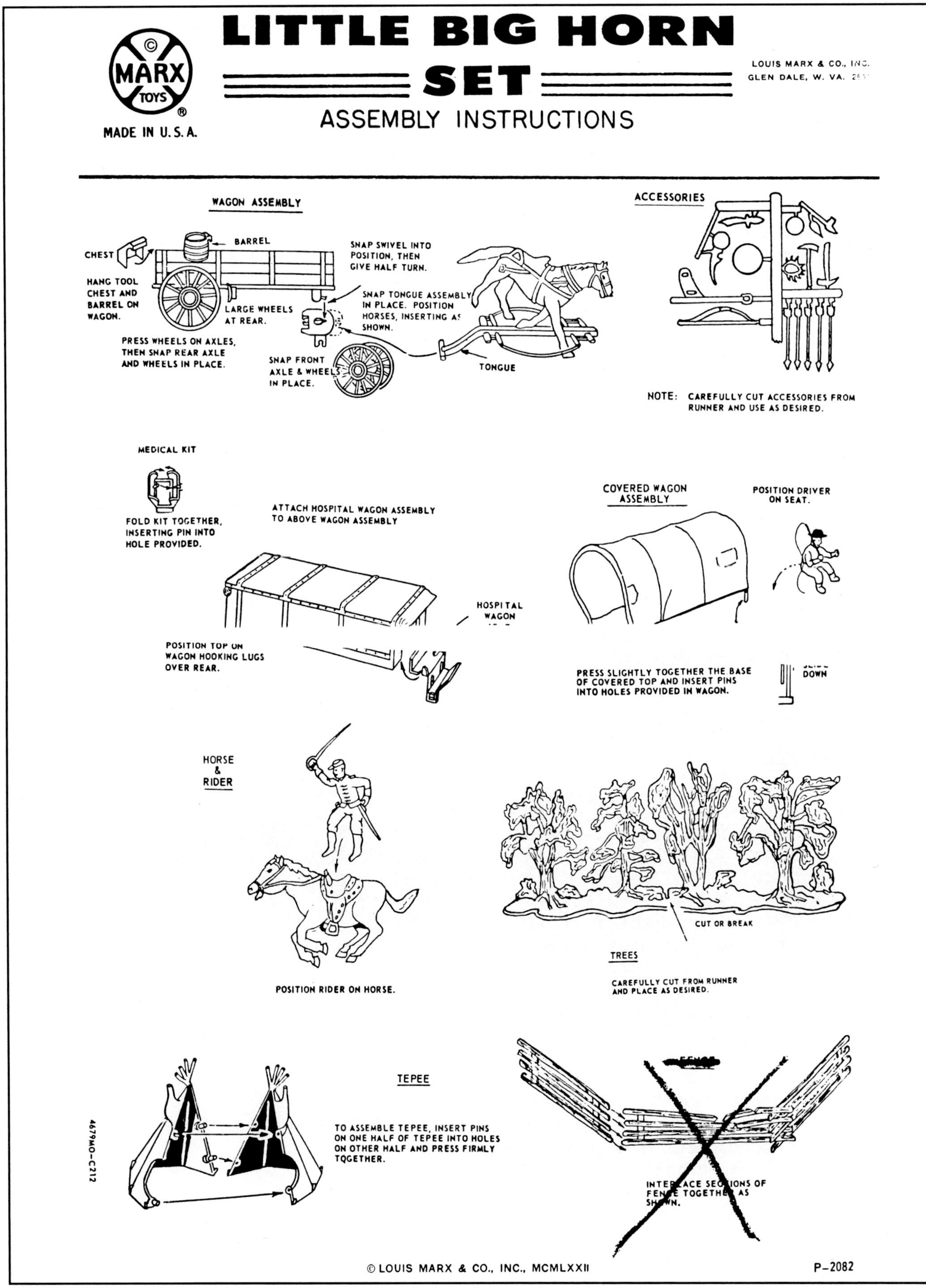

LITTLE BIG HORN SET

ASSEMBLY INSTRUCTIONS

MARX TOYS ®

MADE IN U.S.A.

LOUIS MARX & CO., INC.
GLEN DALE, W. VA.

WAGON ASSEMBLY

CHEST

BARREL

HANG TOOL CHEST AND BARREL ON WAGON.

LARGE WHEELS AT REAR.

PRESS WHEELS ON AXLES, THEN SNAP REAR AXLE AND WHEELS IN PLACE.

SNAP SWIVEL INTO POSITION, THEN GIVE HALF TURN.

SNAP TONGUE ASSEMBLY IN PLACE. POSITION HORSES, INSERTING AS SHOWN.

SNAP FRONT AXLE & WHEELS IN PLACE.

TONGUE

ACCESSORIES

NOTE: CAREFULLY CUT ACCESSORIES FROM RUNNER AND USE AS DESIRED.

MEDICAL KIT

FOLD KIT TOGETHER, INSERTING PIN INTO HOLE PROVIDED.

ATTACH HOSPITAL WAGON ASSEMBLY TO ABOVE WAGON ASSEMBLY

HOSPITAL WAGON

POSITION TOP ON WAGON HOOKING LUGS OVER REAR.

COVERED WAGON ASSEMBLY

POSITION DRIVER ON SEAT.

PRESS SLIGHTLY TOGETHER THE BASE OF COVERED TOP AND INSERT PINS INTO HOLES PROVIDED IN WAGON.

DOWN

HORSE & RIDER

POSITION RIDER ON HORSE.

CUT OR BREAK

TREES

CAREFULLY CUT FROM RUNNER AND PLACE AS DESIRED.

TEPEE

TO ASSEMBLE TEPEE, INSERT PINS ON ONE HALF OF TEPEE INTO HOLES ON OTHER HALF AND PRESS FIRMLY TOGETHER.

INTERLACE SECTIONS OF FENCE TOGETHER AS SHOWN.

4679MO-C212

© LOUIS MARX & CO., INC., MCMLXXII

P-2082

DANIEL BOONE

The dates of documentation suggest that most of the versions of this playset were produced to jump on the bandwagon of the popular TV series starring Fess Parker. However, no set features an official, identifiable Daniel Boone. All are comparatively small, low-priced playsets. The factory specification sheets state that the nine frontier figures could be produced by mold PL-1230 or PL-745A — whichever was available at the time. Collector Gary J. Linden points out that these figures are rare if in mint condition and are examples of the fact that figures designated to be part of a playset often take on special value beyond the set itself.

0631 Daniel Boone Wilderness Scout Playset (99¢ Size) (1964, 1965)
Nine buckskin frontiersmen, seven "Indian Brown" Indians, one beige tepee, reddish brown gate and fence with and without ramps.

0670, 0670D Daniel Boone [Wilderness] Playset (1965)
Features a dark brown blockhouse as well as the beige tepee.

2060, 2060D Daniel Boone, Wilderness Scout (1965)
(See **Larger-scale Playsets**)

2640 Daniel Boone Wilderness Scout Playset ($1.99 Size) (1965)
Featured set; see reproduced documentation and color photos.

3659 Daniel Boone Playset (1965)
Includes dark brown fence with and without ramp, stockade gate, and blockhouse.

4671, 4672 Daniel Boone Frontier Playset (1960)
Lithographed log cabin and plastic blockhouse with miscellaneous figures, wagons, and accessories.

Daniel Boone Wilderness Scout Set #0670, and its blockhouse, tepee, and four Indians and four frontiersmen. Gary J. Linden Collection

XEROX

ITEM NO. 2640
Date Feb. 11, 1965
Customer No.
Replaces Sheet 11/25/64

GLEN DALE DIVISION
SPECIFICATION SHEET

Model No. 7819X
Cost No. 2~~5~~5 C03059

Item DANIEL BOONE WILDERNESS SCOUT PLAY SET ($1.99 size)

Quantity	Part No.	Description	Color
1 ea.	PL-942	Blockhouse w/hot stamp on front	Dark Brown
1 ea.	PL-411	Cannon w/shells	Black
9 pcs.	PL-1230	Frontiersmen	Buckskin
1 set	PL-787	Indians & Totem Pole (16 Pcs.)	Indian Brown
1	PL-692	Indian Horses (1 pc.)	Ivory
1 set	PL-903	Bow & Arrows (4 pcs.)	Brown
1 set	PL-1099	Pack Horses & Acc. (9 pcs.)	Brown
1 ea.	R-76	Rubber Band	
1	P-1601	Instruction Sheet	
	*	Per A. Begg - can use PL-745A if PL-1230 mold is not available.	

REMARKS:— Each in a E Flute box - printed Gold and Blue

DEMONSTRATOR DATA:

SHIPPING CARTON Size— L W H Gross Tare Net Legal

SHIPPING CARTON INFORMATION:—

Individual Carton:—L 14-1/2 W 7-3/4 H 4 Diagonal 16-1/2 Girth 23-1/4 Weight 1 lb. 8-1/2 oz

Description

Master Carton Size—L 24-3/4 W 16 H 15-1/4 Diagonal Girth 62-1/2 Weight

Quantity Packed Per Shipping Carton 1 dozen

Freight Classification Rail - Flex. Plastic - Class 85

Net Weight 13-3/4 Gross Weight 20-1/2 Tare Weight 6-3/4 Legal Weight 18-1/2

Acknowledged by AEB Date 2/16/65

FORT DEARBORN

This was clearly a variation on Fort Apache, to give retailers a fresh offering. Frank Rice reports that the metal stockade offered with this particular playset was produced to compete with toy manufacturers such as T. Cohn. The log cabin shown in the photographs and instruction sheet is part of a number of Western playsets. See Color Photos 6 and 7.

2705, 2705D Fort Dearborn Set With Metal Fort — Bagged (1957)
Featured set; see reproduced documentation.

3688MO "Fort Dearborn" (1972)
Featured set; see reproduced documentation.

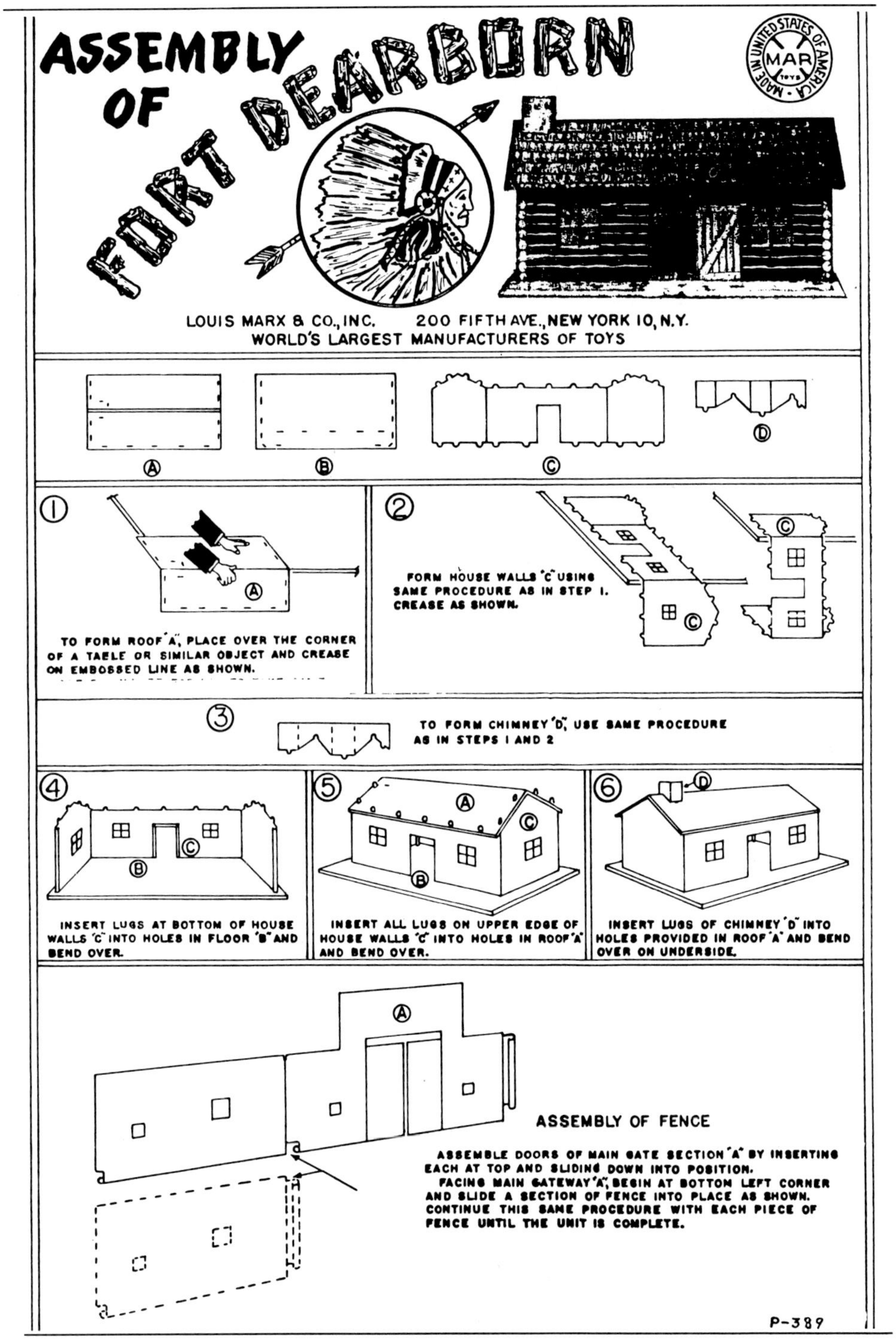

LOUIS MARX & CO.
200 Fifth Ave., New York

GLENDALE DIVISION
7/18/57

NO. 2705 FORT DEARBORN SET WITH METAL FORT - BAGGED

Fort Dearborn, bastion of the frontier, is now available in a 31-piece complete play set packaged in a sturdy sales and storage bag.

The colorfully lithographed steel fort measures 8-3/4" long, 8-3/4" wide and 5-1/2" high. A fort Dearborn sign is lithographed on the archway. Packed in four sections the fort is easily set up. Complete directions with diagram are given on the back of the card closure.

Sturdy plastic accessories supplied with the set include an anvil, a well with pole and bucket, a churn, 2 powder kegs, a cooking pot with campfire, a logpile, a chopping block with axe.

Indians and Cowboys change in constant warfare along the frontier. Six Indian Figures are supplied as well as nine cowboy figures. Two horses with integral saddles are also included.

Fort Dearborn in this complete unit play set is packaged in a clear-view polyethylene plastic bag with a colorful card closure.

PACKED: Each set in transparent polyethylene bag w/cardboard closure.
1 dozen sets to shipping carton,
Weight per carton -

NO. 2705D FORT DEARBORN SET DEMONSTRATOR

Counter demonstrator board with all compenent parts displayed and affixed thereto for display purposes.

PACKED: Each in a shipping carton,
Weight per carton - 8 lbs.

FACTORY SPECIFICATIONS:

Model No. 6464X-1

3 - No. 3500 Sections lithographed Fence -Reg. Fort Apache litho.
1 - Lithographed Archway (no gate)
1 - PL-351 Set Stockade Accessories
1 - PL-443 Set Indians (any six in mold)
2 - PL-610 Horses
1 - PL-833 Set Cowboys (9 pieces)

P-925 Card Closure

JESSE JAMES

Here is an example of Marx aiming to use a legendary personality and his adventures without the need to pay royalties. In his Preface to this book, collector Gary J. Linden asks if any reader has information about the general availability of the Jesse James playset. Although we can reproduce the specification sheets found in the archives, we cannot find any evidence that this playset ever went into mass production.

4218 Official Legend of Jesse James Playset (1966)

See reproduced documentation.

4238 Official Legend of Jesse James Playset (1966)

See reproduced documentation.

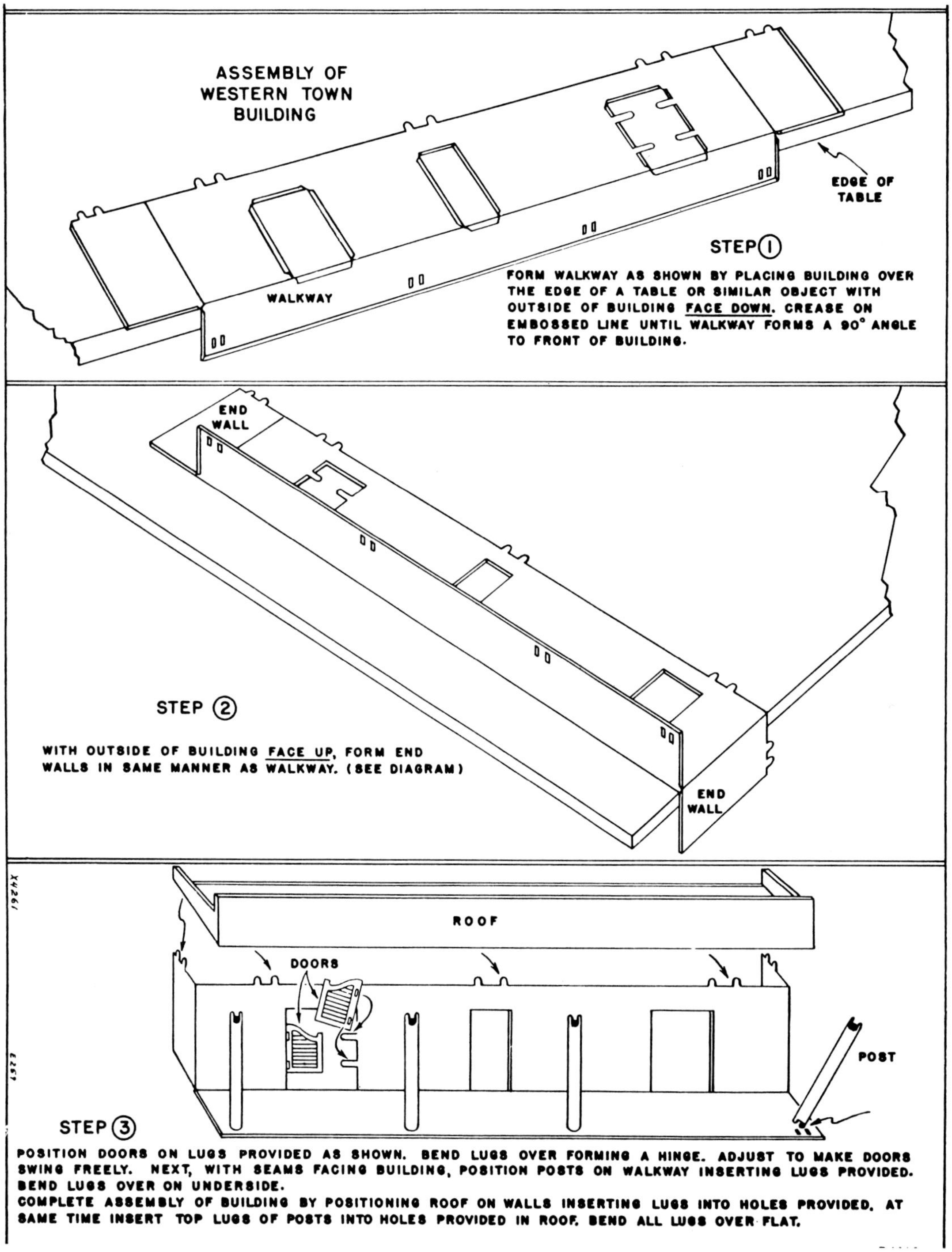

ASSEMBLY OF WESTERN TOWN BUILDING
EDGE OF TABLE
WALKWAY
STEP ①
FORM WALKWAY AS SHOWN BY PLACING BUILDING OVER THE EDGE OF A TABLE OR SIMILAR OBJECT WITH OUTSIDE OF BUILDING FACE DOWN. CREASE ON EMBOSSED LINE UNTIL WALKWAY FORMS A 90° ANGLE TO FRONT OF BUILDING.
END WALL
STEP ②
WITH OUTSIDE OF BUILDING FACE UP, FORM END WALLS IN SAME MANNER AS WALKWAY. (SEE DIAGRAM)
END WALL
ROOF
DOORS
POST
STEP ③
POSITION DOORS ON LUGS PROVIDED AS SHOWN. BEND LUGS OVER FORMING A HINGE. ADJUST TO MAKE DOORS SWING FREELY. NEXT, WITH SEAMS FACING BUILDING, POSITION POSTS ON WALKWAY INSERTING LUGS PROVIDED. BEND LUGS OVER ON UNDERSIDE.
COMPLETE ASSEMBLY OF BUILDING BY POSITIONING ROOF ON WALLS INSERTING LUGS INTO HOLES PROVIDED. AT SAME TIME INSERT TOP LUGS OF POSTS INTO HOLES PROVIDED IN ROOF. BEND ALL LUGS OVER FLAT.

This set was to incorporate a Marx Western playset staple — the Western Town building

ITEM NO. 4218
Date March 15, 1966
Customer No.
Replaces Sheet 3/1/66

GLEN DALE DIVISION
SPECIFICATION SHEET

Model No. 7962X-D
Cost No.

Item OFFICIAL LEGEND OF JESSE JAMES PLAY SET

Quantity	Part No.	Description	Color
1		6892X-6 Western Town Building consisting of:	
	PT-1885	Front Ends & Floor	
	PT-1886	Small Roof	
1	PL-733	Set Bar Room Doors (2 pcs.)	
1	PL-388	Set Outside Accessories	
1	PL-857	Stagecoach.	
1	PL-858	Double Hitch	
2	PL-532	Harness Horses	
3	PL-610	Horses w/Integ. Saddles	
1	PL-833	Set Cowboys (9)	
1	PL-971	Driver w/whip	
1		(2732) Set (3) Jesse James Figures	
1	P___	Inst. Sheet	

REMARKS:—

DEMONSTRATOR DATA:

SHIPPING CARTON Size— L W H Gross Tare Net Legal

SHIPPING CARTON INFORMATION:—

Individual Carton:—L 26-7/8 W 9-5/8 H 4-1/8 Diagonal 28-1/8 Girth 27-1/2 Weight 2 lb. 4 oz.

Description Each set in a die cut (2 print)

Master Carton Size—L 13-1/2 W 10" H 28-1/2" Diagonal 31-1/2 Girth 47 Weight

Quantity Packed Per Shipping Carton 1/4 dozen

Freight Classification

Net Weight ~~Gross~~ approx. Weight 8-1/2 Tare Weight Legal Weight

Acknowledged by A. E. B. Date [redacted]

Rec for W Y but
not signed 3/21

ITEM NO. 4238
Date April 1, 1966
Customer No.
Replaces Sheet

GLEN DALE DIVISION
SPECIFICATION SHEET

Model No. 8076X
Cost No. CO 3165

Item Official Legend of Jesse James Play Set

Quantity	Part No.	Description		Color
1	4218	Western town building consisting of: PT-1885 Front Ends & Floor PT-1886 Small Roof		
1	10 B	Building consisting of: PT-1784 Roof PT-1785 Front & Ends		
1	PL-101C	Set Porch & Chimeny	Hi. Imp.	Brown
5	PL-147	Sections Fence	Hi. Imp.	Brown
1	PL-388	Set Outside Accessories	Hi/ Imp.	Brown
2	PL-1145A	Units Trees	Poly.	Green
2	PL-532	Harness Horses	Poly.	Rust Brown
3	PL-610	Horses w/Integ. Saddles	Poly.	Asst. Colors
1	PL-857	Stagecoach	Hi. Imp.	Bwown
1	PL-858	Double Hitch	Linear.	Brown
1	PL-971	Driver w/whip	Poly.	Ivory
1	PL-833	Set Cowboys (9)	POLY.	Cowboy Tan
1	2732	Set Jesse James Figures (3)		?
1	PL-1014A	Set Frontier Figures (16)	Poly.	Buckskin
1	P	Inst. Sheet		

REMARKS:—

DEMONSTRATOR DATA:

SHIPPING CARTON Size— L [illegible] W [illegible] H [illegible] Gross .... Tare .... Net .... Legal ....

SHIPPING CARTON INFORMATION:—

Individual Carton:—L 25-3/4 W 7-7/8 H 3-15/16 Diagonal 27 Girth 27-1/2 Weight 3 lb. 4 oz.

Description

Master Carton Size—L 13 W 10 H 28-1/2 Diagonal 31-1/4 Girth 46 Weight

Quantity Packed Per Shipping Carton 1/4 dozen

Freight Classification

Net Weight .... Gross Weight approx. 12 Tare Weight .... Legal Weight ....

Acknowledged by AEB Date 4/7/66

JOHNNY RINGO

Marx was always on the lookout for a playset theme that would tie in with a successful television program. The existence of only one version of Johnny Ringo is clear testimony to the short-lived appeal of the series featuring a sharpshooting lawman reminiscent of Matt Dillon of *Gunsmoke*. It has become a very rare set, especially with its red, green, and white box, shown in the photograph on page 9. In contrast to the use of characters in the Gunsmoke playset, Johnny Ringo, played on television by Don Durant, was not accompanied by his girlfriend (Laura) or his deputy (Cully) in this set.

4784 Johnny Ringo Western Frontier Playset (1960)

See reproduced documentation and photo on catalog sheet.

Otherwise lost in the large Johnny Ringo Western Frontier scene (shown in the original catalog photo above), the hero is here poised for action. Gary J. Linden Collection

Date 3/15/60

PACKING INFORMATION

2000 SERIES NO.

Item No. NO. 4784 JOHNNY RINGO WESTERN FRONTIER PLAY SET
How Packed EACH SET IN DIE CUT CORR. BOX.
Quantity Packed 1/4 DOZEN
Wgt. Per Shipping Ctn.
Carton Dimensions L. W. D.

Cartons, Games or Toys, NOIBN, Iron or Steel, 20 ga or thicker, or
Frt. Classification any aggauge KDf
Net Wgt.
Tare Wgt.
Gross Wgt.
Legal Wgt.

FACTORY SPECIFICATIONS

MONTGOMERY Ward
Mail Order and Retail

1 - No. 10B	Ranch Building
1 - PL-1010	Plastic Porch- Light Gray
1 - PL-1057	Gold Mine Accessories- Note: Paint water course on one unit
3 - PL-1030	Wagons w/Accessories- Brown, Lgt. Gray, Red
2 - PL-1035	Wagon Tops- Pastel Blue, Light Gray
6 - PL-532	Horses- Brown, Beige, Ivory
3 -PL-1027 771	Drivers w/Whip- Ivory
1 - Set PL-1014A	Frontier Figures (16 pcs.) Light Gray
1 - Set PL-833	Cowboys (9 pcs.) Ivory and Tan
2 - PL-524	Trees- Light Green Polyethylene
5 - PL-369	Fence- Brown
2 - PL0610	Horses- Brown & Ivory
6 - PL-610	Steer0 Light Gray, Brown and Black
2 - PL-337	Wagon Wheels- Yellpw
3 -PL-148	Cactus- Light Green
1 - PL-864	Tepee- Beige
1 - Set PL-787	Indians (16 pcs.) Copper
1 - PL-692	Indian Poly- Ivory Horse
1 - Model No. 2634	Johnny Ringo Figure- Ivory
1 - P - 1260	Insturction LSheet

JOHNNY WEST RANCH/ROUNDUP

Johnny West was the center figure of a comprehensive series of 11-inch figures and their accessories (see **Larger-scale Playsets**). Reproduced here, complete with product number, is the catalog photo and sales description of a smaller-scale playset, with 3½-inch figures, which, it is widely believed, never went into full production due to insufficient advance orders. We include two other spec sheets found in the archives. It is, in any event, an interesting application of the use of prior molds, as it added Gunsmoke figure molds without using the Gunsmoke license. In a stroke of creative genius, Marx was able to take advantage of the fact that James Arness, who played the lead in *Gunsmoke*, resembles John Wayne, with whom Marx's own Johnny West was identified (see **Johnny West**). The ranch house and gate appeared in other playsets, too.

3978 Johnny West Ranch Set (Sears) (1968)
See reproduced documentation.

3980 Johnny West Roundup (1967)
See reproduced documentation and catalog photo, below, under name Johnny West Ranch.

4194 Johnny West Range Set (1967)
See reproduced documentation.

No. 3980 JOHNNY WEST RANCH

Contained within the 1 1/2" x 3 foot plastic fence the ranch hands of Johnny West, measuring up to 3 1/2" in height are busy with a multitude of chores in characteristic poses. Set includes a variation of scaled action figures - over two dozen in all plus the horses, cattle, trees and bushes as well as ranch yard installation. Featured is a lithographed metal bunkhouse with high impact plastic front porch.

PACKED: Each in a fully illustrated corrugated carton, 6 cartons to a shipper, weighing 21 lbs.
FOB Glendale, W. Va.

LOUIS MARX & CO., INC., 200 FIFTH AVENUE, NEW YORK, NEW YORK, 10010

MAY 24 1967

ITEM NO. 3978

Date February 20, 1968

Customer No.

Replaces Sheet

GLENDALE DIVISION
SPECIFICATION SHEET

Model No. 8366 X

Cost No.

Item Johnny West Ranch Set - Sears

Quantity	Part No.	Description	Color
1	10B	Ranch Bldg. consisting of:	
		1 - PT-1785 Front & Ends	
		1 - PT-1784 Roof	
1	PL-1010	Set Chimney & Porch	Lt. Gray
1	PL-130	Set Outside Accessories	Brown - Tan - Gray
18	PL-147	Sects. Fence	Dk. Brown
1	PL-466	Archway (Hot Stamped)	Dk. Brown
1	PL-1145A	Unit Tree	Green
1	PL-336A	Buckboard with new shaft	Blue
1	PL-532	Horse	Ivory
4	PL-610	Horses	Rust Brown
5	PL-1067	Steers	Assorted
1	PL-833-A	Set Cowboys (9)	Tan
1	PL-891-B	Set Cowboy Accessories	Rust Brown
1	PL-1014-A	Set Figures (16)	Lt. Gray
1		Wire Brace for Ranch Bldg.	
1		Instruction Sheet	

REMARKS:—

DEMONSTRATOR DATA:

SHIPPING CARTON Size— L W H Gross Tare Net Legal

SHIPPING CARTON INFORMATION:—

Individual Carton:—L W H Diagonal Girth Weight

Description Ind. D. C. with Sears Overall print.

Master Carton Size—L W H Diagonal Girth Weight

Quantity Packed Per Shipping Carton 6 to master

Freight Classification

Net Weight Gross Weight Tare Weight Legal Weight

Acknowledged by G P Date 2/28/68

ITEM NO. 3980
Date March 15, 1967
Customer No.
Replaces Sheet

GLEN DALE DIVISION
SPECIFICATION SHEET

Model No. CO-3206
Cost No.

Item JOHNNY WEST ROUNDUP

Quantity	Part No.	Description	Color
1	#10B	Building (no stack)	
1	PL-130	Set Outside Acces.	
18	PL-147	Fence	
1	PL-336A	Buckboard	
1	PL-466	Archway (hot stamped)	
1	PL-891	Indian & Cowboy Access.	
1	PL-1010	Chimney & Porch	
2	PL-1145A	Trees	
1	PL-[illegible]2	Horse	
4	PL-610	Horses	
1	PL-833	Set (9) cowboys	
1	PL____	Set (4) Figures	
1	PL-1014A	Set (16) Figures	
10	PL-1067	Steers	
1	P____	Instruction Sheet	

REMARKS:—

DEMONSTRATOR DATA:

SHIPPING CARTON Size— L W H Gross Tare Net Legal

SHIPPING CARTON INFORMATION:—

Individual Carton:—L approx. 24 W 11 H 3-5/8 Diagonal 26-1/2 Girth 29-1/4 Weight

Description Each in an ind. die cut - litho box

Master Carton Size—L 24 W 11-1/2 H 24-3/4 Diagonal 34-1/2 Girth 67 Weight

Quantity Packed Per Shipping Carton 6 to a master case

Freight Classification approx. 21

Net Weight Gross Weight Tare Weight Legal Weight

Acknowledged by AEB Date 3/20/67

ITEM NO. #4194

Date March 30, 1967

Customer No.

Replaces Sheet

GLEN DALE DIVISION
SPECIFICATION SHEET

Model No. 8198-X

Cost No.

Item JOHNNY WEST RANGE SET

Quantity	Part No.	Description	Color
1	PL-336A	Buckboard	
1	PL-351	Set Access.	
6	PL-939	Fence	
2	PL-1145A	Tree	
4	PL-1383	Corner Blocks	
1	PL-1384	Center Desert Section	
1	PL-1384	Center Lake Section	
1	PL-532	Horse	
3	PL-610	Horses	
1	PL-833	Set (9) Cowboys	
1	PL-1014A	Set (17) Figures	
3	PL-1067	Steers	
1	PL____	Set (2 pcs.) J. West Figures (New Cavity)	
1	P____	Instruction Sheet	

REMARKS:—

DEMONSTRATOR DATA:

SHIPPING CARTON Size— L W H Gross Tare Net Legal

SHIPPING CARTON INFORMATION:—

Individual Carton:— approx. L 24-5/8 W 13 H 5-7/8 Diagonal 27-3/4 Girth 38 Weight 5 lb. 11 oz.

Description 1 pc. per Ind. die cut with partial label

Master Carton Size— approx. L 18-1/4 W 13-1/4 H 25-1/4 Diagonal 31-1/4 Girth 63 Weight

Quantity Packed Per Shipping Carton 3 per Master

Freight Classification

Net Weight Gross Weight approx. 19 lbs. Tare Weight Legal Weight

Acknowledged by AEB Date 4/3/67

LONE RANGER

The masked Texas Ranger and his Indian side-kick Tonto had a long reign via movies and television. One variation of the Lone Ranger playsets is shown in Color Photo 14.

0708 27-Piece Lone Ranger Western Set (1956)
Bagged group with Lone Ranger and Tonto (both in ivory), two horses, saddles and bridles, sixteen assorted action Indians in red and yellow, and three miniature guns.

3696, 3696D Lone Ranger Rodeo (1956)
Featured set; see reproduced documentation and color photo. One of the smallest playsets made, it fit into a pizza-sized box.

3698, 3698D Official Lone Ranger Ranch Set (1956)
Designed for both retail and mail order (Montgomery Ward), this is a complete Western ranch layout where the steel "Bar M" Ranch house replaces the rodeo chute and four assorted horses and one longhorn are included. The trees have been changed to two spreading trees, 5" tall.

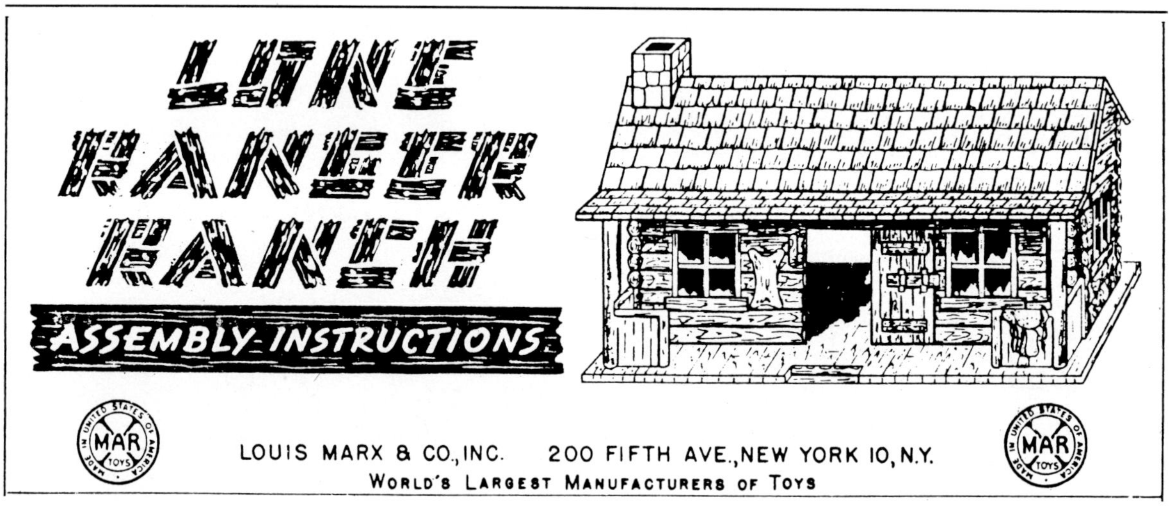

LONE RANGER RANCH
ASSEMBLY INSTRUCTIONS
LOUIS MARX & CO., INC. 200 FIFTH AVE., NEW YORK 10, N.Y.
WORLD'S LARGEST MANUFACTURERS OF TOYS

Compare this illustration with the assembly instruction sheet for Fort Dearborn; the cabin appears in many Marx Western playsets.

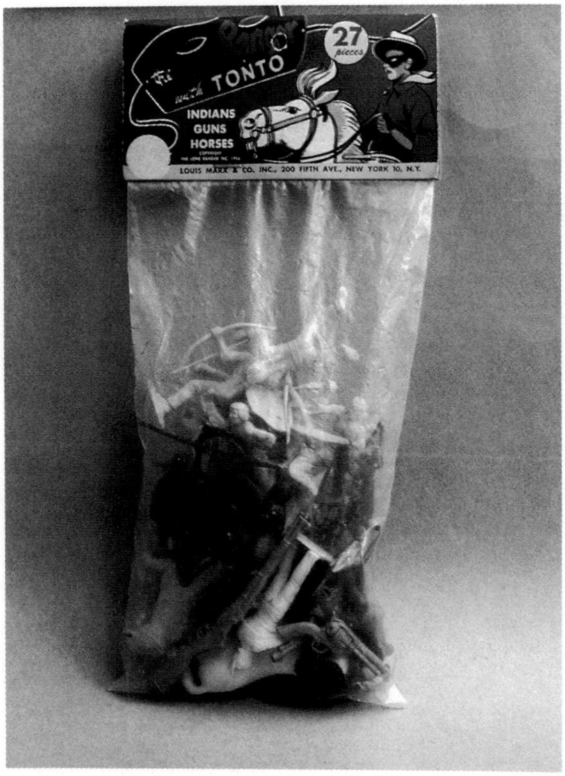

Many Marx Western playset themes included the offering of a bagged set of figures and accessories. Gary J. Linden Collection

LOUIS MARX & CO.
200 Fifth Ave., New York

GLENDALE DIVISION
8/22/56

NO. 3696 LONE RANGER RODEO

Watch the Lone Ranger and his Rodeo come to life! We have actually reproduced the Lone Ranger and Tonto, and with these two famous characters as the stars, we have a Rodeo, complete with a three-stall Rodeo Chute with swinging gates. Rodeo Cowboys with lassos and whips, bucking horses, snorting and bucking steers, with the saddles and reins for the horses actually removable.

There is also a life-like buckboard wagon with a separate hitching harness. All the above is completely enclosed by interlocking fence sections with a Lone Ranger Archway.

RODEO CHUTE: Measures 9-1/4" long, 4-3/4" wide, 4-1/4" high. ~~Madexxxf~~ Molded of sturdy plastic, in authentic detail.

COWBOYS: Eleven rodeo figures, including Lone Ranger and Tonto, bronco riders, cowboy with guns. Molded in life-like vinyl plastic. Standing figure measures 2-3/8" high, others in proportion.

ANIMALS: There are eight rodeo animals including: Bucking Bronco, Rearing Horse, Bracing Cowpony, Snorting Steer, small Calf for Branding.

SADDLE & REINS: There are six removable saddles and reins for horses. Molded of soft vinyl plastic so that theyoung cowhands may put them on, or take them off.

BUCKBOARD: A plastic Buckboard Wagon, with a seat has realistic spoke wheels and is equipped with a vinyl harness to permit hitching and unhitching of the horse.

OUTSIDE ACCESSORIES: Made of plastic, in appropriate color and detail:
2 - Cactus 1 - Flag w/flagpole 1 - Tree

FENCE & ARCHWAY: There are twelve sections of interlocking board fence, which completely enclose the Rodeo. Ranch Archway is included with the fence.

PACKED: Each set in an individual corrugated shipping carton,
1/2 dozen sets to master carton,
Weight per carton - 16 lbs.

NO. 3696D DEMONSTRATOR FOR ABOVE

PACKED: 1 only to shipping carton - Weight per carton - 9-1/2 lbs.

FACTORY SPECIFICATIONS:

1 - PL-356	Rodeo Chute			
1 - PL-463	Cowboys (8)			
1 - PL-496	Lone Ranger Figures (LR Standing, Ridng & Tonto)			
1 - PL-324	Horse		1 - PL-345	Harness
1 - PL-325	Horses and Calf (3)		1 - PL-131	Tree
6 - PL-326	Saddles and ~~Rxxxg~~ Reins		2 - PL-148	Cactus
1 - PL-460	Animals (4)		12 - PL-187	Sections of Fence
1 - PL-336	Buckboard		1 - PL-346	Flagpole
2 - PL-337	Sets of Buckboard wheels		1 -	Lithographed Flag

RIFLEMAN

Again TV inspired Marx. As the documentation says: "Based on the exciting television series, the 'Rifleman' Ranch Play Set finds Lucas McCain and his son, Mark, at the ranch — ready for roundup." See Color Photo 16.

3997, 3998, 3998D "Rifleman" Ranch Playset (1959)

See reproduced documentation. The ranch house used here was picked up for several other playsets. The two characters by the gateway in Color Photo 16 are the Rifleman and his son.

Two of the characters from The Rifleman *are shown here: left to right Flint McCullough and Major Seth Adams of* Wagon Train *and Lucas McCain and Mark McCain of* Rifleman. *Gary J. Linden Collection*

LOUIS MARX & CO.
200 FIFTH AVE. NEW YORK

GLENDALE DIVISION

4/23/59

NO. 3997 "RIFLEMAN" RANCH PLAY SET

NO. 3998 "RIFLEMAN" RANCH PLAY SET

RAnchhouse measures 9" long, 5-1/2" wide, 4-1/2" high.
Bunkhouse measures 8-1/2" long, 4-1/4" wide, 4-1/4" high.

Based on the exciting television series, the "Rifleman" Ranch Play Set finds Lucas McCain and his son, Mark, at the ranch- ready for roundup.

Two buildings, a ranchhouse and a bunkhouse, are constructed of steel lithographed inside and out. The Ranchhouse is equipped with outside chimney and front porch- both in plastic.

Twelve sections of brown board build a corral for eight molded plastic steer. Other special mention features include a buckboard wagon with horse and buckboard harness and a driver.

Lucas McCain, carrying a miniature model of his own special rifle, and his son mark, are also included. There are two detailed plastic figures- exact replicas of the television stars. Other ranch figures include 27 Cowboys in live action poses and 4 horses.

Accessories to the "Rifleman" Ranch Play set include a cactus, tree and a 35 piece set of lariots, carbines, shotguns, canteens, and others.

PACKED: Each in a box,
1/4 dozen to shipping carton,
Weight per carton - 16 lbs.

1/2 dozen to shipping carton,
Weight per carton - 30 lbs.

NO. 3998 D SET UP DEMONSTRATOR

All contents securely fastened on board for counter display purposes.

Packed
Each in a shipper
Weight per carton - 15 lbs.

Rpplaces sheet dated 3/11/59

Acknowledged By: FWD Date 5/7/59

Date 4/23/59

1000 SERIES

PACKING INFORMATION

Item No. 3997 -3998 "RIFLEMAN" RANCH PLAY SET
How Packed EACH IN A BOX
Quantity Packed 1/4 DOZ. 1/2 DOZ.
Wgt. Per Shipping Ctn. 16 lbs. 30 lbs.
Carton Dimensions L. W. D.

Cartons, Games or Toys, NOIBN, Iron or Steel 20 ga or thicker
Frt. Classification or any gauge KDF PJS
Net Wgt.
Tare Wgt.
Gross Wgt.
Legal Wgt.

W FACTORY SPECIFICATIONS DEL

1 - Regular Type Extra Small Log Cabin Building w/stovepipe chimney w/ Log Cabin litho- Basic Yellow Roof
1 - 6966-A Extra Small Cabin Building w/new litho on walls Light Gray shingle litho on roof
1 - PL-1010 Plastic Porch & Chimney- Light Gray to match roof

12 - PL-147 Sections Log Fence (Brown)
1 - PL-146 Ranch Gate & Archway (Brown)
1 - Rifleman Hotstamp in yellow or gold
1 - PL-130 Set Ranch Access. (assorted colors)
3 - PL-833A Sets Cowboys (total 27 pcs.) Yellow- Gray- Buckskin
1 - PL-1015 Set Rifleman Figures (3 pcs.) (Ivory)
4 - PL-610 Horses (Assorted colors)
1 - PL-524 Tree (Green poly)
1 - PL-148 Cactus (Green poly)
8 - PL-610 Steer (Assorted colors)
1 0-PL-891 Set Cowboy Access. on runner (silver metallic poly)
1 - PL-336A Buckboard w/Integral Hitch (blue w/yellvo wheels) PL 337
1 - PL-532 Harness Horses (Ivory)
1 - P - Instr. Sheet

ROY ROGERS

One of the first Western characters especially done for children's viewing in the early years of television was Roy Rogers. Roy, Dale Evans, Pat Brady, the horse Trigger, and Nellybelle the Jeep are all names that Baby Boomers easily recognize. It was thus logical that this was the first license Marx undertook in the early 1950s. Although the dates of the archive documentation for Mineral City and the Roy Rogers Double R Bar Ranch Rodeo are late 1950s, both these sets were featured in the 1952 Sears Christmas catalog. They appear on the same page as Super Circus, also stemming from television programming, and Tom Corbett's Space Academy. Frank Rice reports that the Roy Rogers playset was created in the second year of Marx playsets, under Ed Hjelte.

0707 27-Piece Roy Rogers Cowboy Set (1956)

Bagged set featuring Roy Rogers and wife Dale Evans, in ivory (see photograph), and cowboys in yellow, green, beige, and silver.

0770 Roy Rogers & Frontier Figure with Accessories (1956)

4"-high Roy and frontiersman and seventeen items of clothing and equipment in bagged set.

0788 Roy Rogers and Indian Riders on Horse (1956)

Bagged set of 6¾" horse, PL-724 set of cowboy and Indian riders, and PL-725 set of riding equipment.

3981, 3981D, 3982, 3982D Roy Rogers Ranch Set (1962)

Features lithographed steel ranch building with plastic porch and chimney, white Roy Rogers archway, and red miniature of Pat Brady's jeep, "Nellybelle," according to factory specification sheet.

3985, 3985D Roy Rogers Double Bar Rodeo Ranch Set (1956)

Featured set; see reproduced documentation. Note the notation to eliminate string: some Western playset accessories included short lengths of string meant to represent rope.

3986, 3986D Roy Rogers Double Bar Rodeo Ranch Set (1956)

Essentially the same as #3985, the factory documentation of which is dated one month earlier; #3986 includes one cactus and one tree.

3989, 3989D "Roy Rogers" Double-R Ranch Set (1959)

In comparing the original Marx promotional description of this playset with that for #3985, we note that it features a new lithographed steel ranch house (same one used in Rifleman). Roy, Dale, Pat, and Bullet, eighteen cowboys, and thirty-five-piece set of cowboy accessories on runner. Over ninety pieces in this set.

3990 Happi-Time Roy Rogers Rodeo Ranch Set (Sears) (1954)

This early playset features an all-steel bunk house. See Color Photos 21 and 22.

3992, 3992L Roy Rogers Rodeo Ranch Set (1955)

One of the two separate factory specification sheets for #3992, titled "Rodeo Ranch Set," indicates it was a Sears item. The other specifies a Happi-Time box (#3992L was to be packaged in a "plain box"). As in #3990, there is a lithographed steel bunk house. The "Nellybelle" jeep is included.

3996 New Roy Rogers Rodeo Ranch (Sears) (1957)

Featured set; see reproduced documentation.

4216, 4216SD "Roy Rogers" Mineral City (Sears) (1958)

This and the remaining Roy Rogers playsets listed feature a large two-story Western town "street" building — with small variations. Compared with the documented set, #4258, its building houses the jail, newspaper office, and dry goods store; includes outside and cowboy accessories, no inside furnishings. See Color Photos 19 and 20 for this simpler building set-up.

4255, 4255SD "Roy Rogers" Mineral City (1958)

Distinguished from similar sets by including only one character figure, Roy Rogers himself.

4257, 4257D Roy Rogers Western Town (1957)

No apparent difference from #4258, below.

4258 Roy Rogers Mineral City Western Town (1956)

See reproduced documentation and Color Photos 17 and 18.

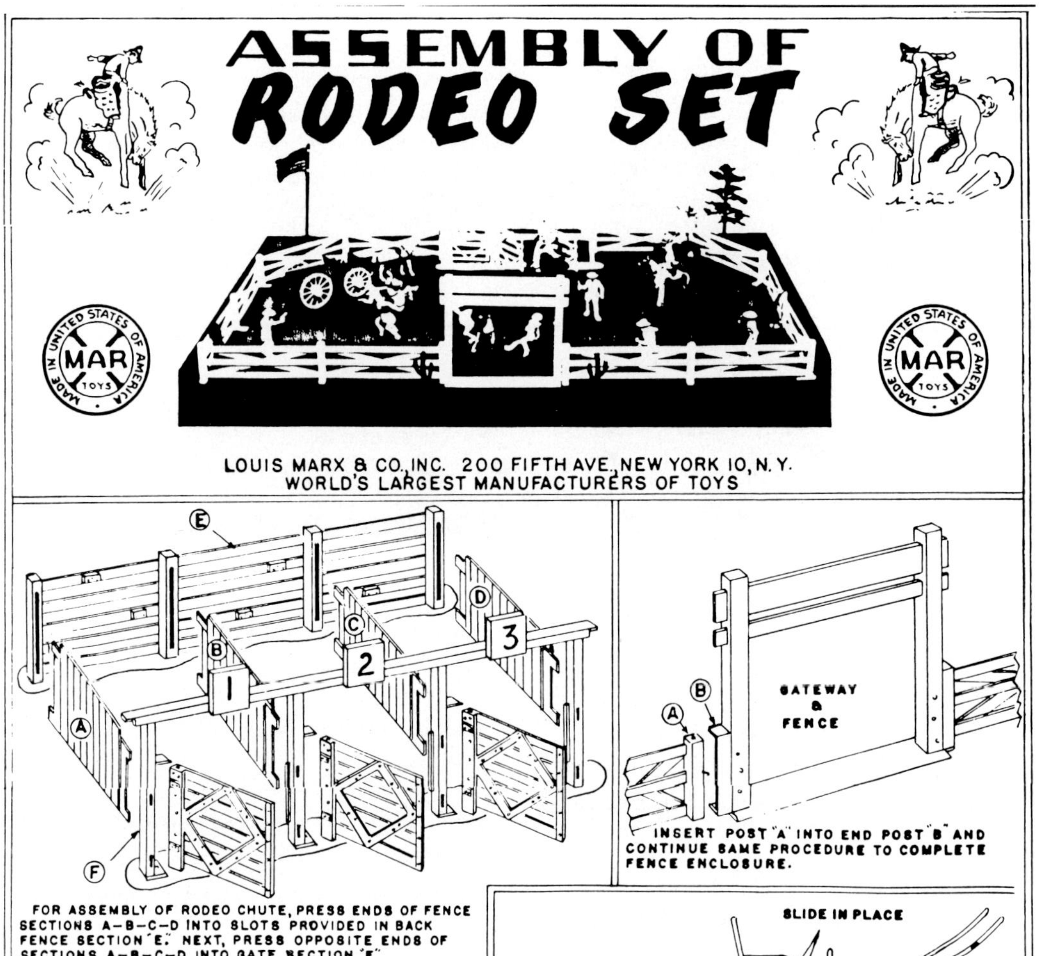

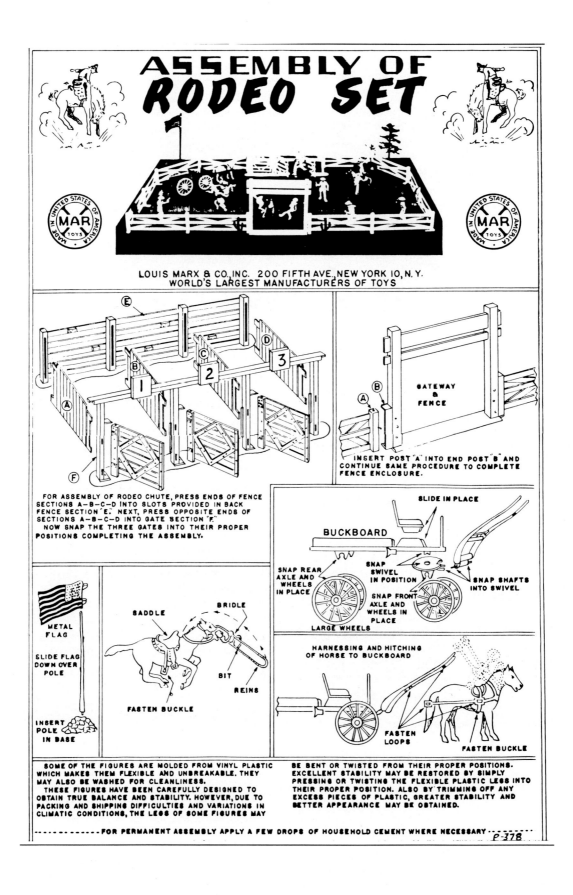

ASSEMBLY OF RODEO SET

LOUIS MARX & CO., INC. 200 FIFTH AVE., NEW YORK 10, N.Y.
WORLD'S LARGEST MANUFACTURERS OF TOYS

INSERT POST "A" INTO END POST "B" AND CONTINUE SAME PROCEDURE TO COMPLETE FENCE ENCLOSURE.

FOR ASSEMBLY OF RODEO CHUTE, PRESS ENDS OF FENCE SECTIONS A-B-C-D INTO SLOTS PROVIDED IN BACK FENCE SECTION "E." NEXT, PRESS OPPOSITE ENDS OF SECTIONS A-B-C-D INTO GATE SECTION "F."
NOW SNAP THE THREE GATES INTO THEIR PROPER POSITIONS COMPLETING THE ASSEMBLY.

SOME OF THE FIGURES ARE MOLDED FROM VINYL PLASTIC WHICH MAKES THEM FLEXIBLE AND UNBREAKABLE. THEY MAY ALSO BE WASHED FOR CLEANLINESS.
THESE FIGURES HAVE BEEN CAREFULLY DESIGNED TO OBTAIN TRUE BALANCE AND STABILITY. HOWEVER, DUE TO PACKING AND SHIPPING DIFFICULTIES AND VARIATIONS IN CLIMATIC CONDITIONS, THE LEGS OF SOME FIGURES MAY BE BENT OR TWISTED FROM THEIR PROPER POSITIONS. EXCELLENT STABILITY MAY BE RESTORED BY SIMPLY PRESSING OR TWISTING THE FLEXIBLE PLASTIC LEGS INTO THEIR PROPER POSITION. ALSO BY TRIMMING OFF ANY EXCESS PIECES OF PLASTIC, GREATER STABILITY AND BETTER APPEARANCE MAY BE OBTAINED.

FOR PERMANENT ASSEMBLY APPLY A FEW DROPS OF HOUSEHOLD CEMENT WHERE NECESSARY

P-378

All the leading characters of "Roy Rogers," in the 4-inch-high person scale. Gary J. Linden Collection

ROY ROGERS'
MINERAL CITY
$5.98
Roy spotted you in the corral and signaled for help as the jail door burst open. The rustlers have broken out and are racing to join their Indian gang camped outside town! It's up to you and Roy to stop them, and there's not much time to do it. Six gun in hand, you mount and gallop down Main Street. . . .
JAIL
HAY-FEED
MINERAL CITY

Reproduced from the Marx brochure Toyland Adventures, of 1958.

LOUIS MARX & CO.
200 Fifth Ave., New York

GLENDALE DIVISION
10/8/56

NO. 3985 ROY ROGERS DOUBLE BAR RODEO RANCH SET

This set is complete with rodeo, three stall rodeo chutes with swinging gates, cowboys with lassos and whips, bucking horses, snorting and bucking steers, complete with ten sections of log style fence and a Roy Rogers Archway entrance.

Ranch building measures 11" wide, 7" deep, 6-1/8" high, and is made of beautifully lithographed metal, and designed both inside and out to represent a western motif.

A complete set of ranch accessories are also included and these have been scaled in the utmost detail.

RODEO CHUTES: Three chutes measuring 9-1/4" long, 4-3/4" wide, 4-1/4" high, molded in exact authentic detail with three swinging gates.

COWBOYS & FIGURES: Accurate reproduction of Rodeo figures, Roy Rogers, bronc riders, cowboys in various positions, all made of detailed sculptured flexible plastic, Includes one authentic Roy Rogers figures.

FENCE: Consists of ten sections of log-type fence with an entrance Archway, "Roy Rogers" hot stamped thereon.

There are other western items included such as extra outside ranch accessories including a fireplace, a chopping block, anvil, pump, empty barrels, etc.

PACKED: Each set in a corrugated shipper,
1/2 dozen to shipping carton,
Weight per carton - 19-3/4 lbs.

NO. 3985D ROY ROGERS DOUBLE BAR RODEO RANCH SET DEMO.

A demonstrator that is completely set up for display purposes.

PACKED: One only to shipping carton,
Weight per carton - 10 lbs.

FACTORY SPECIFICATIONS:

1 - Metal Building w/board & batten-type litho.
1 - PL-130 Set of outside ranch accessories
1 - PL-337 Separate buckboard wheel
1 - PL-416 Roy Rogers figure
1 --PL-463 Set of Rodeo Cowboys (8 pcs.)
1 - PL-610 Set of Western animals
10 -PL-147 Sections of Log Fence (White)
1 - PL-356 Set of 3 Rodeo chutes (White)
1 - PL-466 Roy Rogers Archway w/hot stamp
See our letter of 3/10/54 - Re. figures
2/23 Eliminate string.

LOUIS MARX & CO.
200 Fifth Ave., New York

GLENDALE DIVISION
3/13/57

NO. 3996 NEW ROY ROGERS RODEO RANCH

This complete new Double-R-Bar Ranch layout combines all the action and realism of a big Western Ranch layout. Over Seventy (70) pieces in all, this Ranch features a rodeo chute, new horses with separte saddles, "Nellybelle" the Jeep, and an authentic stage with team of horses, plus the official miniature figures of Roy Rogers, Dale Evans, Pat Brady & Bullet.

The lithographed Bunk House measures 11" long, 6-1/8" wide, 6" high to top of chimney. Constructed of steel with all edges rolled for extra strength. Attractively and authentically lithographed in a Western Ranch motif, shipped flat and exceptionally easy to set up without the use of tools. Roy Rogers Ranch name lithographed on roof.

STAGE COACH: with team of harness horses, measures 3-1/2" high, 6-1/2" long and 3-1/4" wide. Authentic marking and detail are molded into the coach body. The two harness horses readily snap into appropriate hitching shaft for easy assembly.

RODEO CHUTE: 9-1/4" long, 4-3/4" wide, 4-1/4" high. Molded in sturdy plastic with authentic detail. Gates actually swing open.

NELLYBELLE JEEP: Authentic replica of Pat Brady's famous Jeep, molded in sturdy high-impact plastic with easy rolling wheels. Measures 4-1/4" long, 2" wide, 2" high to top of wire tumble bar.

COWBOYS: In addition to Roy, Dale, Pat and Bullet, there are eighteen (18) polyethylene figures of cowhands with lasso, bullwhips, etc., badmen with masks, riders with drawn pistols, etc. There are twenty-two (22) figures in all, including Bullet. Standing figures measure 2-1/4" high, others in proportion.
WESTERN ANIMALS: Six (6) new Horses in lifelike action poses, plus two snorting Longhorn Steer, all molded in colorful unbreakable polyethylene.

SADDLES & REINS: Six(6) separate Saddles and six (6) Reins add hours of play in saddling the horses. Molded in soft brown vinyl, these accessories are easily assembled by the young cowhand.

RANCH ACCESSORIES: Completely enclosed by sixteen (16) sections of interlocking fence, this ranch boasts an authentic Roy Rogers Double-R-Bar Ranch Archway. Realistic ranch equipment to round out the set include the following:

1 - Hitching Rail	1 - Pump with Pail
1 - Gringing Stone	1 - Forge
1 - Chopping Block	1 - Well
1 - Pile of Logs	1 - Anvil
2 - Trees	2 - Cactus
1 - Rain Barrel	2 - Extra Wagon Wheels

PACKED: Each set in a box,
1/2 dozen sets to shipping carton,
Weight per carton - 30 lbs.

(continued.....

- 2 -

FACTORY SPECIFICATIONS:

Sears Exclusive - 1957
Model No. 6355X

1 -	Roy Rogers Ranch Bldg. w/wire support, no base (board and batten type litho)
1 --PL-130	Set Outside Ranch Accessories
1 --PL-857	Stage Coach - Model No. 6236X w/double hitch unit PL-858
2 - PL-532	Harness Horses
4 - PL-879	New Roy Rogers Figures - Model No. 2513
2 - PL-524	Trees
2 - PL-158	Cactus
16 - PL-147	Sections Log Fence (white)
2 - PL-337	Extra Buckboard wheels
1 - PL-356	Rodeo Chute
1 - PL-366	Roy Rogers Archway
2 - PL-610	Steer
1 - PL-694	Nellybelle Jeep
PL-521	Necessary wheels
2 - PL-833	Sets New Cowboys (total 18 pieces)
6 - PL-865	Horses
6 - PL-326	Saddles & Bridles
1 - P-	Instruction sheet

LOUIS MARX & CO.
200 Fifth Ave., New York

GLENDALE DIVISION
10/24/56

NO. 4258 ROY ROGERS MINERAL CITY WESTERN TOWN

Exact replica of a Western Town, complete with buildings, horses, cowboys, Roy Rogers figures, including Roy, Dale Evans and their Dog, Bullet.

BUILDING UNIT: Metal lithographed building measures 27-1/2" long, 6" wide, 9" high. Consists of Hotel, Express Office, Barber Shop, Stage-coach, ~~Waiting~~ Waiting Room, Barroom. Each unit well lithographed in appropriate color and design. Shipped knocked down and easy to assemble without tools. "MINERAL CITY" sign lithographed over hotel.

INSIDE FURNITURE: Twenty-five detailed, plastic accessories, to be set up in various units, such as bedroom furniture for hotel. Teller's cage and slated-type table for bank, Barber chair, clothes tree and bench for Barber Shop; Dry Goods counter, flour sack and cider barrel for general store; bar, round table, two swinging doors for bar--room. All furniture appropriately detailed and designed.

OUTSIDE ACCESSORIES: Nineteen outside accessories including; hitching rails, lamp post, tool garden, racks, barrel, feed sack, bench, crate, with rifles, water trough, lantern, etc.

COWBOYS: Cowboys in various action like positions, including: Standing cowboy measuring 2-5/8" high, others in proportion. There are running, shooting, riding cowboy w/lasso, fist fighter, a sheriff, bank robber being arrested, etc.

HORSE & CALVES: Running, rearing, bucking and standing horse, a draft horse and two calves to be branded.

SADDLES & BRIDLES: Six western saddles and bridles, made of flexible plastic, well detailed and designed.

FENCE: Two section of log-type fence.

TREES: Two trees, measuring 5" tall.

CACTUS: Two realistic looking cactus plants.

BUCKBOARD: Buckboard wagon with two large, spoke wheels. Furnished with a separate soft vinyl plastic harness, for hitching and unhitching horses.

PACKED: Each set in a box 1/4 dozen sets to shipping carton
Weight per carton - 15 lbs.

FACTORY SPECIFICATIONS:

1 - 4250	Western Town Bldg.	
14 - PL-389	Cowboys	Yellow
5 - PL-329	Cowboys	Tan
1 - PL-324	Set horses(2) & calf (1)	Brown
1 - PL-325	Set Horses (2) & calf (1)	Light gray
1 - PL-324	Standing Horse	Brown
6 - PL-326	Saddles & Bridles	Brown
1 - PL-336	Buckboard	Blue
2 - PL-337	Buckboard wheels	Yellow
1 - PL-386	Set Inside Furn.	Brown
1 - PL-388	Set outside Access.	Brown
3 - PL-416	R. Rogers Figures: Roy, Dale, Bullet,	Ivory
2 - PL-131	Trees	Light Green
2 - PL-148	Cactus	Light Green
2 - PL-147	Fence	Brown
1 - PL-345	Harness	Black

WAGON TRAIN

In this group we have both "generic" wagon train playsets and those that latched, once again, onto the popularity of a TV series (*Wagon Train,* starring Ward Bond as Major Seth Adams and Robert Horton as Flint McCullough). The focus was the trail of brave pioneers crossing the country to participate in the 1850 Gold Rush. See also **Larger-scale Playsets**, which used a wagon mold in various settings.

4104 Red River Gang (1978)

Featured set; see reproduced documentation and Color Photo 10.

4777 Official "Wagon Train" Playset (Montgomery Ward) (1958)

Apparently the earliest variation, it differs from featured set #4805, which was designed as a Sears exclusive, in a number of ways: this includes three buckboards without harness shaft instead of four wagons with hitches and one tepee instead of two.

4785, 4785D, 4786, 4786D Wagon Train Playset (1960)

Playsets with these numbers and the ones immediately following are basically the same. Comparing them with the specifications for the featured set, #4805, we note that *absent* from these smaller sets are a wagon with oxen hitch and two oxen (now considered very rare), a second set of Indians and totem pole, a set of cowboys and cowboy accessories, Indian camp accessories, three steer, a set of small animals, two cowboy horses, and a second cactus; also, the mountains specified in #4805 have been replaced by a "mound unit." See description following.

4788, 4788D Official "Wagon Train" Playset (1960)

See above. One change in this "official" set is a change in the type of wagon and accessories. According to the March 3, 1960 documentation for this playset, a "new" wagon is to be used. (Gary Linden believes this is the hard plastic, or high-impact styrene, buckboard with soft plastic, or low-density polyethylene, cover and accessories.) Also, the specified colors for the cavalry figures are here pastel blue and beige, whereas they were pastel blue and light gray for the previous sets.

4805 Official Wagon Train Playset (Sears) (1960)

Featured set; see reproduced documentation. Advertised in the 1959 Sears Christmas catalog; exclusive 235-piece set, with 100-piece set also offered.

4997, 4997D, 4998, 4998D Mammoth Western Wagon Set (1960)

Living up to its name, this is a large set, with two wagons (green and brown), one red and gray stagecoach, eight horses, a set of Covered Wagon Accessories and one of Chuck Wagon Accessories, and various figures and their accessories.

G. Almond · F. Mueller · T. Dudek
D. Barnett · D. Sigler · M. Yankoski
E. Peck · J. Strope · G. Vi
F. Pavalko · T. Gayvont · J. His.
M. Fleming · J. Meyers · B. Turberville
B. Brak · B. Terrill · Bob Jennings
E. Sollenberger · E. Livingston

BILL OF MATERIALS

PART NO.	1	2	3	4	5	6	PURC	DRAWING NO.	PART NAME	MATERIAL OR SIZE	COLOR NO.	REMARKS
✓ 4104	1/6						P		Master Carton	See Packing Specifications	18 5/8 X 9 5/16	X12
✓ 8540		2					P		Tape -Kraft	See Packing Specifications	3X27-	To seal Master Carton
✓ 4104			1				P		Individual Box	See Packing Specifications	8 3/4 X 2 5/16	X 11 3/4
✓ PL-11002				1				C-1925	Top (PL-1615)	Plastic	PMS-165 Orange	PL-1615
✓ 8715						x	P		Shrink Film	See Packing Specifications	60 Ga.	15"X16 1/2"
✓ P-0030			1				P		Tepee	(Paper)		
✓ 7646			3				P		Poly Bag	8 x 8 x .002 w/1" Lip	-	Wagon & Access.
PL-11106				1					Wagon Body	Hi Density Poly	PMS-470 Brown	PL-1030
PL-11107				1					Swivel Axle	Hi Density Poly	PMS-470Brown	PL-1030
PL-11108				1					Seat	Hi Density Poly	PMS-470 Brown	PL-1030
PL-11109				1					Wagon Tongue	Hi Density Poly	PMS-470 Brown	PL-1030
PL-11110				2					Front Wheel	Hi Density Poly	PMS-470 Brown	PL-1030
PL-11111				2					Rear Wheel	Hi Density Poly	PMS-470 Brown	PL-1030
PL-11112				1					Tool Box	Hi Density Poly	PMS-470 Brown	PL-1030
PL-11113				1					Water Barrel	Hi Density Poly	PMS-470 Brown	PL-1030
PL-11114				1					Bucket	Hi Density Poly	PMS-470 Brown	PL-1030
PL-11115				1					Tub	Hi Density Poly	PMS-470 Brown	PL-1030
✓ P-0042				1			P		Instruction Sheet			

REV	NO.	CHANGE DESCRIPTION	BY	DATE	REV.	NO.	CHANGE DESCRIPTION	BY	DATE

MARX TOYS: ERIE · GIRARD · GLEN DA
CAT. # 4104 · MODEL #
TOY NAME Red River Gang
ISS'D BY FM · APPR. BY
DATE 2/7/78 · PAGE 1 OF 5

G. Almond · F. Mueller · T. Dudek · Mike Marra
D. Barnett · D. Sigler · M. Yankoski · J. John Schroeder
E. Peck · J. Strope · G. Vincent · Al Beddy
F. Pavalko · T. Gayvont · J. Hissom
M. Fleming · J. Meyers · B. Turberville
B. Brak · B. Terrill
E. Sollenberger · E. Livingston · Jimmy Ray

BILL OF MATERIALS

PART NO.	1	2	3	4	5	6	PURC	DRAWING NO.	PART NAME	MATERIAL OR SIZE	COLOR NO.	REMARKS
PL-11116				1					Lantern	Hi Density Poly	PMS-470 Brown	PL-1030
PL-10999				2				B-1297	Axle	Hi Density Poly	PMS-470 Brown	PL-1030
PL-1031									Covered Wagon Top	Poly	~~PMS-155C~~ Beige	PL-1031(A) 50% run Black
PL-11117									Old Style Steer or Running Steer or Walking Steer		Ivory & Black	"Ivory PL-1037
								Note: Group Cowboys as follows -	Use one group only			
E-7646			1						Poly Bag	8 x 8 x .002 w/1" Lip		Cowboys
PL-11124				1					Running w/Strong Box	L. D. Poly	Buckskin Tan 5688S	PL-1528
PL-11180				1					Holding Rifle	L. D. Poly	"	PL-1528
PL-11121				1					Riding Bandit	L. D. Poly	"	PL-1528
PL-11123				1					w/Branding Iron	L. D. Poly	"	PL-1528
PL-11122				1					w/Pistols in both Hands	L. D. Poly	"	Sold HG PL-1528
PL-11181				1					Standing Sheriff	L. D. Poly	"	PL-1528
PL-11120				1					Rider w/Lasso	L. D. Poly	"	PL-1528
PL-11182				1					Walking w/Rifle	L. D. Poly	"	PL-1528
PL-11183				1					Drawing Pistol	L. D. Poly	"	PL-1528
PL-11184				1					Fighting w/Hat	L. D. Poly	"	PL-1528
PL-11185				1					Shooting Pistol	L. D. Poly	"	PL-1528
PL-11125				1					Sitting	L. D. Poly	"	PL-1528

REV	NO.	CHANGE DESCRIPTION	BY	DATE	REV.	NO.	CHANGE DESCRIPTION	BY	DATE
A	87	Add PMS-155C color for Wagon Top PL-1031	FM	3/20/78					

MARX TOYS: ERIE · GIRARD · GLEN DAL
CAT. # 4104 · MODEL #
TOY NAME Red River Gang
ISS'D BY FM · APPR. BY
DATE 2/7/78 · PAGE 2 OF 5

BILL OF MATERIALS

PART NO.	LEVEL & QTY. 1	2	3	4	5	6	PURC	DRAWING NO.	PART NAME	MATERIAL OR SIZE	COLOR NO.	REMARKS
				1					Front. w/gold bags	L. D. Poly	Buckskin Tan 5688S	PL-1528
				1					Figure w/bull whip	L. d. Poly	"	PL-1528
				1					Riding Sheriff	L. D. Poly	"	PL-1528
				1					Front. w/shovel	L. D. Poly	"	PL-1528
								GROUP #2				
PL-11124				1					Running w/Strong Box	L. D. Poly	Buckskin Tan 5688-S	PL-1528
PL-11180				1					Holding Rifle	L. D. Poly	5688-S Buckskin Tan	PL-1528
PL-11121				1					Riding Bandit	L. D. Poly	"	PL-1528
PL-11123				1					w/Branding Iron	L. D. Poly	"	PL-1528
PL-11122				1					w/Pistols in both hands	L. D. Poly	"	PL-1528
PL-11181				1					Standing Sheriff	L. D. Poly	"	PL-1528
PL-11120				1					Rider w/Lasso	L. D. Poly	"	PL-1528
PL-11186				1					Walking w/Rifle & Lantern	L. D. Poly	"	PL-1528
PL-11183				1					Drawing Pistol	L. D. Poly	"	PL-1528
PL-11187				1					Fighting without hat	L. D. Poly	"	PL-1528
PL-11188				1					w/Coonskin cap & rifle	L. D. Poly	"	PL-1528
PL-11185				1					Shooting Pistol	L. D. Poly	"	PL-1528
				1					Front. w/gold bag	L. D. Poly	"	PL-1528

REV	NO.	CHANGE DESCRIPTION	BY	DATE	REV.	NO.	CHANGE DESCRIPTION	BY	DATE

MARX TOYS
ERIE GIRARD GLEN DALE
CAT. # 4104 MODEL #
TOY NAME Red River Gang
ISS'D BY FM APPR. BY
DATE 2/7/78 PAGE 3 OF 5

C. Almond, D. Barnett, E. Peck, F. Pavalko, M. Fleming, B. Brak, E. Sollenberger, F. Mueller, D. Sigler, J. Strope, T. Gayvont, J. Meyers, B. Terrill, E. Livingston, T. Dudek, M. Yankoski, G. Vincent, J. Hissom, B. Turberville, Jimmy Ray, Mike Marrs, J. John Schroeder, Al Beddy

BILL OF MATERIALS

PART NO.	LEVEL & QTY. 1	2	3	4	5	6	PURC	DRAWING NO.	PART NAME	MATERIAL OR SIZE	COLOR NO.	REMARKS
				1					Front. carrying Lantern	L. D. Poly	Buckskin Tan 5688S	PL-1528
				1					Front. Panning Gold	L. D. Poly	"	PL-1528
				1					Front. Fur Trader	L. D. Poly	"	PL-1528
PL-11126				2					Wagon Horse	L. D. Poly	Rust Brown 50798-S	PL-532 A
E7646				1			P		Poly Bag	8 x 8 x .002 1" Lip		Indians
PL-10728				2				6-1855	Indian #1	Plastic	PMS-172 Red	PL-787
PL-10729				2				6-1885	Indian #2	Plastic	"	"
PL-10730				1				6-1885	Indian #3	Plastic	"	"
PL-10731				1				6-1885	Indian #4	Plastic	"	"
PL-10732				1				6-1885	Indian #5	Plastic	"	"
PL-10733				1				6-1885	Indian #6	Plastic	"	"
PL-10734				1				6-1885	Indian #7	Plastic	"	"
PL-10735				1				6-1885	Indian #8	Plastic	PMS-172 Red	"
PL-10736				1				6-1885	Indian #9	Plastic	PMS-172 Red	"
PL-10737				1				6-1885	Indian #10	Plastic	PMS-172 Red	"
PL-10738				1				6-1885	Indian #11	Plastic	PMS-172 Red	"
PL-10739				1				6-1885	Indian #12	Plastic	PMS-172 Red	"

REV	NO.	CHANGE DESCRIPTION	BY	DATE	REV.	NO.	CHANGE DESCRIPTION	BY	DATE
A	98	Chg. color PL-11126 to Rust Brown 50798-S, was Brown 5793S	FM	4/6/78					

MARX TOYS
ERIE GIRARD GLEN DALE
CAT. # 4104 MODEL #
TOY NAME Red River Gang
ISS'D BY FM APPR. BY
DATE 2/7/78 PAGE 4 OF5

G. Almond, D. Barnett, E. Peck, F. Pavalko, M. Fleming, B. Brak, E. Sollenberger, M. Yankoski, F. Mueller, John Rusinko, J. Strope, T. Gayvont, J. Myers, G. Vincent, T. Dudek, J. Hissom, A. Podratsky, J. Ray, M. Marra, J. John Schroeder, A. Beddy, E. Livingston

BILL OF MATERIALS

PART NO.	LEVEL & QTY. 1	2	3	4	5	6	PURC	DRAWING NO.	PART NAME	MATERIAL OR SIZE	COLOR NO.	REMARKS
PL-10740				1				6-1885	Indian #13	Plastic	PMS-172 Red	PL-787
PL-10741				1				6-1885	Totem Pole	Plastic	"	"
PL-11139				2					Horse w/Saddle	L.D. Poly	Black GP-225	PL-610 (A)
PL-11140				1					Wagon Driver	L.D. Poly	PMS-136 Orange	PL-971
PL-11073				4					Fence	F.H.I. Styrene	Brown GP-7130	PL-147
PL-10722 PL-10722A				1				B-1173	Indian Pony	Plastic	GP-563 Random Ivory	PL-692 (B)
8650				1			P		Ground Sheet	Poly. .0025 thk 18 x 24	Printed	

REV.	NO.	CHANGE DESCRIPTION	BY	DATE	REV.	NO.	CHANGE DESCRIPTION	BY	DATE
A	124	Chg. qty to (2), was (3)	MM	6/12/78					
B	124	Add One(1) PL-692 Pony	"	"					

MARX TOYS
ERIE GIRARD GLEN DALE

CAT. # 4104 MODEL #

TOY NAME Red River Gang

ISS'D BY FM APPR. BY

DATE 2/7/78 PAGE 5 OF 5

Date 2/23/60

2000 SERIES PACKING INFORMATION

Item No. 4805 OFFICIAL WAGON TRAIN PLAY SET
How Packed EACH IN A DIE CUT CORRUGATED BOX
Quantity Packed 1/4 DOZEN
Wgt. Per Shipping Ctn.
Carton Dimensions L. W. D.

Cartons, Games or Toys, NOIBN, Iron or Seel, 20 ga or thicker
Frt. Classification or any gauge KDf
Net Wgt.
Tare Wgt.
Gross Wgt.
Legal Wgt.

FACTORY SPECIFICATIONS

Exclusvie Sears Roebuck 1960

2 - PL-864 Tepees- Light Gray & Buckskin
2-PL-524 Trees- Light Green POlyethylene
1 - PL-1030-A Wagon W/Oxen Hitch- Brown
3- PL-1030 Wagons w/Horse Hitch -Beige, Gray & Blue
6 - PL-532 Horses- Asstd. Colros, 2 Lgt, Gray, 2 Beige 2 Ivory
5 - PL-1031 Wagon Tops - L Beige, 2 Li. Gray, 1 Pastel Blue
4 - PL-971 Wagon Drivers- Ivory
2 - Pcs. Model No. 2612 Oxen-Light Gray
1 - Set PL-787 Indians & Totem Pole- Copper
1 - Set PL-919 Indians & Totem Pole- Yellow
2 - PL-974 Wagon Train Figure- Ivory
2 - Sets PL-745 Cavalry Figures(20 Pcs.0 1 Set Beige, 1 Set Pastel Blue
1 - Set PL-833 Cowboey, Asstd cOlors, Beige & Light Gray
4 - PL-779 Cavalry Horses- 2 Brown, 2 Beige
2 - PL-610 Western Horses- 1 Ivory, 1 Beige
2 - PL-692 Indian Horses- 1 Ivory, 1 Beige
1 - PL-850 Dead Horse- Brown
4 - Pcs. PL-1018 Prehistorick Mountains- Brown w/Silk Screen on Pool
1 - Set PL-891 Indian Accessories - Red
1 - Set PL-891 Cowboy Accessories- Silver Metallic
3 - PL-610 Steer- Beige, Gray & Black
3 - PL-895 Indian Camp Accessories- Brown, Saddle Brown Polyethylene
1 - Set PL-878 Small Animals- Ivory
1 - PL-903 Bow & Arrow- Red
2 - PL-148 Cactus- Light Green
1 - P - Instruction Sheet

WESTERN RANCHES

We here group three playsets that atypically feature no character, but rather demonstrate still other combinations of Marx Western playset components. The settings clearly distinguish them from the Western Towns group, below. Note that there is a ranch set in the "O" gauge suitable for use with some of the Marx train sets (see **Crossover Items: Trains and Playsets**).

3956, 3956D Wild West Ranch Set (1955)

Featured set; see reproduced documentation.

3999, 3999D Ranch Set (Sears) (1963)

A typical example of Marx modifying an existing playset to create an exclusive 100-piece set for a mail-order customer. The specifications sheet, which is too faded to reproduce here, indicates that the white archway is to be produced by eliminating the Roy Rogers sign. Contains a lithographed ranch building, No. 10-B, twenty-seven cowboys in tan, rust, brown, and gray, sixteen other figures, fifteen head of steer, six horses, a single-hitch wagon, and accessories.

4260 Western Playset (Sears) (1965)

Featured set; see reproduced documentation and mold sheet below.

PL-1528

Item: Western Play Set (Cowboy) Mold

Model No. 8782X

No. of Cavities: 32 cav.

No. of Sets: 1 set

Cost: $4500.00 (GlenDale Estimate) Card 9091 Act Cost 5709.21

Made By: Glen Dale

Date Ordered: 12/29/71

Delivery Date:

Date Received: Samples 3-14-72

Machine:

Average Per Hour:

Gross Per Day:

Weights: Per Shot-

Per Piece-

Per M-

8
9
10
5
32

Mold Contains: (Note - Cav. from PL-833 & PL1014 combined for new mold)

From PL-833	From PL-1014		
2 - w/strong box	1 -	Frontiersman walking	w/rifle
2 - holding rifle	1 -	"	w/rifle & lantern
2 - riding bandits	2 -	"	w/gold bags
2 - w/branding irons	1 -	"	w/shovel
2 - w/pistol in hands	2 -	"	drawing pistols
2 - standing Sheriff	1 -	"	fighting w/hat
- Riders w/Lasso	1 -	"	without hat
1 - W/Bull Whip	1 -	"	carrying lantern
1 - Riding Sheriff	1 -	"	w/coonskin cap & rifle
	1 -	"	panning gold
	2 -	"	shooting pistols
	1 -	"	sitting
PL-800	1 -	"	Furtrader

A new mold was created for set #4260 by combining cavities from two earlier molds.

LOUIS MARX & CO.
200 Fifth Ave., New York

GLENDALE DIVISION
2/7/55

NO. 3956 WILD WEST RANCH SET

1 - Log Cabin w/ Stovepipe Chimney
1 - Set of Outside Equipment
8 - Sections Fence
1 - Buckboard Wheel
8 - Cowboys
1 - Tree
4 - Animals

PACKED: Each set in a box
1/2 dozen to shipping carton
Weight per carton - 16 lbs.

NO. 3956D DEMONSTRATOR

Measures 16" x 24".

FACTORY SPECIFICATIONS:

Model 5376-X Log Cabinw/Stovepipe Chimney
PL-130 Set of Outside Equipment
PL-147 8 Sections Fence
PL-337 Buckboard Wheel Molded in Yellow
PL-463 8 Cowboys.
PL-524 Tree
PL-610 4 Animals.

ITEM NO. 4260
Date March 17, 1965
Customer No. ____
Replaces Sheet ____

GLEN DALE DIVISION
SPECIFICATION SHEET

Model No. 70[illegible]X
Cost No. CO-3[illegible]

Item WESTERN PLAY SET - SEARS

Quantity	Part No.	Description	Color
	# 1	Ranchers Bldg. consisting of:	
1	PT-1785	Front & Ends - Yellow Board and Batten	
1	PT-1784	Roof w/o Smokestack - Yellow Shingles litho	
1	PL-1010	Set Porch & Chimney	
1	PL-388	Set Outside Acc.	Brown
3	PL-148	Cactus	Green
1	PL-332A	Set Dead Tree & Stumps	Gray
2	PL-337	Wheels (any two from mold)	Yellow
1	PL-524	Tree	Green
1	PL-857	Set Stagecoach	Gray
1	PL-858	Double Hitch	Brown
1	PL-1030A	Wagon w/ Oxen Hitch	
1	PL-1057	Set Gold Mine Acc.	Brown
2	PL-532	Harness Horses	Black
2	PL-610	Horses	Beige
1	PL-833	Set Cowboys (9)	
1	PL-1014A	Set Frontier Fig. (16)	
1	PL-1056	Set Oxen (2)	
1	PL-1067	Set Steers (6)	
1	VF____	Vac. Formed Base	
1		Wire Brace for Bldg.	
1	P____	Inst. Sheet	

REMARKS:— Pack in an Ind. Glo cut w/ S. O. A. P. [illegible] +/8 oz

DEMONSTRATOR DATA: ....

SHIPPING CARTON Size— L .... W .... H .... Gross .... Tare .... Net .... Legal ....

SHIPPING CARTON INFORMATION:—

Individual Carton:—L 33-3/4 W 27-3/4 H 3-5/8 Diagonal 43-1/2 Girth 62-3/4 Weight 7 lbs.

Description Ind. 1 pc. Glo cut w/ S. O. A. P.

Master Carton Size—L 28-1/8 W 11-1/4 H 34-1/2 Diagonal 44-1/2 Girth 78-3/4 Weight ....

Quantity Packed Per Shipping Carton 1/4 dozen

Freight Classification Approx.

Net Weight .... Gross Weight 23 lb. Tare Weight .... Legal Weight ....

Acknowledged by AEB Date 3/26/65

The above specifications have been retyped for legibility.

WESTERN TOWNS

As mentioned previously, one of the earliest known Western playsets produced by Marx was Mineral City, described under **Roy Rogers**, page 139. In offering it in its 1952 Christmas catalog, Sears declared: "New! The stage is set for year-round enjoyment . . . three-dimensional model sets in sturdy metal and durable plastic . . . straight from the wonderlands of excitement and adventure. Never before, in all our toy history, has such accurate scaling and lifelike detail been offered at such low prices." In the following years Marx brought out a number of variations of the Western Town. Some are shown in the color photos in the Album of Marx Western Playsets.

Contrary to our usual method of listing playsets by number, the listings below are organized alphabetically according to name of playset, with variations of each listed by number. See also **HO-scale Playsets** and Color Photos 16-24.

4229 Old Western Town Set (1954)
Featured set; see reproduced documentation.

4219 Silver City Frontier Town (1956)
Featured set; see reproduced documentation.

4220 Silver City Frontier Town (1956)
This differs from #4219, above, in that there are three additional character figures: General Custer, Daniel Boone, and Kit Carson.

4256 Silver City Western Town (Montgomery Ward) (1954)
This early playset is distinguished primarily by the inclusion of a set of Inside Furniture (twenty-five detailed plastic accessories), and there are, in comparison with #4219, twenty-two cowboys but no character figures. The factory's specification sheet notes that this will be exactly the same as #4258, Roy Rogers Mineral City, except that the sign will read "Silver City", and the three Roy Rogers figures are to be replaced by three generic cowboys.

4268 Silver City Western Town with Painted Figures (1956)
Similar to #4219, but there are eight painted cowboys, plus four cowboy riders and horses and four Indian riders and horses, a tree, two cactus, and four fence sections.

4262, 4262D "Tales of Wells Fargo" Western Town with Dale Robertson (Montgomery Ward) (1959)
Featured set; see reproduced documentation. The actor Dale Robertson portrayed that guardian of law and order, Jim Hardie.

4264, 4264D "Tales of Wells Fargo" Western Town with Dale Robertson (1958, 1959)
Larger set than #4262, above: includes two sets of cowboys, three steer, one additional horse, two cactus, and a thirty-five-piece set of accessories on a runner.

3983 "Western Cattle Drive" (also known as Cattle Drive) (1972)
See Color Photo 9. As the catalog description puts it, "two fully lithographed steel buildings as well as a full complement of outdoor accessories provide the town setting." Includes log cabin and one-story Western Town building.

4265, 4265D, 4266, 4266D Western Mining Town Playset (1960)
Featured set; see reproduced documentation. Note the comment about it not being an official "Gunsmoke" item. The reference seems actually to be to "The Rifleman" — the ranch building was, as you see, the one used in that playset, #3397/8 — but that building is also the one used in #4268, Official Gunsmoke Western Town, and in #4784, Johnny Ringo Western Frontier Playset (which also has Gold Mine Accessories); the date of the factory specification sheet for the Johnny Ringo and the Western Mining Town is the same — March 15, 1960.

4680 Western Town (Sears) (1964)
See reproduced documentation and original catalog glossy photo.

4226, 4226SD "Wyatt Earp" Dodge City (1958)
Featured set; see reproduced documentation.

4228 Official Wyatt Earp Dodge City (Montgomery Ward) (1957)
This differed from the set featured in that it included not a buckboard but a plastic stagecoach with double hitch, two harness horses, and saddle horses of a different type. Also, instead of Indian Accessories and Cowboy Accessories, it included Outside Accessories.

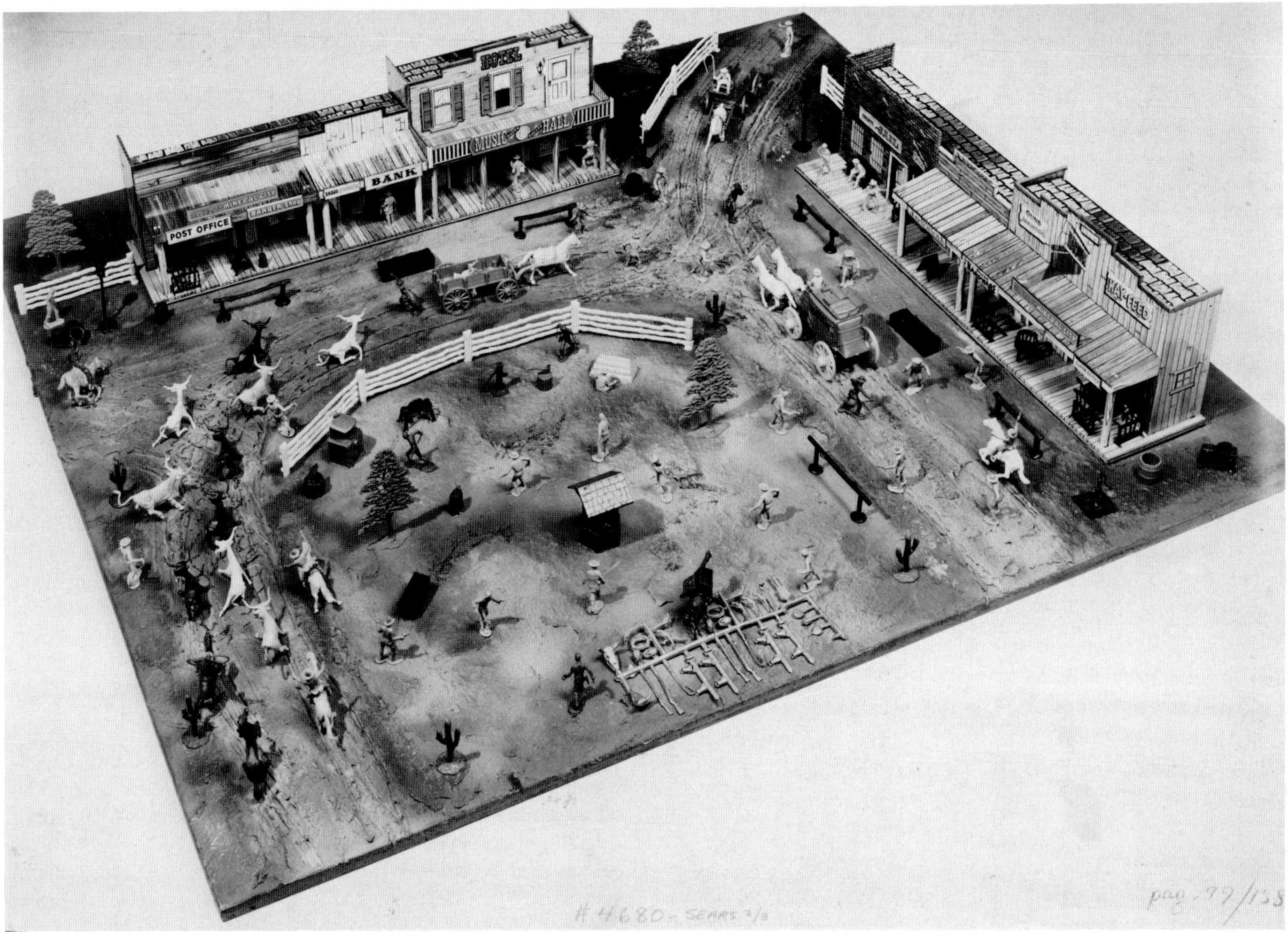

Marx promotional glossy photo for #4680, Sears' Western Town

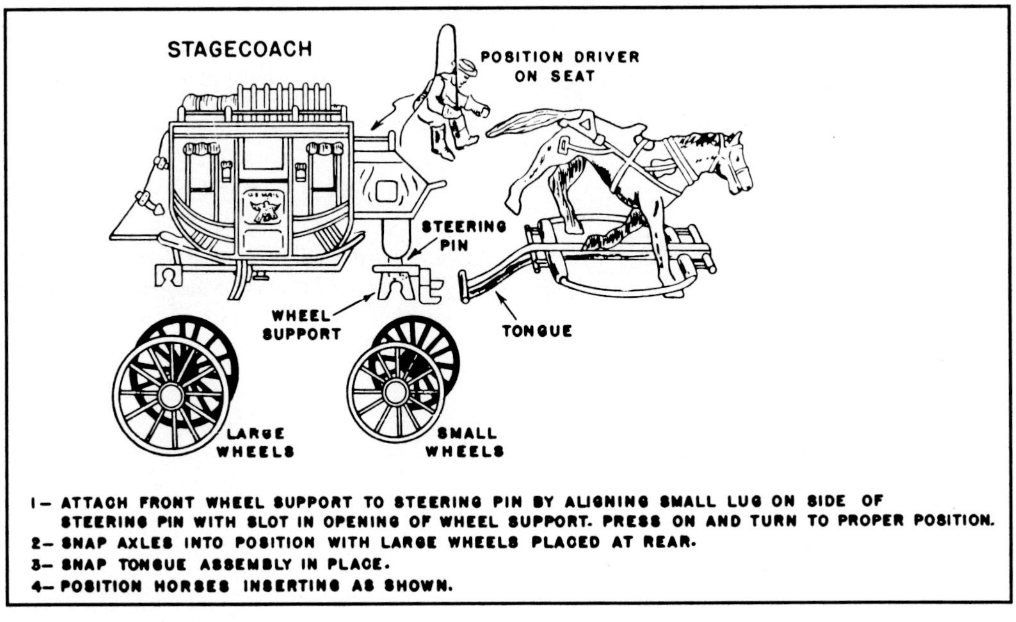

From the instruction sheet

LOUIS MARX AND COMPANY
200 FIFTH AVE., NEW YORK

GLEN DALE DIVISION
5/6/54

NO. 4229 OLD WESTERN TOWN SET

This set is an exact replica of the "Old West" complete with jail, general store, journal and law office, cowboys, horses, etc. Contents are as follows:

BUILDING UNIT: 9	Metal lithographed building measures 27 1/2" long, 6" wide, 9" high. This unit consists of a general store, jail, law office, journal. Each unit is well lithographed in appropriate design and color. Shipped knocked down, and easy to assemble without tools.
INSIDE FURNITURE	Twenty-three detailed plastic accessories to be set up in the various units such as the dry goods counter, food sacks, flour sacks, barrels, crate of rifles, display rack with guns, counter scales for the general store, roll top desk type cabinet, printing press and straight chair for the journal and law office and sherrif's desk table with books, bench, cot, wash stand with pail, and wash basin in the jail. All furniture appropriately detailed and designed.
OUTSIDE ACCESSORIES	Nineteen outside accessories made of durable plastic, appropriately colored. Included are the following: hitching rails, lamp post, garden tool racks, barrel, feed sack, bench, crate with rifles, watering trough, lantern, etc.
COWBOYS:	Twenty two cowboys made of plastic in various realistic action life like positions. Standing cowboys measure 2 5/8" high, others in proportion. There are running cowboys, cowboys shooting, riding cowboys with lasso, fist fighter, bank robber being arrested, sherrif, etc.
HORSES:	Also included in this set are five horses made of sturdy plastic in appropriate colors. There is a running horse, a draft horse, rearing horse, bucking horse and standing horse.
SADDLES AND REINS	Included in the set are six western saddles and bridles made of plastic. Well detailed and designed.
BUCKBOARD:	Plastic buckboard wagon with large spoke wheels.
FENCE:	Two sections of log type fence also supplied.
PACKED:	Each set in a box 1/2 dozen sets to shipping carton Weight per carton - 33 3/4 lbs.

LOUIS MARX AND COMPANY
200 FIFTH AVE., NEW YORK

2

GLEN DALE DIVISION
5/6/54

NO. 4229 OLD WESTERN TOWN SET

FACTORY SPECIFICATIONS:

Contents as follows:

1		Metal lithographed building
2	PL-324	Horses
2	PL-325	Horses
6	PL-326	Western saddles and bridles
1	PL-336A	Buckboard
8	PL-329	Standing cowboys
14	PL-389	New bowboys
1	PL-387	Inside furniture
1	PL-388	Outside furniture
2	PL-147	Log type fence sections
2 sets	PL-337	Wheels
1	PL-532	Horse

No harness FXR 5/6/54

LOUIS MARX & CO.
200 Fifth Ave., New York

GLENDALE DIVISION
10/8/56

NO. 4219 - SILVER CITY FRONTIER TOWN

Replica of a western frontier town, complete with buildings, horses, cowboys, Indians, Tepee, Buckboard, and equipment, and featuring exact miniature figures of Sitting Bull and Buffalo Bill.

BUILDING UNIT: Metal lithographed building measures 27-1/2" long, 6" wide, 9" high, consists of a Hotel, Express Office, Barber shop, Stagecoach, Waiting Room, B rroom. Each unit well lithographed in appropriate color and design. Shipped knocked down and easy to assemble, without the use of tools. Lithographed "SILVER CITY" sign on porch roof.

OUTSIDE ACCESS: Nineteen outside accessories included: Hitching rails, lamp post, tool garden racks, barrel, feed sack, bench, crate w/rifles, water trough, lanterns.

FIGURES: Total of twenty-two figures. Authentic replicas of Buffalo Bill and Sitting Bull, mounted on integral platform, embossed with name and date of birth. Other figures include fourteen Cowboys, six Indians in various fighting and action poses. Standing figures measure approximately 2-5/8" high. Others in proportion.

HORSES & STEER: Five western animals consisting of: Four horses in various action poses, one snorting steer.

BUCKBOARD: Buckboard Wagon with large, spoke wheels, hitching shaft for hitching and unhitching horse.

PACKED: Each set in a box,
1/4 dozen sets to shipping carton,
Weight per carton - 18 lbs.

FACTORY SPECIFICATIONS:

1 - Basic Western Town Building w/"Silver City" sign.
1 - PL-388 Set outside accessories
1 - PL-336A Buckboard w/integral harness
1 - PL-368 Indian Tepee
2 - PL-337 Sets wheels
1 - PL-310 Set Indians (6 pcs.)
1 - PL-389 Set Cowboys (14 pcs.)
1 - PL-733 Bar Room Doors (2 pcs.)
2 - PL-687 Figures: Sitting Bull & Buffalo Bill

1 - PL-532 Harness Horse
1 - PL-610 Set Western Animals (4 pcs.)

NOTE: Buffalo Bill figure substituted for Davy Crockett figure
See letter to S.E. Liden 5/18/56

This item possibly worked up for the Department Stores with a Catalog allowance.

Date 8/1/59

PACKING INFORMATION

2000 SERIES
Item No. 4262 "TALES OF WELLS FARGO" WESTERN TOWN W/DALE ROBERTSON
How Packed EACH IN A BOX
Quantity Packed 1/4 DOZEN SETS
Wgt. Per Shipping Ctn. 12 LBS.
Carton Dimensions L. W. D.

Frt. Classification
Net Wgt.
Tare Wgt.
Gross Wgt.
Legal Wgt.

FACTORY SPECIFICATIONS

Montgomery Ward - 1959

1-	Western Town Building, #18, w/4 Posts
1-Set PL-733	Swinging Doors (2 pieces)
1-#3678	Stable Building w/Litho Sign (Use Wells Fargo name)
1-PL-857	Stage Coach - Tan
4-PL-337	Wheels-Yellow
1-PL-858	Double Hitch - Tan
2-PL-532	Harness Horse - Ivory
1-PL-971	Driver Figure - Ivory
1-Set PL-388	Outside Accessories - Assorted
1-Set PL-833	Cowboy Figures (9 pieces) - Lt. Gray & Tan
1-Set PL-787	Indians & Totem Poles (16 pcs.) 2 colors-Yellow & Copper
3-PL-610	Horses (Assorted colors)
1-PL-147	Fence - Brown
1-PL-524	Tree - Green
1-PL-1006	Dale Robertson Figure (Ivory)
1-P1110	Instruction Sheet

Date 3/15/60

NO SERIES NO.

PACKING INFORMATION

Item No. 4265 & 4266 WESTERN MINING TOWN PLAY SET
How Packed EACH IN A DIE CUT CORRUGATED BOX
Quantity Packed 1/4 DOZEN
Wgt. Per Shipping Ctn. 13 LBS.
Carton Dimensions L. W. D.

Frt. Classification CARTONS, GAMES OR TOYS, NOIBN, Iron OR STEEL, 20 GA. OR THICKER, OR ANY GAUGE, KDF
Net Wgt.
Tare Wgt.
Gross Wgt.
Legal Wgt.

FACTORY SPECIFICATIONS

1-No. 4264	Western Town Building
1-Set PL-733	Swinging Doors
1-No. 10-B	Rifleman Ranch Building (see note below)
1-PL-1010	Plastic Porch (see note below)
1-Set PL-1057	Gold Mine Setting---Brown Mottle with silk screen on water unit
1-Set PL-1014A	Frontier Figures - 16 pcs.
1-Set PL-1030	Wagon--Maple
2-PL-532	Horses--Ivory
1-Set PL-388	Outside Accessories--Brown
1-PL-524	Tree---Light Green Polyethylene
2-Sections PL-147	Fence--Brown
1-Set PL-833	Cowboys--9 pcs. Pastel Blue & Beige
2-PL-610	Horses--1 Brown, 1 Black
6-PL-1067	Steer---Assorted Colors, Brown, Beige & Ivory
1-P--	Instruction Sheet

Note: This is "not" an Official Gunsmoke item. Only the Sers item No. 4260 is official.

Date ~~February 5, 1964~~ Mar 4,

Item Number 4680 WESTERN TOWN SEARS

How Packed Each in a die cut w/sears overall print

Quantity Packed 1/4 dozen in a master

Wgt. per Shipping Ctn.

Carton Dimensions L. W. D.

Frt. Classification

Net Wgt. Gross Wgt.

Tare Wgt. Legal Wgt.

FACTORY SPECIFICATIONS

MODEL #CO 3018

1 4250 Hotel Bldg. PT-1060 Fr. & Ends. PT-1061 Base

PT-1066 (left) Large Roof, PT-1062 (Right) Hotel Roof, PT-1062 Hotel Sec. Flr., PT-1063 Hotel end & part., PT-1069 lg. Part. PT-1070 Long Posts (4), PT-1071 Short Posts (4), PT-1068 Hotel Porch, PT-1065 Bank & Trad. Post., Porch Roof, PT-1067 Gen. Store Sign.

1 4229 Jail Bldg. -PT-1060 Fr. & Ends, Pt-1061 Base PT-1066 Large Roof (left), PT-1062 (Right) Gen. Store Roof, PT-1062 Genl. Store Sec. Flr., PT-1064 Porch Roof, PT-1063 Genl. Store End & Part., PT-1067 Genl. Store sign, PT-1069 Partition, PT-1070 Long Posts (4)

1 set	PL-130	Outside Acc. dark brown ok – 96	
8 sects	PL-147	Log fence light brown ok. 96	
6	PL-148	Cactus green no	
1 set	PL-337	Wheels (4) gray ok 73	
1 set	PL-386	W.T. Hotel, Bank & Barroom Furn. brown ok	
1 set	PL-387	W.T. Inside Furn. brown ok	
1 set	PL-388	W.T. Outside Furn. light brown ok	
4	PL-524	Trees green ok – 96 —	
2	PL-733	Doors dark brown no.	
1 set	PL-857	Stagecoach-dbl. hitch tan ok	
2 sets	PL-1030C	Buckboards w/sgl. hitch gray ok 94 2h apache	
6	PL-532	Horses Ivory ok	
6	PL-610	Horses black & brown sold	
3 sets	PL-833A	Cowboys (27) 2 sets tan 1 set copper ok 23	
1 set	PL-891	Indian & Cowboy Acc. copper ok 81	
1	PL-971	Driver ivory ok 94-23	
1 set	PL-1014A	Frontier Figs. (16) gray ok 16	
10	PL-1067	Steers black & brown	1 pc. Wire Hook 1-5/8" ok 13+15
1 set	PL-1099	Pack Train brown	1 pc. Inst. Sheet Sred

LOUIS MARX & CO.
200 Fifth Ave., New York

GLENDALE DIVISION
2/28/58

NO. 4226 "WYATT EARP" DODGE CITY

Our "Wyatt Earp" Dodge City is a big play set that has all the color and fire of the lawless west, the west of the frontier.

The Western Town measures 27-1/2" long, 6" wide and 9" high, is constructed of steel lithographed inside and out. Here are reppoduced the Bank, the All-important Fargo Express Office and the Silver Dollar Hotel and Music Hall complete with swinging doors.

Detailed flexible plastic 3-dimensional figures include 18 Cowboys, 15 Indians and U. S. Marshall, Wyatt Earp. There are also 6 Horses - each with integral saddle, and a Buckboard with Harness Horse to pull it.

Accessories include a Totem Pole, 3 section of Log Fence, a Tree, two Cactus, a General Store Sign and 2 General Store Racks, a Rifle Crate, and 2 Hitching Rails, 3 Cuspidors, a Feed Sack, a Lamp Post and 3 Lamps, a Tavern Chain, two Benches, 2 Boardwalk signs, a Tavern Chair and a Barrel.

There is also a 35-piece set of Cowboy Equipment including such ~~items~~ items as Carbines, Shotguns, Pistols, and Lariots, and a 35-piece set of Indian Equipment including Tom-toms, Tomahawks, and Bows and Arrows.

PACKED: Each in a box, 1/4 dozen to shipper,
Weight per carton - 18 lbs.

NO. 4226SD DEMONSTRATOR

The above item completely set up for display purposes.

PACKED: Each in a shipper, Weight per carton - 17 lbs.

FACTORY SPECIFICATIONS:

1 -	Western Town - Hotel Unit (Dodge City Sign)
2 - PL-733	Plastic Swinging Doors
3 - PL-147	Sections Log Fence
2 - PL-148	Cactus
1 - PL-388	Set of Outside Accessories
1 - PL-524	Tree
1 - PL-336A	Buckboard w/integral hitch
1 - PL-891	Set Indian Accessories on runner
1 - PL-891	Set Cowboy Accessories on runner
1 - PL-532	Harness Horse
6 - PL-610	Horses w/Integral Saddles
15 - PL-787	Indians & 1 Totem Pole (16 pcs.)
18 - PL-833	Cowboys
1 - PL-897	Wyatt Earp Figure
1 --P	Instruction sheet

1000 Series

ZORRO

Remembered for the "Z" brazenly slashed across television screens during the opening of this series' episodes, *Zorro* was still another program that inspired the Marx experts to combine old molds with new concepts. The hacienda and palm trees it required do not appear in any other Marx Western playset. As shown also in the 1958 Sears catalog, the playset included a tin litho building with hard (H.I.S) plastic roof and porch and six character figures: Zorro, Don Diego, Don Alejandro, Bernardo, Sergeant Garcia, and the commandant. Note the unusual hill with cave entrance to the right in Color Photo 2.

In addition to the many Zorro-inspired toys and children's costume-play items, Marx offered a larger-scale Zorro figure, with detachable cape and hat, and horse, 12½ inches long from hoof to tail.

3758 Zorro Playset (1966)
Featured set; see reproduced documentation.

As Color Photo 2, the Zorro playset appears in the Album of Marx Western Playsets; here, the rear view of the hacienda.

ITEM NO. 3758
Date July 7, 1966
Customer No.
Replaces Sheet 6/9/65

Dargit
GLEN DALE DIVISION
SPECIFICATION SHEET

Model No. 7931X
Cost No.

Item Zorro Play Set

Quantity	Part No.	Description	Color
		Contains:	
1	PT-1145	(3754) Alamo Building	LITHO
1	PL-967	Plastic Roof	RED
1	PL-967A	Plastic Porch	BROWN
1	PT-1054	Zorro Litho Flag	LITHO
1	PL-346A	Set Flag Pole and Base	GRAY
1	PT-1057	(3754) Gate Section	LITHO
2	PT-1059	(3754) Gate Doors	LITHO
6	PT-1026	(#16) Fence Sections (#4800)	LITHO
1	PL-130	Set Ranch Acc. (12) ok	ASST LT & DK BROWN
4	PL-148	Cactus NO	GREEN
1	PL-760	Set Palm Tree and Fern Tops (11) no	GREEN
1	PL-761	Set Palm Tree Trunks and Fern Bases (9) no	BROWN
1	PP-34	Vacuum Formed Cave	
1	PL-411	Cannon w/Shells	BLACK
1	PL-610-7	Set Horses (7)	ASST BROWN BEIGE/BLK.
1	PL-968	Zorro Figure w/Cape	BLACK
1	PL-969	Set Zorro Characters (5)	IVORY
1	PL-970	Set Mexican Soldiers (24)	BLUE
1	P-1051	INstruction Sheet	

REMARKS:— Ind. Box to be printed (no label)

DEMONSTRATOR DATA:

SHIPPING CARTON Size— L W H Gross Tare Net Legal

SHIPPING CARTON INFORMATION:—

Individual Carton:—L 24-5/8 W 15-3/8 H 4-3/4 Diagonal 28-1/2 Girth Weight 4 lb. 6 oz.
Description Each set in an individual die cut w/2 prints (W.E.N. 6/29/66)
Master Carton Size—L W H Diagonal Girth Weight
Quantity Packed Per Shipping Carton 1/4 dozen
Freight Classification
Net Weight Gross Weight approx. 15 lb. Tare Weight Legal Weight

Acknowledged by Date

Returned fr. N. Y.
but not signed 7/14/66

CIVIL WAR PLAYSETS

The creation of the Civil War sets, especially the famous "Blue and Gray," represented a highly effective and enduringly interesting use of the Western playset to depict a major historical event — on its centennial. The time was right — it was far enough in the past to be historic but vivid enough to still have strong feelings harbored generation to generation. No license or royalties were necessary — we learned about it all in school each year — and Marx put much money and care into building an entire set of new molds, with the detail and precision found in some works of art.

We consider the following sets to fit into the Western category as well as the Military. The Civil War brought with it the greatest number of casualties of any war involving the United States. It also brought the possibility that the country (as we know it) would not survive. Therefore, the outcome of the events depicted in this playset were far more significant than any other battle recreated in any Marx playset. Public interest in the battle between the Blue and the Gray remains high to this day. See also **HO-scale Playsets.**

Marx steadily worked to refine figures and accessories. Some, such as Boy Scout Accessories (PL-765) and Revolutionary War Accessories (PL-875) were clearly picked up from other playsets. Most commonly found in the Civil War sets are the following:

Standard Union Foot Soldiers Set (PL-847)

4 Marching with rifle
2 With ramrod across waist
2 Running with rifle at waist
2 Lying with rifle
1 Standing with firestick
1 Standing and shooting rifle
1 With pistol and flag
1 Charging with bayonet on rifle
1 Officer with extended left arm and pistol
1 Bugler with pistol

Standard Confederate Foot Soldiers Set (PL-848)

4 Marching with rifle
2 Running with rifle in right hand
2 Kneeling shooting rifle
2 Rifle overhead in left arm
1 Loading rifle
1 Charging with bayonet on rifle
1 Charging with sword overhead
1 Standard being waved
1 Wounded soldier dropping pistol
1 Standing shooting rifle

Civil War Medical Figures (PL-1093)

1 Wounded figure for stretcher
2 Stretchers
3 Stretcher bearers
1 Soldier swinging rifle overhead
1 Injured figure to lean against tree
2 Soldiers stabbing with rifle and bayonet
1 Officer kneeling with field glass
1 Officer charging with sword and pistol
2 Soldiers crawling with rifle and bayonet
1 Drummer boy
1 Wounded figure holding head
1 Running solider with bore swab and bucket
1 Charging soldier, just shot

Civil War Accessories (PL-909)

2 Broken wheels
2 Chevaux-de-frise (spike barricades)
1 Trench mortar
1 Trench mortar base
1 Stack of four mortar shells
2 Stacks of rifles
1 Blanket roll
1 Snare drum
1 Ammo box
1 Powder keg
1 Sandbag emplacement
1 Crate of rifles
1 Dispatch table
1 Wooden washtub
2 Buckets with handle
1 Barrel with legs
2 Three-legged stools
1 Jockey-type hitching post

Miniature Civil War Accessories On Runner (PL-908); this is illustrated in Chapter Three.

5 Swords
2 Cavalry-type bugles
3 Belts with cavalry-type holsters
5 Cavalry-type revolvers and pistols
3 Cavalry-type carbines
3 Belts with scabbards
1 Cavalry-type guidon
1 Pair folded cavalry gloves to fit over belt
2 Wooden Confederate-type canteens
1 Camp fire
1 Coffee pot
1 Frying pan
1 Dish with cup
2 Pair field glasses
2 Dispatch cases

THE BLUE AND THE GRAY

1715 104-Piece Blue and Gray Soldiers with Accessories (1957)

Bagged set of Generals Grant and Lee, sixteen Confederate and sixteen Union soldiers, with two sets of Cowboy Accessories (see list, page 82).

2258 Blue and Gray Civil War (1975)

Factory bill of materials sheet indicates this should include a random assortment of sixteen battlefield accessories from twenty-four named, a cavalry horse and rider, and twelve each of Confederate and Union soldiers. This fifty-piece set came with printed plastic layout sheet and was packaged in a snap-top storage box.

2646, 2646D Battle of the Blue and the Gray (1960, 1962)

Basically sixteen each of Confederate and Union soldiers, with tents, one cannon, two flagpoles with lithographed flags, and a set of PL-908 accessories, the 1962 specifications indicate a few changes: a brown mound unit has been added, Confederate President Jefferson Davis has joined President Lincoln and Generals Grant and Lee, and the "Boy Scout" tents have changed to all beige from a mixture of beige and light gray to distinguish large tent from the pup tents.

4644 Battle of Blue and Gray (1965)

Among features of this playset are the tan Blue and Gray ruin and bunker and two sets (thirty-two pieces) of Civil War medical figures.

4655 Blue and Gray Set (Sears) (1968)

The Colonial mansion and portico and the medical figures are distinguishing features.

4657, 4657D, 4658, and 4658D Blue and Gray Battleground (also known as the Centennial Set) (1962)

One of the more complete sets, with thirty-two each of Confederate and Union soldiers and Civil War Accessories, Cavalry Accessories, and PL-1091 Battlefield Accessories, it is especially treasured for the falling horse and rider. See original catalog glossy photo.

4668 Blue and Gray Set (Sears) (1962, 1965)

In addition to the Fallen Horse and Rider and the mansion, this playset is notable for a three-piece exploding bunker in addition to the ruin and bunker.

4744 Montgomery Ward Set (1963)

See original catalog glossy photo. Distinguished by bridge and two boulders as well as exploding bunker.

4745, 4745D (500 and 750 Series), R-4745, R4745D Battle of the "Blue and the Gray" Playset (1959)

Featured set; see reproduced documentation.

4758 Happi-Time Mammoth Centennial Civil War Set (Sears) (1961)

Compared with #4763/64, below, it lacks the hospital wagon and medical figures, battlefield accessories and shell-shooting mortar, and wagon and accessories (and therefore includes only four horses). Does not include the record of battle sounds, booklet, nor paint set.

4760 "Battle of the Blue and Gray" (1956, 1959)

Similar to #4745, but has double the number of soldiers, has a set of bridge and boulders, Cavalry Accessories as well as Civil War Accessories, and a silver caisson cannon.

4763, 4763D, 4764, 4764D Giant Blue and Gray Battle Set (1960, 1961)

Featured set; see reproduced documentation. Included were a record and a booklet explaining how to use "materials you'll find in any park or vacant lot. Follow these simple instruction and you can make a miniature movie set just like they do in Hollywood." For example, pebbles can be utilized for a stream bed, a bomb-and-crater effect can be produced by putting talcum powder into a small balloon, which is slightly blown up and covered with sand to create a mound (which when pricked will scatter sand and talcum smoke).

4765 Sears American Heritage Set (1972)

The factory instructions for preparation of this playset indicate that the cannon and the mortar are to have no shells or firing springs. This was a safety measure dictated by new child-safety legislation, but it is also interesting to note that those connected with the Marx company in the late 1960s and early 1970s recall an increased resistance to weaponry following the assassination of Robert Kennedy. The set included a Blue and Gray Historical Booklet.

4766 Civil War Set (Montgomery Ward) (1962)

No other information available from archives.

FIGURES

The following two sets were part of the American Heroes Series.

3063 General Grant with Civil War Union Soldiers (1955)

Figure of General Grant, in white plastic, on platform with name on front and birth date on rear, measure approximately 2¾" high. Grant is accompanied by nine pastel blue soliders: soldier standing shooting rifle, dispatch carrier, rider with sword, bugler, rider with flag, kneeling shooting soldier, soldier charging with rifle, and two marching with rifles.

3064 General Lee with Civil War Confederate Soldiers (1955)

Similar to above. Lee is with soldier riding with drawn sword, soldier charging with rifle and bayonet, soldier loading rifle, cannoneer, soldier saluting, soldier standing shooting, officer standing, and two soldiers marching with rifles.

Above, #4658, with more than sixty-five soldiers in action poses; below, #4744. Both are original catalog photos.

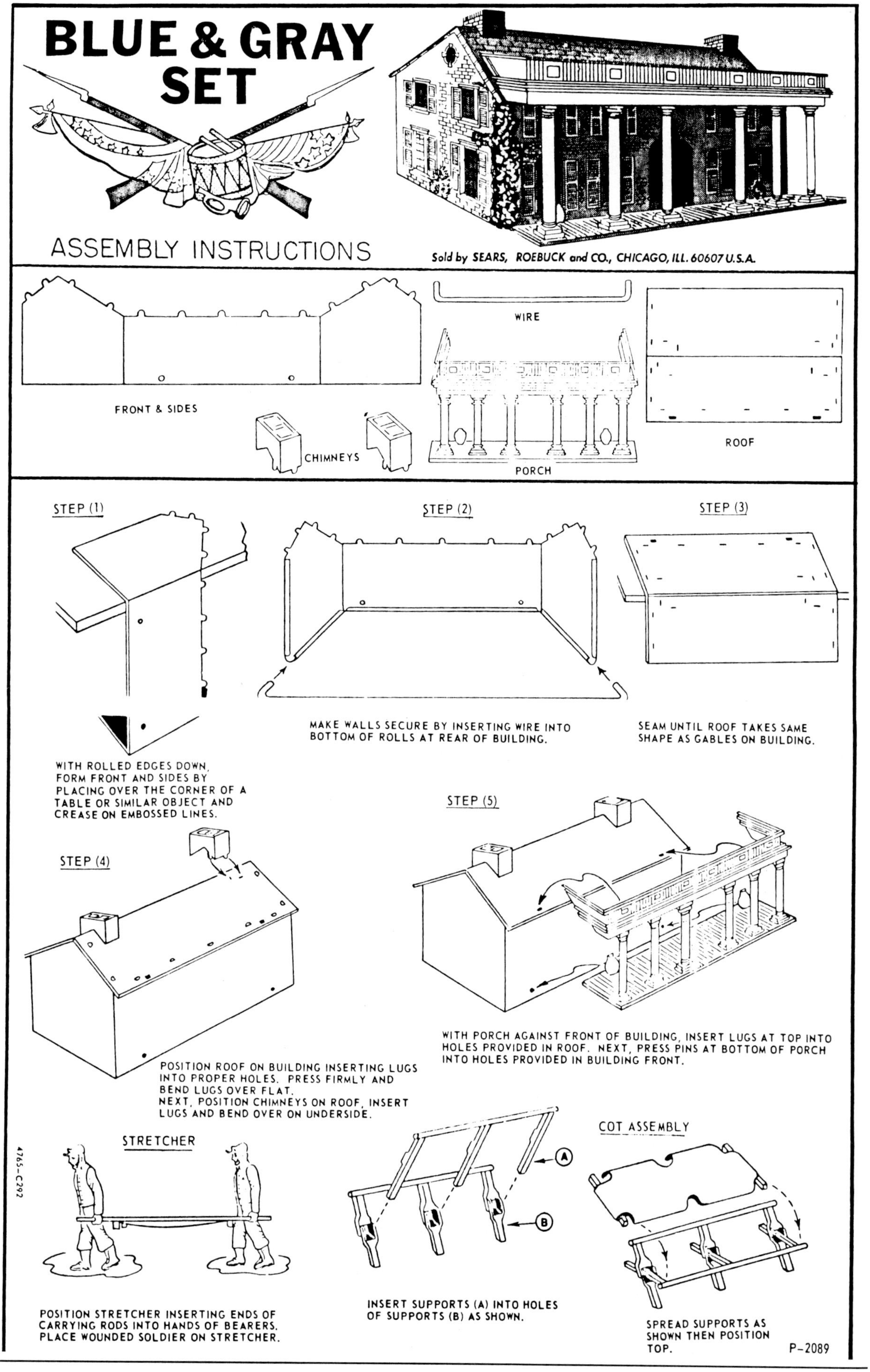
BLUE & GRAY SET
ASSEMBLY INSTRUCTIONS
Sold by SEARS, ROEBUCK and CO., CHICAGO, ILL. 60607 U.S.A.
FRONT & SIDES
WIRE
PORCH
CHIMNEYS
ROOF
STEP (1)
WITH ROLLED EDGES DOWN, FORM FRONT AND SIDES BY PLACING OVER THE CORNER OF A TABLE OR SIMILAR OBJECT AND CREASE ON EMBOSSED LINES.
STEP (2)
MAKE WALLS SECURE BY INSERTING WIRE INTO BOTTOM OF ROLLS AT REAR OF BUILDING.
STEP (3)
SEAM UNTIL ROOF TAKES SAME SHAPE AS GABLES ON BUILDING.
STEP (4)
POSITION ROOF ON BUILDING INSERTING LUGS INTO PROPER HOLES. PRESS FIRMLY AND BEND LUGS OVER FLAT.
NEXT, POSITION CHIMNEYS ON ROOF, INSERT LUGS AND BEND OVER ON UNDERSIDE.
STEP (5)
WITH PORCH AGAINST FRONT OF BUILDING, INSERT LUGS AT TOP INTO HOLES PROVIDED IN ROOF. NEXT, PRESS PINS AT BOTTOM OF PORCH INTO HOLES PROVIDED IN BUILDING FRONT.
STRETCHER
POSITION STRETCHER INSERTING ENDS OF CARRYING RODS INTO HANDS OF BEARERS. PLACE WOUNDED SOLDIER ON STRETCHER.
4765-C292
A
B
INSERT SUPPORTS (A) INTO HOLES OF SUPPORTS (B) AS SHOWN.
COT ASSEMBLY
SPREAD SUPPORTS AS SHOWN THEN POSITION TOP.
P-2089

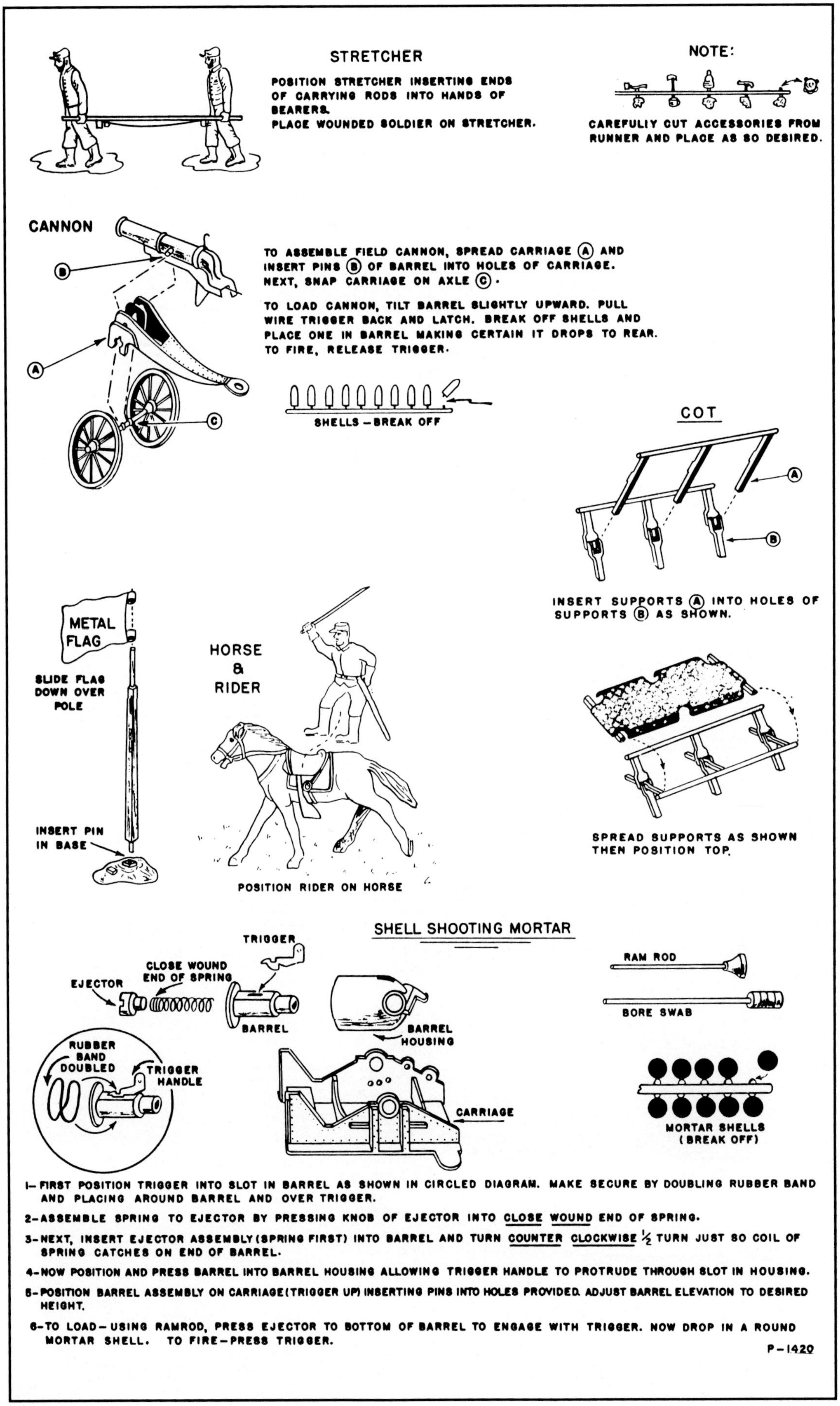

STRETCHER

POSITION STRETCHER INSERTING ENDS OF CARRYING RODS INTO HANDS OF BEARERS.
PLACE WOUNDED SOLDIER ON STRETCHER.

NOTE:

CAREFULIY CUT ACCESSORIES FROM RUNNER AND PLACE AS SO DESIRED.

CANNON

TO ASSEMBLE FIELD CANNON, SPREAD CARRIAGE (A) AND INSERT PINS (B) OF BARREL INTO HOLES OF CARRIAGE. NEXT, SNAP CARRIAGE ON AXLE (C).

TO LOAD CANNON, TILT BARREL SLIGHTLY UPWARD. PULL WIRE TRIGGER BACK AND LATCH. BREAK OFF SHELLS AND PLACE ONE IN BARREL MAKING CERTAIN IT DROPS TO REAR. TO FIRE, RELEASE TRIGGER.

SHELLS – BREAK OFF

COT

INSERT SUPPORTS (A) INTO HOLES OF SUPPORTS (B) AS SHOWN.

METAL FLAG

SLIDE FLAG DOWN OVER POLE

INSERT PIN IN BASE

HORSE & RIDER

POSITION RIDER ON HORSE

SPREAD SUPPORTS AS SHOWN THEN POSITION TOP.

SHELL SHOOTING MORTAR

TRIGGER

CLOSE WOUND END OF SPRING

EJECTOR

BARREL

BARREL HOUSING

RAM ROD

BORE SWAB

RUBBER BAND DOUBLED

TRIGGER HANDLE

CARRIAGE

MORTAR SHELLS (BREAK OFF)

1– FIRST POSITION TRIGGER INTO SLOT IN BARREL AS SHOWN IN CIRCLED DIAGRAM. MAKE SECURE BY DOUBLING RUBBER BAND AND PLACING AROUND BARREL AND OVER TRIGGER.

2– ASSEMBLE SPRING TO EJECTOR BY PRESSING KNOB OF EJECTOR INTO CLOSE WOUND END OF SPRING.

3– NEXT, INSERT EJECTOR ASSEMBLY (SPRING FIRST) INTO BARREL AND TURN COUNTER CLOCKWISE ½ TURN JUST SO COIL OF SPRING CATCHES ON END OF BARREL.

4– NOW POSITION AND PRESS BARREL INTO BARREL HOUSING ALLOWING TRIGGER HANDLE TO PROTRUDE THROUGH SLOT IN HOUSING.

5– POSITION BARREL ASSEMBLY ON CARRIAGE (TRIGGER UP) INSERTING PINS INTO HOLES PROVIDED. ADJUST BARREL ELEVATION TO DESIRED HEIGHT.

6– TO LOAD – USING RAMROD, PRESS EJECTOR TO BOTTOM OF BARREL TO ENGAGE WITH TRIGGER. NOW DROP IN A ROUND MORTAR SHELL. TO FIRE – PRESS TRIGGER.

P – 1420

LOUIS MARX & CO.
200 FIFTH AVE. NEW YORK

GLENDALE DIVISION
7/6/59

No. R-4745 Battle of the "Blue and the Gray" Play Set

This exciting play set based on Civil War days features a Southern Colonial Mansion constructed of lithographed steel with plastic columns and portico measuring 11" long, 7-1/4" wide, 5-1/2" high.

Under the eye of his Commander-in-chief, President Abraham Lincoln, General Ulysses S. Grant leads 24 Union Soldiers against General Robert E. Lee's gray clad 24-man Confederate Army. Each side also includes a Cavalry Horse and Rider. A third horse, victim of battle, lies on its side. All figures are molded with integral weapons and costume.

Mid-19th Century heavy artillery includes two Shell-Shooting Cannons with shells, a Trench Mortar with mortar balls.

Terrain accessories are molded in high detail in plastic. Among the many and varied accessories supplied are two rifle stacks, two chevaux de frise (spike barricades), two lithographed steel flags on poles, three Pup Tents, one Army Tent, an Army cot, and a sand bag implacement.

The Battle of the "Blue and the Gray" play set spells historic adventures.

Packed: Each in a box
1/4 dozen to shipping carton
Weight per carton - 18 lbs.

No. R-4745D Set Up Demonstrator

The above item completely setup. All items securely affixed to board for counter display purposes.

Packed Each in a shipper
Weight per carton - 19 lbs.

Acknowledged By: F.W.D. Date 8/7/59

Date 7/6/59

PACKING INFORMATION

750 Series

Item No. R-4745 The Battle of the Blue & Gray

How Packed Each in a box — Demo.

Quantity Packed 1/4 dozen — 1 only

Wgt. Per Shipping Ctn. 18 lbs. — 19 lbs.

Carton Dimensions L. W. D.

Demo 40-1/4 24-1/2 12-1/2

Frt. Classification Demo. Class 85

Net Wgt. 12

Tare Wgt. 7

Gross Wgt. 19

Legal Wgt. 16

FACTORY SPECIFICATIONS

1 - No. 11 Civil War Building
1 - PL-930 Plastic Porch w/Column - White

1 - PL-765 Scout Tents (Light Gray Poly.)

1-1/2 sets PL-847 Union Soldiers (24 pcs. - Pastel Blue)
1-1/2 sets PL-848 Confederate Soldiers (24 pcs. - Light Gray)
2-PL-849 Riders for Horses (Note: Shut off Caisson Riders)
1-PL-902 Historical Figures: Grant, Lee, Lincoln (Ivory)

2-PL-779 Cavalry Horses (Assorted Colors)
1-PL-850 Lying Down Horse (Brown)

2-PL-346A Flagpole w/Base
1- Litho, Flag-Union
1- Litho. Flag-Confederate

2-PL-411 Shell Shooting Cannons (1-Silver, 1-Black)

2-PL-524 Trees (Light Green polyethylene)

1 - PL-909 Civil War Accessories (Assorted colors)

Display Board- 24" x 40"

1 - P1112 Instruction Sheet

LOUIS MARX & CO.
200 FIFTH AVE. NEW YORK

GLENDALE DIVISION
3/2/61

NO. 4763 GIANT BLUE & GRAY BATTLE SET

NO. 4764 GIANT BLUE & GRAY BATTLE SET

This exciting Play Set containing over 300 pieces based on the Civil War Days, features miniature repàicas of the equipment used in themid-19th century. All of the heavy artillery equipment plus the light armor of these times are depicted in the set.

A Southern Colonial Mansion measuring 11" long, 7-1/4" wide, made of lithographed steel with plastic columns and portical.

There are trench sections molded realistically [redacted] out of plastic also ruins of buildings, cannon and caisson set drawn by four [redacted] horses, also a hospital wagon horse drawn, also included is an exploding bunker position with a realistic sheāl shoöting mortor.

The Confederate troops, all three dimensional minutely detailed and in all action positions are lead by General Lee and Jeff Davis. President Lincolns figure also prominent while the figure of General Grant.

Torain accessories are molded in high detail in plastic. There are 2 lithographed flags and various pup tants, army tnets and cavalry gear.

PACKED: Each set in a box,
1/4 dozen to shipping carton
Weight per carton- 22 lbs.

NO. 4763 D SETUP DEMONSTRATOR

NO. 4764 D SETUP DEMONSTRATOR

Packed
Each in shipper,
Weight per carton- 20 lbs.

Replaces sheet dated 2/9/61

Acknowledged By: FWD Date 4/5/61

Date 3/21/61

PACKING INFORMATION

Item No. 4763-64 GIANT BLUE AND GRAY BATTLE SET
How Packed EACH IN DIE CUT CORRUGATED BOX
Quantity Packed 1/4 DOZEN
Wgt. Per Shipping Ctn. 22 LBS.
Carton Dimensions L. W. , D.

Cartons, Games or Toys, NOBN, Iron or Steel, 20 ga or thicker,
Frt. Classification or any gaUge KDF
Net Wgt.
Tare Wgt.
Gross Wgt.
Legal Wgt.

FACTORY SPECIFICATIONS

Model #7433X

1- Lithographed Southern Colonial Building No. 13
1- PL-930 Plastic Portico- White
3- Sets PL-847 Union Soldiers (total 48 pcs.) Pastel Blue
3- Sets PL-848 Condederate Soldiers (total 48 pcs.) Light Gray
10- PL-849 Cavalry Figures- 4 Gray, 6 Pastel Blue
10--Set PL-902 A Historical Figures (4 pcs.) Ivory
1- Set PL-1093 Civil War Medical Figures- Light Gray

2- Sets PL-765 Scout Tents- Beige
1- Lithographed Confederate Flag
1- Lithographed Union Flag
2- PL-346-A Flagpoles- Light Gray
1- Set PL-332A- Dead Tree & Stumps- Dark Gray
2- PL-524 Trees- Bright Green

1- Set PL-917 Civil War Cannon & Caisson w/Extra Hitch- Silver Metallic
6- PL-532 Harness Horses-2 Ivory, 2 Black, 2 Brown
8- PL-779 Cavalry Horses- 2 Black, 2 Brown, 2 Ivory, 2 Biege
1- PL-850 Lying Down Horse- Ivory
1- Set PL-1030 B Wagon & Accessories- Light Gray
1- PL-1084 Hospital Wagon & Acces. Light Gray w/Red Cross Hotstamp
1- Set PL-944 Bridge & 2 Boulders- Mottle Gray
4- Sections PL-1092 Split Rail Fence- Brown

2- SetPL-908 Cavalry Accessories on runner- 1 Soft Black- 1- Silver
1- Set PL-909 Civil War Accessories-Tan and Dark Gray to the set
1- Set PL-1091 Battlefield Accessories- (2 pcs.) Brown Mottle
1- Set PL-1056 Exploding Machine Gun Nest w/Revised Target- Borwn Mottle
1- PL-1085 Shell Shooting MOrtar w/Shells- Black

1- PL-411 Shooting Cannon- Dark Gray
1- J-5253 Miniature die cast shooting Pistol w/Bullets

1- Civil War Record
1- Civil War ½ Booklet (sound effects explained)
1- Set Paint & Paint burshes-consisting of 3 Bottles, Black, Red and White
1- P -1331 Instruction Sheet

CROSSOVER ITEMS: TRAINS AND PLAYSETS

By the end of the 1930s, Marx was identified with the low end of the market for train sets. There are two distinct levels of train sets with Western themes, listed below. See Color Photo 25 for a ranch set (#3792) believed designed for Marx's O-gauge trains.

2873 Old-Fashioned B. & O. [Baltimore & Ohio] Train — Wild West Set (1959)

This is a comparatively simple set, where a small selection of cowboy and Indian figures, a tepee, and various accessories from other Western playsets joined a battery-powered train on eight sections of two-rail track (see photograph on the catalog sheet). The Western town strip includes a Wells Fargo office in the middle. The black plastic locomotive was Marx #1 William Crooks, which pulled two lithographed tin cars.

X-4261 Wells Fargo Wild West Town from Glendale [manufacturing plant] for use with #54752 Electric Train (1959)

See photo on catalog sheet. It was a larger, more sophisticated set, with transformer. The archive documentation is too faded for reproduction here; the following items are listed:

1 Model #6892-X, New Western building
1 Set PL-733, Swinging doors
1 PL-857, Stage coach
1 Set PL-336, Buckboard wheels
1 PL-858, Double hitch
2 PL-532, Harness horses
1 PL-971, Driver
1 PL-524, Tree
1 Set PL-833, Cowboys, 9 pieces
1 Set PL-787, Indians and totem pole, 16 pieces
3 PL-610, Horses
1 PL-1006, Dale Robertson (Jim Hardie) figure
1 Set PL-388, Outside accessories
1 Instruction sheet

X-4262 Wells Fargo Wild West Town from Glendale for use with Girard [manufacturing plant] #54762 Train (1959)

Same contents as above, with the addition of Wells Fargo Stable Building, with sign, and one PL-147 Fence.

The William Crooks Locomotive was a major innovation in the Marx locomotive line and reflected the intense interest in the approach of the centennial of the Civil War in the late 1950s. H. Diehl Collection, M. Feinstein photograph.

A stylized William Crooks in a nostalgic setting. H. Diehl Collection, M. Feinstein photograph.

LOUIS MARX & CO.
200 FIFTH AVE. NEW YORK

GIRARD DIVISION
F.O.B. Factory—Girard, Pa.

No. 54752 OFFICIAL "TALES OF WELLS FARGO" 4-UNIT SMOKING PASSENGER SET WITH ACCESSORIES

12 50 ea

This old-time "Wells Fargo" Smoking Train set is complete with figures, a western building, accessories and 50-watt transformer.

Train measures: 31" long overall. Track measures: 27" x 36".

Circumference of track: 102" oval.

PACKED: Each set in a box
¼ doz. sets per shipping carton
Weight per carton – 28 lbs.

No. 2873 OLD FASHIONED B.O. TRAIN—WILD WEST SET

The B/O train runs around on a circle of track and surrounded by a complete setup of western cowboys, Indians and accessories.

PACKED: Each set in a box
½ doz. to shipping carton
Weight per carton – 17 lbs.

2 45 ea

FORM #519

HO-SCALE PLAYSETS

The Marx Toys archives could not produce documentation on the miniature playsets because they were manufactured in Hong Kong, during the 1960s. We have some information on these unusual and sought-after playsets, however. Reproduced here is a catalog photo from the announcement of an assortment of the HK Series, which included the Western Town. We are indebted to collector Gary Linden, who allowed us to photograph his Alamo (Border Battle) set and Blue and Gray set, included in the color section, Album of Marx Western Playsets, and for the list of HO-scale playsets. Note the color detailing, which was featured in the promotion of the miniatures.

The Marx technology allowed changes of scale without the expense and delay of creating newly crafted figures, and most of the miniature sets employed this expertise. These sets may have been small in scale but were large in volume: Custer's Last Stand included 181 pieces, with thirty-three Indians, forty-seven cavalry soldiers, and fourteen cowboys.

There were also the Miniature Masterpieces, and although figure sets are generally beyond the subject of this volume, we have included a few color photos (26 and 27) of such sets to provide an idea of their presentation. Also, Color Photo 36 dramatically illustrates the range of scale, down to the miniature 1 inch, provided by Louis Marx & Co., Inc.

The Western theme HO-scale playsets include:

- Blue and the Gray, #HK-6109
- Covered Wagon Attack
- Custer's Last Stand
- Fort Apache (probably three variations, including #HK-7526 and HK-8078)
- Western Town, #HK-8933

The Western Town miniature playset, top and upper left, contains minutely detailed hand-painted figures measuring up to 1¼ inches high and accessories. Each set measures 9½ inches long, 4½ inches wide, and 2¾ inches high. Each was packed in a see-through box. Others pictured with the Western Town are the farm set, knights and vikings, and knights and castle. See Color Photo 24 for another small-scale Western Town.

LARGER-SCALE PLAYSETS

JOHNNY WEST AND THE BEST OF THE WEST

The existence of the Johnny West Circle X Ranch justifies the inclusion in this book of the large assortment of poseable figures and accessories in the Johnny West series (there was also a chipboard Fort Apache Fighters unit, described under #1875, below).

Heavily promoted in television advertising, the collection added characters (members of the Johnny West family, cavalrymen, Indians, and cowboys) as well as accessories from 1965 to 1976, according to the Marx archives. From time to time the name of the series would change, or certain figures would be promoted as "Fort Apache Fighters" or "Heroes of the West." The cavalry action figures and accessories were promoted as "Fort Apache Defenders." In later years the lines between such distinct sets blurred and they all became "friends" of Johnny West. Other Western-theme figure sets were of the same scale and construction: #2060, for example, is Daniel Boone Wilderness Scout, with a full range of accessories.

In the 1975 promotion, "Johnny West Adventure" was the name chosen for the line that then introduced "quick-draw action," complete with gunshot sound, in the shootout between Johnny West and Sam Cobra. Interestingly, Cobra represents the adaptation of Marx molds into new products: his head was taken from a figure called Noble Knight. As mentioned earlier, it appears that Johnny West was modeled generally after John Wayne, with whom he shares initials. All the adult figures measure 11½ inches, the scale of Barbie dolls and G. I. Joe. The figures were injection molded of solid poly plastic; the faces, which have realistic character details, and the hands were pliable vinyl.

Many duplicate molds were made and the product found its way into homes around the globe — especially in England and Mexico. The line transcended the Marx ownership change and is currently being produced in England and Ecuador. Note that in addition to the reproduction (Color Photo 28) of the color catalog sheets for the line, we have included illustrations of some items featured in television promotion in Chapter Two.

The following listings give the basic numbers for each item; other numbers or number-and-letter combinations (especially using "C") would have been used in various assortments of figures and accessories. Not included in the listings are various Best of the West Assortments of figures and their display variations (documented in archive records from 1973 and 1974). See Color Photo 28 for illustrations of most of the items listed below.

1061 "Pancho" (1975)
12½"-long Welsh pony, for West youngsters. PL-1417 is an eight-piece set of pony accessories.

1062A and 1062B Jamie West and Jay West (1974)
Two all-American boys; each may have eleven extra pieces of Western clothing and range gear.

1067A and 1067B Janice West and Josie West (1974)
Teenaged cowgirls; clothes for chores and for dressup; ten accessories each.

1861A (matte brown), 1861B (beige), 1861CMO "Comanche" (1975)
Articulated horse (with thirteen pinned/hinged joints), rideable by 11½" figures. Fifteen pieces comprised the full set of horse accessories (PL-1272).

1862 Zeb Zachary (?)
Cavalry Sgt. Zachary was an experienced Indian fighter.

1863 Fighting Geronimo (1974)
This Indian figure, with headband, could be accompanied by thirty-six accessories.

1864 Fighting Eagle (1974)

1865 Captain Tom Maddox (1974)
In cavalry uniform, he was given full range of personal and military accessories.

1866 General Custer (1974)
With distinctive hat and the set of accessories that could be found with Captain Maddox.

1867 Fighting Indian's Teepee (?)
Colorfully printed vinyl over six poles.

1870D, GD Fort Apache and Johnny West Demo (1967)
The West family, Geronimo, Chief Cherokee, and Captain Maddox with accessories and three animals on printed pressed board display.

1875 Fort Apache (1967)
Lithographed chipboard fort, 23" high, with 13¾"-high fence surrounding; headquarters building over 2 feet long. See illustration on page 180.

2033 Buffalo (1967)

2035, 2056 Buckskin (1975)
Horse with movable head.

2049 D Best of the West and Fort Apache Fighters Display (1968, 1975)
42"-long, 39"-high, 18"-deep chipboard unit, with seven figures and fourteen horses wired on.

2057 Jed Gibson (1974)
Black scout for cavalry.

2061 Thundercolt (1975)
Range stallion with saddle and accessories.

2062 Johnny West (1974)
Basic figure of the hero of the series. (See also #5062.)

2063 Chief Cherokee (1974)
Like #1863, could come with three dozen pieces of ceremonial gear.

2067 Jane West (1974)
Her twenty-seven pieces of accessories included utensils as well as clothing.

2071 Smoke Cloud (1975)
Indian horse.

2072 Sam Cobra (1974)
The outlaw could come with "complete array of twenty-five sinister accessories."

2085 Sheriff Garrett (1974)

2097 Princess Wildflower (1975)
Indian girl in buckskin pants.

4424 Johnny West Buckboard and Horse (1967, 1976)
Included wheeled horse. (See photo.)

4427 MO Sears Western Set (1969)
Jamie West and accessories, wagon, and Comanche, his horse.

4434 Covered Wagon and Horse (1968, 1974)
Wagon is a buckboard. (See photo.)

4550 Johnny West Ranch Set (1966)
Consists of jeep, horse trailer, Johnny West with accessories, and Thunderbolt and accessories.

4560 Johnny West Camping Set (1973)
Includes jeep, tent, sleeping bag, camp fire set, cot.

5062 Quick-Draw Johnny West (1974)
Button at rear raises arm and "shot" is fired; arm must be lowered manually.

5072 Quick-Draw Sam Cobra (1975)
See above; the bad guy is ready for a shoot-out with our hero.

5085 Quick-Draw Sheriff Garrett (1975)
See above.

5275, 5275 MO Johnny West Circle X Ranch (1966)
See photo on page 180; lithographed chipboard bunkhouse with furniture, porch, water trough, barn, and corral, ready for addition of figures and accessories.

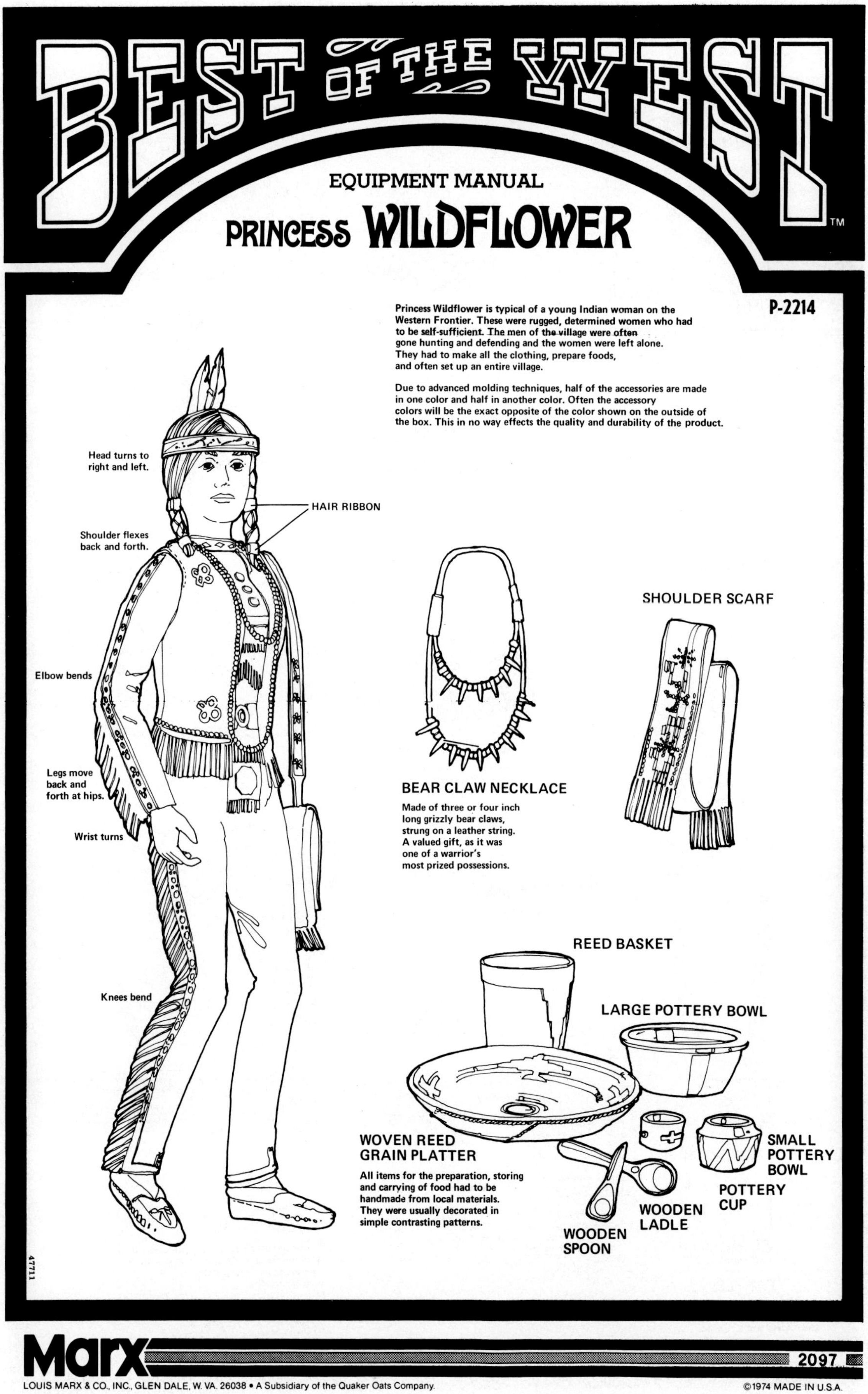

BEST OF THE WEST™

EQUIPMENT MANUAL

PRINCESS WILDFLOWER

P-2214

Princess Wildflower is typical of a young Indian woman on the Western Frontier. These were rugged, determined women who had to be self-sufficient. The men of the village were often gone hunting and defending and the women were left alone. They had to make all the clothing, prepare foods, and often set up an entire village.

Due to advanced molding techniques, half of the accessories are made in one color and half in another color. Often the accessory colors will be the exact opposite of the color shown on the outside of the box. This in no way effects the quality and durability of the product.

Made of three or four inch long grizzly bear claws, strung on a leather string. A valued gift, as it was one of a warrior's most prized possessions.

All items for the preparation, storing and carrying of food had to be handmade from local materials. They were usually decorated in simple contrasting patterns.

Marx 2097

LOUIS MARX & CO., INC., GLEN DALE, W. VA. 26038 • A Subsidiary of the Quaker Oats Company.

©1974 MADE IN U.S.A.

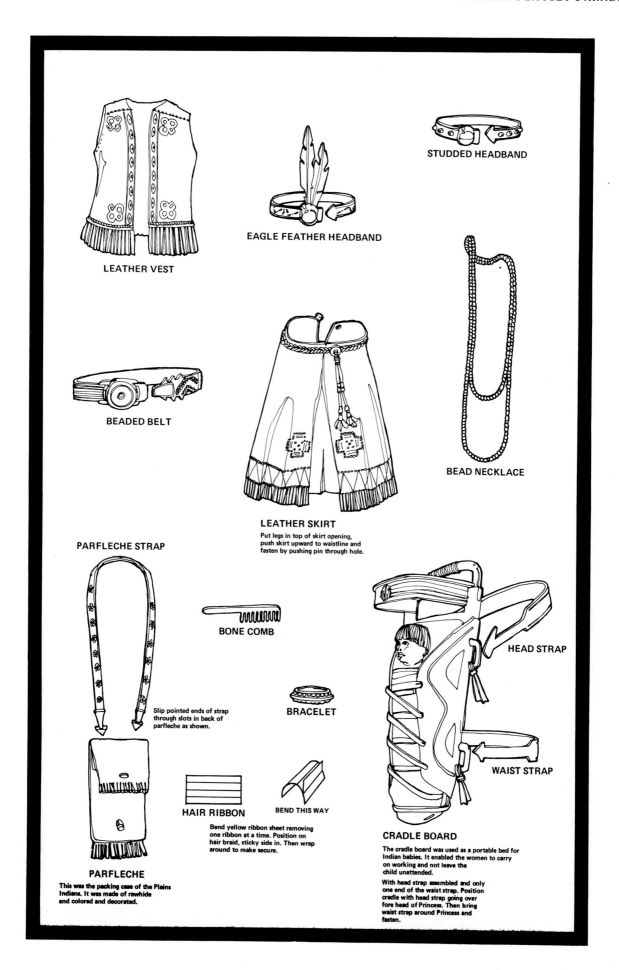

LEATHER VEST

EAGLE FEATHER HEADBAND

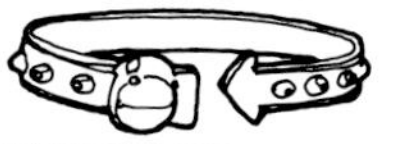

STUDDED HEADBAND

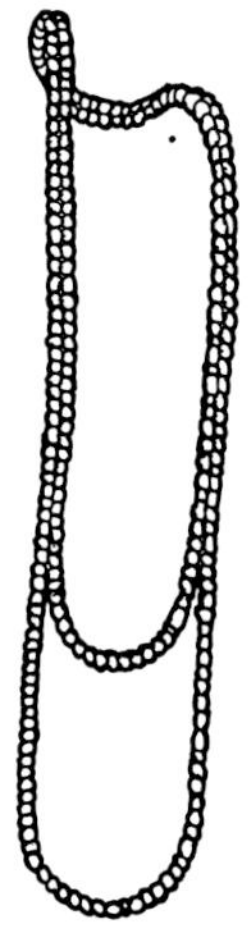

BEAD NECKLACE

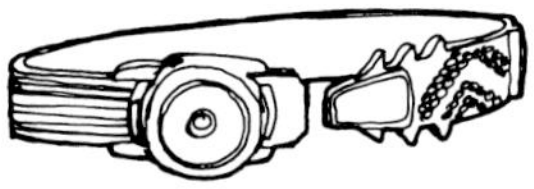

BEADED BELT

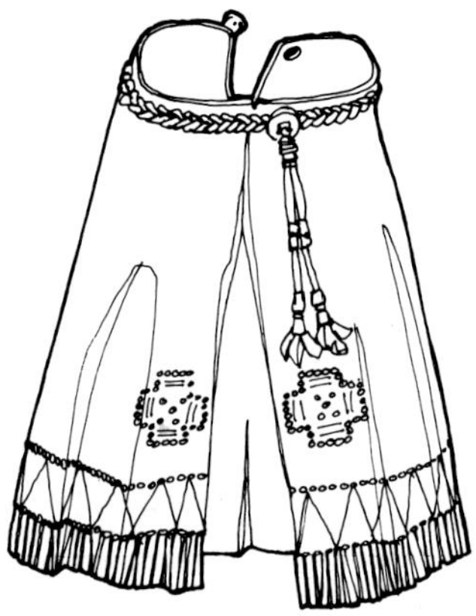

LEATHER SKIRT

Put legs in top of skirt opening, push skirt upward to waistline and fasten by pushing pin through hole.

PARFLECHE STRAP

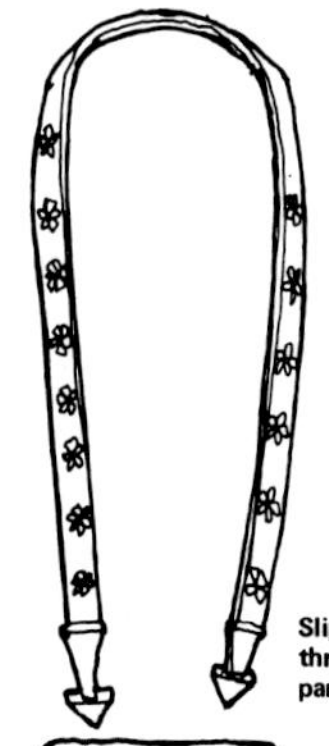

Slip pointed ends of strap through slots in back of parfleche as shown.

PARFLECHE

This was the packing case of the Plains Indians. It was made of rawhide and colored and decorated.

BONE COMB

BRACELET

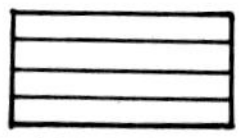

HAIR RIBBON

BEND THIS WAY

Bend yellow ribbon sheet removing one ribbon at a time. Position on hair braid, sticky side in. Then wrap around to make secure.

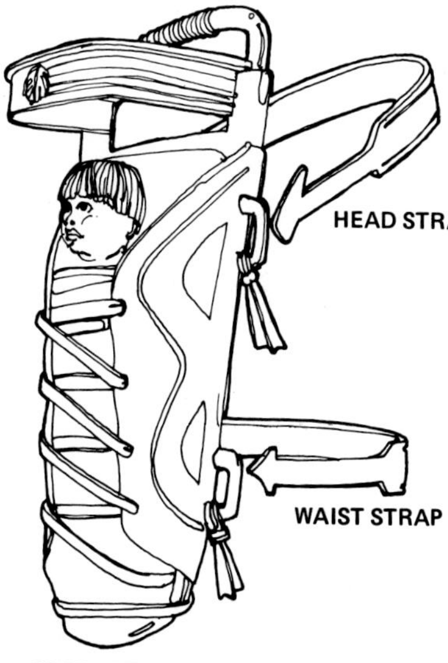

CRADLE BOARD

The cradle board was used as a portable bed for Indian babies. It enabled the women to carry on working and not leave the child unattended.

With head strap assembled and only one end of the waist strap. Position cradle with head strap going over fore head of Princess. Then bring waist strap around Princess and fasten.

Chipboard Fort Apache

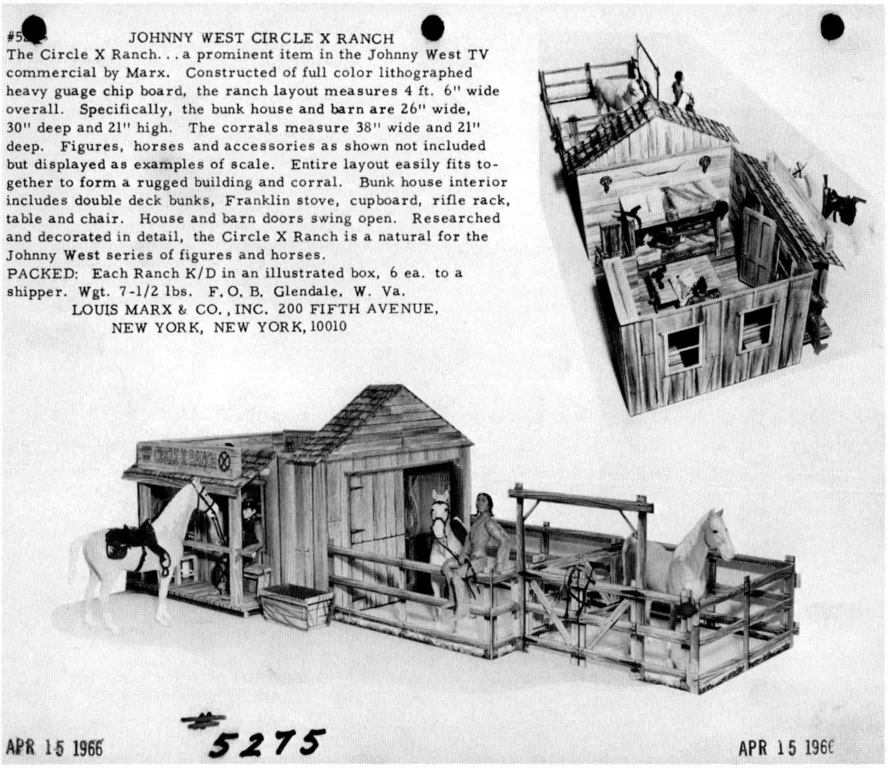

#5 JOHNNY WEST CIRCLE X RANCH
The Circle X Ranch. . . a prominent item in the Johnny West TV commercial by Marx. Constructed of full color lithographed heavy guage chip board, the ranch layout measures 4 ft. 6" wide overall. Specifically, the bunk house and barn are 26" wide, 30" deep and 21" high. The corrals measure 38" wide and 21" deep. Figures, horses and accessories as shown not included but displayed as examples of scale. Entire layout easily fits together to form a rugged building and corral. Bunk house interior includes double deck bunks, Franklin stove, cupboard, rifle rack, table and chair. House and barn doors swing open. Researched and decorated in detail, the Circle X Ranch is a natural for the Johnny West series of figures and horses.
PACKED: Each Ranch K/D in an illustrated box, 6 ea. to a shipper. Wgt. 7-1/2 lbs. F. O. B. Glendale, W. Va.
LOUIS MARX & CO., INC. 200 FIFTH AVENUE,
NEW YORK, NEW YORK, 10010

APR 15 1966 #5275 APR 15 1966

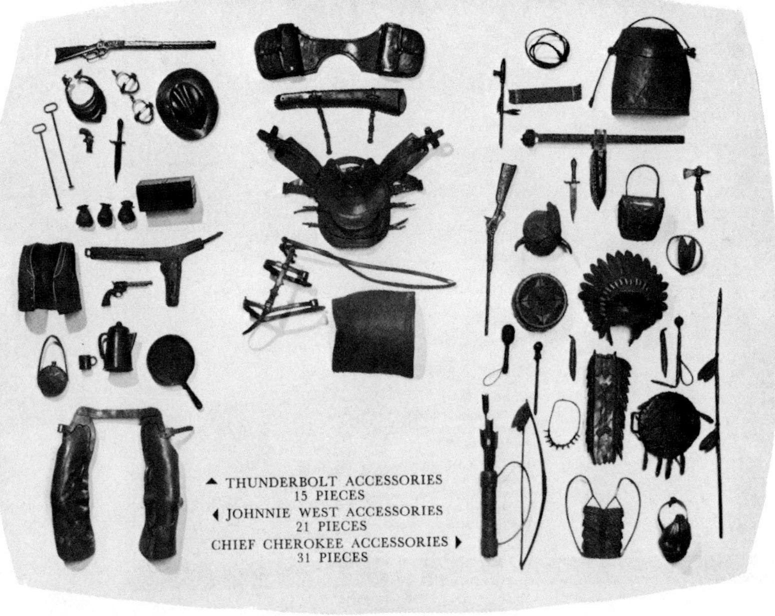

See page 34 for other accessories and figures in this scale.

THE READY GANG

This is the only Western playset made in this odd 9½-inch size. Quaker originated this and the Safari Set in the same scale as an attempt to regain the share of the market that Marx had enjoyed ten to twenty years earlier. See Color Photo 30 for catalog illustration.

1703 The Ready Gang (1977)
Featured set; see reproduced documentation.

[redacted] PARTS LIST

PART NO.	LEVEL & QTY. 1	2	3	4	5	6	PURC	DRAWING NO.	PART NAME	MATERIAL OR SIZE	COLOR NO.	REMARKS
9507	1/3						P		Master Carton	See Packing Specifications		
9508		1					P		Individual Top	See Packing Specifications		
9509		1					P	F-1403	Individual Bottom	See Packing Specifications		
9510			1				P		Label	See Packing Specifications		
							P		Poly Bag	See Packing Specifications		
E-1987			4				P		Tape	See Packing Specifications		
8540		2					P		Tape	See Packing Specifications		
9522				1			P	F-1404	Main Facade	Chipboard		
9523				1			P	C-2097	Bank Roof	Chipboard		
9524				1			P	C-2098	Front Balcony Floor	Chipboard		
9519				1			P	D-1402	Rear Balcony Floor	Chipboard		
9516				1			P	C-2094	Bank & Hotel Wall	Chipboard		
9517				1			P	C-2095	Hotel & Jail WAll	Chipboard		
9518				1			P	C-2096	Jail Wall	Chipboard		
9514				1			P	B-1732	Tellers Cage Facade	Chipboard		
9515				1			P	B-1733	Beer Sign	Chipboard		

REV.	NO.	CHANGE DESCRIPTION	BY	DATE	REV.	NO.	CHANGE DESCRIPTION	BY	DATE
		G. Almond E. Sollenberger D. Barnett Ed Peck D. Zigler J. Strope T. Gayvont					F. Pavalko J. Rusinko F. Mueller M. Fleming B. Brak B. Terrill J. Hale — E. Livingston T. Dudek M. Yankoski G. Vincent J. Hissom B. Turberville		

MARX TOYS
ERIE GIRARD GLEN DALE

CAT. # 1703	MODEL # Y-5096
TOY NAME Ready Gang	
ISS'D BY RF	APPR. BY
DATE 3/25/77	PAGE 1 OF 3

[redacted]

PARTS LIST

PART NO.	LEVEL & QTY. 1	2	3	4	5	6	PURC	DRAWING NO.	PART NAME	MATERIAL OR SIZE	COLOR NO.	REMARKS
PL-11688				4				C-2087	Post	Plastic		
PL-11687				2				C-2086	Saloon Door	Plastic		
PL-11697				2				B-1734	Door Hinge Bracket	Plastic		
PL-11683				1				D-1401	Rear Bannister-Wall Side	Plastic		
PL-11684				1				D-1401	Rear Bannister-Break Section	Plastic		
PL-11685				1				D-1401	Rear Bannister-Step Side	Plastic		
PL-11686				4				C-2085	End Bannister	Plastic		
PL-11692				1				B-1730	Jail Window	Plastic		
PL-11689				1				C-2088	Safe Front	Plastic		
PL-11690				1				C-2089	Safe Back	Plastic		
PL-11691				1				B-1729	Safe Door	Plastic		
PL-11679				1				C-2083	Front Bannister	Plastic		
PL-11680				1				C-2084	Tellers Cage	Plastic		
PL-11681				1				C-2090	Jail Door	Plastic		
PL-11682				1				D-1400	Rear Stairs	Plastic		

REV.	NO.	CHANGE DESCRIPTION	BY	DATE	REV.	NO.	CHANGE DESCRIPTION	BY	DATE

MARX TOYS
ERIE GIRARD GLEN DALE

CAT. #	MODEL # Y-5096
TOY NAME Ready Gang	
ISS'D BY RF	APPR. BY
DATE 3/25/77	PAGE 2 OF 3

[redacted]

PARTS LIST

PART NO.	LEVEL & QTY. 1	2	3	4	5	6	PURC	DRAWING NO.	PART NAME	MATERIAL OR SIZE	COLOR NO.	REMARKS
PL-11693				1				C-2091	Jail Bars	Plastic		
PL-11694				1				C-2092	Hotel Window-Right	Plastic		
PL-11695				1				C-2093	Dresser	Plastic		
PL-11696				1				B-1731	Hitching Rail	Plastic		
9521				1			P		String	14" Long		For Beer Sign

REV.	NO.	CHANGE DESCRIPTION	BY	DATE	REV.	NO.	CHANGE DESCRIPTION	BY	DATE

MARX TOYS
ERIE GIRARD GLEN DALE

CAT. #	MODEL # Y-5096
TOY NAME Ready Gang	
ISS'D BY RF	APPR. BY
DATE 3/25/77	PAGE 3 OF 3

WESTERN STAGECOACH AND WAGON SETS

1383 Covered Wagon Set (1966)
Featured set; see reproduced documentation. Horses and some accessories same as those pictured in photo of #3814, below.

1393 Daniel Boone Frontier Set (1965)
Featured set; see reproduced documentation.

1395 Western Stagecoach Set (1965)
See #3814; this earlier set is similar but slightly smaller in terms of contents: there are three Indians and three cowboys, and only one driver. Paper tepee not included. Illustrated here by original catalog glossy photo.

3814 New Western Playset with Stage Coach (1972)
Featured set; see reproduced documentation.

3816MO Stage and Covered Wagon Western Set (1972)
Twelve Indians, six cowboys, and wagon accessories accompany this set that would be assembled by mail order customer.

#1395 Western Stagecoach Set, with mockup of 1965 packaging

Length__________
Width__________
Height__________
Dia.__________

Date August 16, 1966

LOUIS MARX & CO.

GLEN DALE, W. VA.

Item No. 1383
Model No. 2599-4
File No.__________
Authorized__________

SPECIFICATIONS FOR 1383 Covered Wagon Set

PART NO.	PCS.	PART NAME	MATERIAL	COLORS	DEL. DATE
PL-987	5	(1) Wagon Body	Poly	Brown	
		(1) Seat	"	"	
		(1) Swivel Axle	"	"	
		(1) Wagon Tongue	"	"	
		(1) Wagon Tongue Wheel	"	"	
PL-987A	2	Wheels for Horses	"	"	
PL-988	4	(2) Large Wheels	"	Yellow	
		(2) Small Wheels	"	"	
PL-989	11	(1) Lantern	"	Brown	
		(1) Tub	"	"	
		(1) Carbine	"	"	
		(1) Crate	"	"	
		(1) Barrel	"	"	
		(1) Barrel Rack	"	"	
		(1) Flour Sack	"	"	
		(1) Storage Box	"	"	
		(1) Shovel	"	"	
		(1) Bucket	"	"	
		(1) Bucket Handle	"	"	
PL-990	2	(1) Left Horse	"		
		(1) Right Horse	"		
P-41	2	Reins (23" Long)	"		
FP-242	1	Cloth Cover	15½" x 13½"		
	1	Front Axle	Wire	5/32" x 6 11/16"	
	1	Rear Axle	Wire	5/32" x 6 11/16"	
	2	Cover Wires	Wire	.120	
P-1741	1	Inst. Sheet	11" x 17" (Inside)		
M-236	4	Palnuts			
	1	Kr. Bag (For Palnuts, axles, & Wires)			

XERO COPY

ITEM NO. 1393

Date 2/12/65

Customer No.

Replaces Sheet

GLEN DALE DIVISION
SPECIFICATION SHEET

Model No. 7849X Rev.

Cost No.

Item DANIEL BOONE FRONTIER SET - LINE

Quantity	Part No.	Description	Color
1	PL-987/F (987)	Set Wagon Body ok (To be the covered wagon)	Brown
2	PL-987A	Wheels for Horses	Brown & Ivory
4	PL-988	Wagon Wheels ok	~~Gray~~ Yellow
1	PL-990	Set Horses (2) ok	1-Ivory, 1-Gray / 1 Brown
1	PL-991	Set Driver & Whip ok	Buckskin ~~Ivory~~
1	PL-989	Set Accessories ok	Gray
1	PL-1225	Set Frontiersmen (6)	Buckskin
1	PL-1217	Set Indians (6)	Indian Brown
2		Wire (Cover) Stays	
1	PL-21	Set Vinyl Reins 23"	
1	P-	Cloth Cover (New Print) Dan'l. Boone Print	
1	P-1612	Instruction Sheet	
4	P-238	Pushnuts for wagon wheels	
2		5/32" dia. x 6 21/32" Long axle axles	

REMARKS:—

~~Each in an Ind. Die Cut~~ (2 print design)

DEMONSTRATOR DATA: 1 each to a shipping carton

SHIPPING CARTON Size— L .... W .... H .... Gross .... Tare .... Net .... Legal ....

SHIPPING CARTON INFORMATION:—

Individual Carton:—L 24-3/8 W 12-3/4 H 3-7/8 Diagonal 27-1/2 Girth .... Weight 3# 13 oz.

Description an Ind 1 pc die cut - 2 print design

Master Carton Size—L .... W .... H .... Diagonal .... Girth .... Weight ....

Quantity Packed Per Shipping Carton 1/4 dozen

Freight Classification ....

Net Weight .... Gross Weight .... Tare Weight .... Legal Weight ....

Acknowledged by .... A. P. .... Date 2/26/65

Length ______
Width ______
Height ______
Dia. ______

Date 6/13/72
Replaces 8/24/71

LOUIS MARX & CO.
GLEN DALE W. VA.

Item No. 3814
Model No. 8737X
File No. ______
Authorized ______

SPECIFICATIONS FOR "New Western Playset w/Stage Coach"

PART NO.	PCS.	PART NAME	MATERIAL	COLORS
PL-987A	4	Wheels - (Horses)	Plastic (Poly.)	Brown & Ivory
PL-988	1Set	Wheels (2 Large - 2 Small)	Plastic (Poly.)	Yellow
PL-990	2Sets	Horses - (4 pcs.)	Plastic (Poly.)	Brown & Ivory
PL-991	2	Driver & Whip	Plastic (Poly.)	Tan
PL-1049	8	StagecoaCH _ (Snap Together)	Plastic (Poly.)	Red
PL-1049A	1	Stagecoach Roof	Plastic (Poly.)	Gray
PL-1217	6	Indians - (5½")	Plastic (Poly.)	Bittersweet
PL-1219	6	Cowboys - (5½")	Plastic (Poly.)	Tan
M-238	4	Pushnuts	5/32"	Chrome Plated
M-370	1	Speednut		
	1	Rear Axle - (LARGE)	5/32" X 6¼"	Bright Finish
	1	Front Axle - (SMALL)	5/32" X 5½"	Bright Finish
PP-41	2	Vinyl Reins - (40")	Plastic Vinyl	Black
FP-239	1	Tepee	Paper	Printed
P-2113	1	Inst. Sheet		Printed
		IND. CORR. DIE CUT w/LABEL		
		Inside size: 24" X 15" X 4"		
		Outside size: 24-3/4" X 15-3/8" X 4¼"		
		Diag; 29"		
		Wt: 4 lbs. - 10 ozs.		
		MASTER CARTON: 6 pcs. per master carton.		
		Inside size: 25-3/4" X 15½" X 25"		
		Outside size: 26" X 15-3/4" X 25½"		
		Diag: 36½"		
		Wt: 29 lbs.		
		Cube: 4.2		

WESTERN ACTION FIGURE SETS

In order to provide you with as much information as possible, we have scrutinized the archive collection of Marx catalogs, year by year. The 1976 catalog includes "Western Action Figure playset" — #3653. It should be noted that this number was used by the original Louis Marx & Co., Inc. for a 1956 product known as "Army Truck with Searchlight Trailer."

The later product was really a line of figures, structures, and Western accessories; each playset contained five or six figures, several vehicles or animals, buildings, terrain pieces and accessories, and a 30-inch-square vinyl layout sheet. It was an attempt by Quaker Oats to modernize the playset concept with detailed articulated figures. The themes offered were Construction, Police Rescue, and Military, as well as Western.

3653, 3653F "Domes" Western Set (1976)

The blueprint of one of the figures shown in the catalog photo is reproduced on the following page. We have not been able to determine the significance of "Domes," which appears in the name on the factory documentation. Below is the list of the items included in the line of articulated plastic figures (Orient purchases), cardboard buildings, and plastic accessories:

Lawman
Bandito
Indian
Mountain man
Bounty hunter
Draw horses (2)
Riding horse
Mule horse
Stable building
Bank building
Saloon building
Tepee
Mine shaft
Girder
Stagecoach, partially assembled, harness
Buckboard, partially assembled, harness
Steamer trunk
Poison sign
Strong box
Camp fire
Buffalo skull
Longhorn skull
Small suitcase
Large suitcase
Cactus (4)
Well pump
Bucket
Fire stand
Kettle
Mule pack
Mine entrance
Rock mounds (4)
Cement bags (3)
Fallen trees (2)
Table
Chairs (4)
Lanterns (2)
Picks (2)
Shovels (3)
Dynamite box (1)

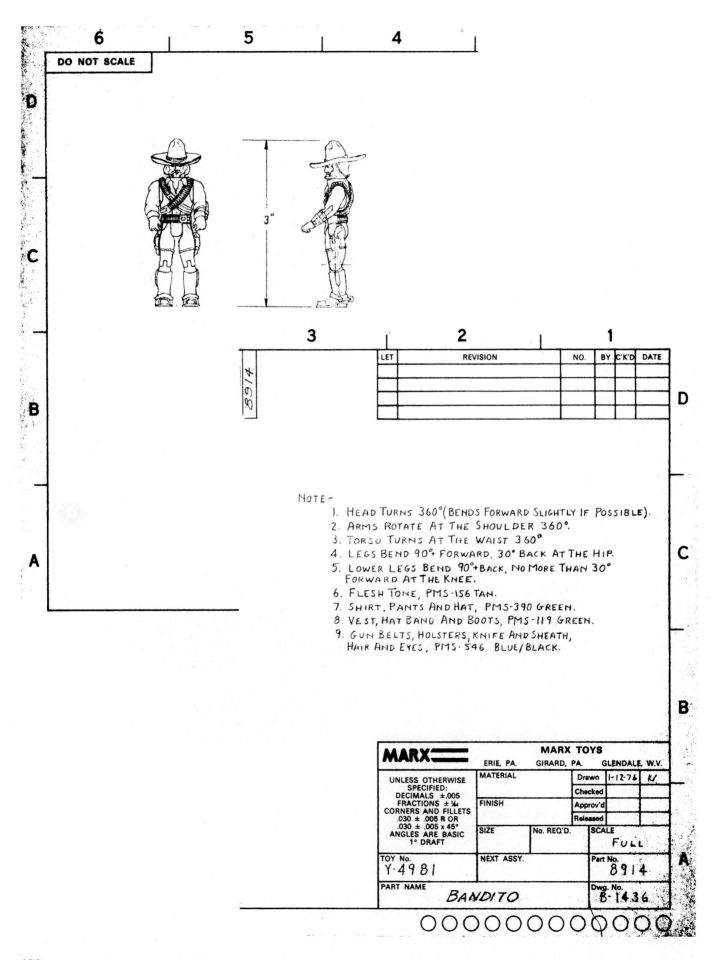

6 5 4

DO NOT SCALE

D

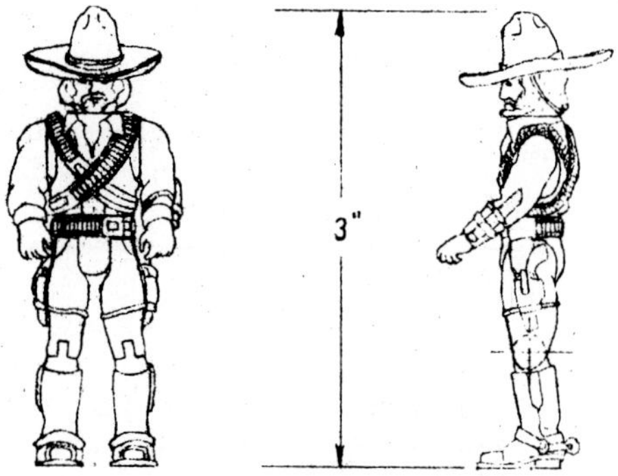

C

B

A

3 2 1

8914

LET	REVISION	NO.	BY	C'K'D	DATE

D

NOTE-

1. HEAD TURNS 360°(BENDS FORWARD SLIGHTLY IF POSSIBLE).
2. ARMS ROTATE AT THE SHOULDER 360°.
3. TORSO TURNS AT THE WAIST 360°
4. LEGS BEND 90°+ FORWARD, 30° BACK AT THE HIP.
5. LOWER LEGS BEND 90°+BACK, NO MORE THAN 30° FORWARD AT THE KNEE.
6. FLESH TONE, PMS-156 TAN.
7. SHIRT, PANTS AND HAT, PMS-390 GREEN.
8. VEST, HAT BAND AND BOOTS, PMS-119 GREEN.
9. GUN BELTS, HOLSTERS, KNIFE AND SHEATH, HAIR AND EYES, PMS-546 BLUE/BLACK.

C

B

A

MARX — MARX TOYS — ERIE, PA. GIRARD, PA. GLENDALE, W.V.

UNLESS OTHERWISE SPECIFIED: DECIMALS ±.005 FRACTIONS ±1/64 CORNERS AND FILLETS .030 ± .005 R OR .030 ± .005 x 45° ANGLES ARE BASIC 1° DRAFT	MATERIAL	Drawn 1-12-76	KJ
		Checked	
	FINISH	Approv'd	
		Released	
	SIZE / No. REQ'D.	SCALE FULL	
TOY No. Y-4981	NEXT ASSY.	Part No. 8914	
PART NAME BANDITO		Dwg. No. B-1436	

MARX VINTAGE COLLECTOR SERIES

In 1990, for the first time in over a decade, a new Marx product was introduced and a collector club was formed. Produced from the original Marx molds to exact specifications, this "Gold Rush" was, as all in the collector series will be, a limited edition, numbered and registered. To eliminate confusion with the original Marx production, principal parts were marked "XC," indicating a 1990 product, and smaller parts were identified by stamping the runner "XC"; if this proved not feasible, colors other than those of antique Marx toys were used. All the thrills of the Old West were brought to new life in a 1992-vintage Fort Apache.

4500 Fort Apache (1992)

This deluxe collectors' set includes 286 pieces, with 142 pieces of accessories — most of them not included in the recently released Fort Apache distributed by Toy Street (shown on page 92). The 2¼" figures include five brown and twelve blue cavalrymen, sixteen Indians, eighteen pioneers, six frontiers people, plus blockhouse and stockade, headquarters building, two tepees. The accessories include spears, peace pipes, and numerous other items, all three-dimensional and produced to scale.

4790 The Gold Rush Playset (1990)

Featured set; see reproduced documentation.

Color Photo 13 shows the set in its full potential: the Western town facade was offered to be used if the purchaser desired; an exploding mountain complete with a spring mechanism was intended as a component, but was not initially available due to problems with its manufacture in Asia; it could be purchased separately. Note the reproduction of a Louis Marx & Co., Inc. mold sheet on the following page. The Vintage Collector Series continues the imaginative use of the original molds in new combinations. The set includes a map, a booklet providing a brief history of the Gold Rush period, and a "claim deed."

These goldminers show the close attention to figure detail identified with Marx; to the right, mine entrance and accessories.

PL- 1163

Item: Exploding Mountain

Model No. 2674-5

No. of Cavities: 8

No. of Sets: 2

Cost: $4550.00 (50.00 model)

Made By: Ferriot

Date Ordered: 11/17/61

Delivery Date: 10 weeks

Date Received: 1/25/62

Machine: 8 oz.

Average Per Hour: 180

Gross Per Day: Hi

Weights: Per Shot- 123.5

Per Piece- 51.6

Per M- 113.8

Mold Contains:

2 Bases
2 Large Mountain Sections
2 Small Bottom Sections
2 Samll Top Sections

FP 249 caplmech.
E 449. fasten

PL - 500

MARX TOYS

LOUIS MARX & CO.

1990

BILL OF MATERIALS

MARX VINTAGE COLLECTABLE PLAY SET

Ref: 4790 Product Name: Gold Rush Play Set

Mold #	Part	Machine	Cav.	Sets	Wt	Mat	Color
MX1057	Gold Mine	250	8	1	174	HIS	Earth Tan
MX1047	Chuck Wagon	200	16 2 -- 18	1	30	LDPE	Light Brown
MX1168	Dynamite Hill	200	8	2	51	HIS	Coppertone
MX174	Fence	200	10	2	40	LDPE	Medium Brown
MX881	Rocks	150	(9-4)5	1	32	HIS	Med Gray
MX388	Outside Furniture	200	21	1	91	HIS	Dark Brown
MX857	Stage Coach	250	6	2		HDPE	Red
MX325	Horse	150	8	3		PE	White
MX1099	Pack Horse	150	9	1	62	HDPE	Black
MX610	Horses	200	8	4	32	LDPE	White
MX1528	Figures	250	32	1	184	LDPE	Powder Blue
MX337	Wheel	150	24	6		HDPE	Black
MR-1616	Western Town Front	300	1	1	91	PPL	Yellow

Tel: (305) 625-9000
FAX: (305) 621-9063
Cables: AMPLAST NMIA
Telex: 803943 AMPLAST NMIA

T.M. "MAGIC MARXIE"

1130 N.W. 159th Drive
Miami, Florida 33169

ABOUT THE AUTHOR

Jay Horowitz was born on June 28, 1946, in Brooklyn, New York, and raised in the Hollis Hills section of Queens. After graduating from Martin Van Buren High School, he attended New York University, School of Commerce, where he held various positions including class president. Jay remains an active alumnus.

Following his college education, he taught briefly in the New York City school system, until deciding to start his own company. While Jay was growing up, he gained experience in his family's retail and wholesale toy business. Toy manufacturing was his dream. But at age twenty-two, he had no capital, contacts, or know-how; competing with giant corporations such as Marx seemed like an impossible task.

So Jay traveled to Colombia, South America, in the mid-1960s, when it was a virtual paradise for entrepreneurs. He observed that toy manufacturing there was rudimentary, and the Colombian government, trying to protect or create its own infant industries, had closed off imports on nonessential consumer goods such as toys. To Jay, Colombia offered the right opportunity for a young, inexperienced, but energetic, individual desiring to establish a new toy factory.

In February 1969 he began operations in a 2000-square-foot garage, using the brand name "Juguetes Toyco." By employing the business methods that Jay had seen succeed in the United States during the 1950s and 1960s, the fledgling company prospered. Toyco was the first toy company in Colombia to make modern toys, apply bright colors, create attractive packaging, offer marketing incentives, and employ television advertising.

This last strategy helped skyrocket the company to the number one position in the national market. As the Andean Pact common market took effect, Toyco opened marketing branches in neighboring Ecuador and Peru. Later, it did some business in Venezuela and Chile. Jay also founded and was president of the Colombian Toy Manufacturers Association.

As the political and economic climate in Colombia changed in the mid-1970s, personal safety became a priority. The family fell prey to such atrocities as robbery, kidnapping, extortion, and even attempted murder. Having lived in Colombia for a decade, Jay felt it was time to move on. Leaving his business affairs in good order, Jay returned with his family to the United States and relocated to the Miami Beach area.

Then thirty-two, faced with the need for a new business and a new life in the United States, Jay considered his options. The aspect of Toyco that he had found most interesting was new product development. Toyco had built its success by purchasing existing molds and rights that were no longer active from American companies. Jay reasoned that if he needed new product molds on an annual basis, wouldn't all of the other Latin American plastic manufacturing companies also need them?

This concept formed the basis for his new business: In April 1978 Jay established American Plastic Equipment, Inc. to provide molds, technology, and machinery to factories in developing nations. This was the road that led him to purchase the assets of Marx Toys in 1982, and to secure the Marx patent, trademark, and rights from the Chemical Bank of New York in 1988. American Plastic, today the world's largest mold dealer, also holds the molds and the rights of many of the other well-known toy companies of yesterday. American Plastic now serves factories around the world. Among its other activities, it is actively developing its Marx Vintage Collector Series to meet the demands of toy collectors and enthusiasts.

Jay Horowitz with a playset mold